Praise for *The Unexpected War*

"Janice Gross Stein and Eugene Lang's new book, *The Unexpected War*, brilliantly recounts how Canada became engaged in Afghanistan and particularly Kandahar. Unexpected indeed!"

—*The Globe and Mail*

"*The Unexpected War* is about the challenges of political decision-making and how Canada's capacity for effective policy choice is waning. It is the product of fruitful collaboration between one of the country's best analysts of international security (Stein) and a former adviser to two Canadian defence ministers (Lang) ... As the authors rightly note, this is a story 'that belongs to Canada's citizens.' We need to hear it now."

—Jennifer Welsh, *The Globe and Mail*

"*The Unexpected War* ... is a revelation, an inside account of how things work in government. You won't be surprised to learn that it's a messy business, fraught with competing agendas and internecine wars, and heavily influenced by personality ... [Stein and Lang] are also unsparing in their descriptions of dysfunction in Ottawa. Few people come off particularly well in this account, with the exception of the men and women in uniform ... Not surprisingly, a lot of people are hopping mad about this book."

—Margaret Wente, *The Globe and Mail*

"In a riveting new book, Janice Gross Stein, the University of Toronto's wise international thinker, and Ottawa policy insider Eugene Lang document how Canada slipped unwittingly into a war in a country it knew nothing about."

—James Travers, *Toronto Star*

"*The Unexpected War* is a fine piece of work—well written, engaging, informative, and thorough (supported by inside information and insightful personal interview material). For anyone interested in a first-hand account of Canada's road to Kandahar—and the political and bureaucratic machinations that accompanied it—this book is a must read."

—*Ottawa Citizen*

PENGUIN CANADA

THE UNEXPECTED WAR

JANICE GROSS STEIN is the Belzberg Professor of Conflict Management in the Department of Political Science and the director of the Munk Centre for International Studies at the University of Toronto. She is a fellow of the Royal Society of Canada, a member of the Order of Canada, and an honorary foreign member of the American Academy of Arts and Sciences. She was the Massey Lecturer in 2001, has been a Trudeau Fellow, and was awarded the Molson Prize by the Canada Council for an outstanding contribution by a social scientist to public debate.

EUGENE LANG, a public policy consultant and writer, served as chief of staff to two ministers of national defence from 2002 to 2006. A 2006–2007 visiting fellow at the Munk Centre for International Studies at the University of Toronto and a former Chevening Scholar at the London School of Economics, Lang is a frequent contributor to *The Globe and Mail* and the *Toronto Star*, and is co-author (with Philip DeMont) of *Turning Point: Moving Beyond Neoconservatism*. He lives in Ottawa with his wife and two children.

THE
UNEXPECTED
WAR
CANADA IN
KANDAHAR

JANICE GROSS STEIN & EUGENE LANG

PENGUIN
CANADA

PENGUIN CANADA

Published by the Penguin Group

Penguin Group (Canada), 90 Eglinton Avenue East, Suite 700, Toronto, Ontario, Canada M4P 2Y3
(a division of Pearson Canada Inc.)

Penguin Group (USA) Inc., 375 Hudson Street, New York, New York 10014, U.S.A.
Penguin Books Ltd, 80 Strand, London WC2R 0RL, England
Penguin Ireland, 25 St Stephen's Green, Dublin 2, Ireland (a division of Penguin Books Ltd)
Penguin Group (Australia), 250 Camberwell Road, Camberwell, Victoria 3124, Australia
(a division of Pearson Australia Group Pty Ltd)
Penguin Books India Pvt Ltd, 11 Community Centre, Panchsheel Park, New Delhi – 110 017, India
Penguin Group (NZ), 67 Apollo Drive, Rosedale, North Shore 0632, New Zealand
(a division of Pearson New Zealand Ltd)
Penguin Books (South Africa) (Pty) Ltd, 24 Sturdee Avenue, Rosebank, Johannesburg 2196, South Africa

Penguin Books Ltd, Registered Offices: 80 Strand, London WC2R 0RL, England

First published in a Viking Canada hardcover by Penguin Group (Canada),
a division of Pearson Canada Inc., 2007
Published in this edition, 2008

1 2 3 4 5 6 7 8 9 10   (WEB)

Manufactured in Canada.

LIBRARY AND ARCHIVES CANADA CATALOGUING IN PUBLICATION

Stein, Janice
The unexpected war : Canada in Kandahar / Janice Gross Stein & Eugene Lang.

Includes bibliographical references and index.
ISBN 978-0-14-305537-2

1. Afghan War, 2001– —Participation, Canadian.   2. Canada—Armed Forces—
Afghanistan.   3. Canada—Military policy.   I. Lang, J. Eugene   II. Title.

DS371.412.S74 2008   958.104'7   C2008-902708-6

Visit the Penguin Group (Canada) website at **www.penguin.ca**

Special and corporate bulk purchase rates available; please see
www.penguin.ca/corporatesales or call 1-800-810-3104, ext. 477 or 474

To our children—Leah, Joshua, Isaac, and Gabriel
May they make wise decisions.

CONTENTS

PROLOGUE
ONE DAY IN KANDAHAR

Kandahar, Afghanistan, July 2002

It was about nine o'clock in the morning when the lumbering C-130 Hercules approached the airfield a few kilometres outside Kandahar City. The C-130s—or Hercs as the military call them—are the work-horses of the Canadian Air Force. Many of these planes are three and four decades old. They were *the* vital supply link to the eight hundred members of the Princess Patricia's Canadian Light Infantry (PPCLI), an army regiment with a long and rich history. The "Patricias" had been based at Kandahar airfield for the previous six months.

Every day, the soldiers received supplies from the Hercs that flew into Kandahar from an undisclosed base in another country several flying hours away. But on this day, the Herc was also transporting a special visitor: the minister of national defence, John McCallum.

McCallum, a former academic and bank economist, was new to his post and unschooled in matters military. He had been given his latest job only two months previously when Prime Minister Chrétien uncere-moniously fired Art Eggleton, the longest-serving defence minister in fifty years, after the prime minister learned that the former mayor of Toronto had granted an untendered contract to a former girlfriend.

Eggleton had visited Kandahar earlier that year. Shortly after he became minister, McCallum raised with his generals the prospect of a trip to Kandahar. They were adamantly opposed: The mission was almost over, the troops were packing up to return home at the end of the summer. There was no need for the minister to visit them. He would be in the way.

Shortly thereafter, McCallum had dinner with his colleague New Brunswick Member of Parliament Dominic LeBlanc, and LeBlanc's friend Alexandre "Sasha" Trudeau, son of the former prime minister. The young Trudeau is an intrepid documentary filmmaker who has travelled to many of the world's hotspots. Over dinner, he asked McCallum point-blank, "When are you going to Afghanistan?" McCallum replied that his officials opposed the trip. "He looked at me with those piercing Trudeau eyes as if I was a total wimp," McCallum recalled. "Then Trudeau said, 'You are the minister, tell them you are going ... you need to see this first-hand.'" The following day, McCallum broke the news to his generals that he was going to Afghanistan and that they had better start arranging the trip.

A visit to Kandahar in summer is no walk in the park. Two weeks prior to departure, McCallum's chief of staff received a call from Brigadier General Michel Gauthier, the officer overseeing the Canadian Forces in Afghanistan, and based at U.S. Central Command (CENTCOMM) in Tampa, Florida, the headquarters for coalition military operations in southwest Asia. Gauthier, in an effort to prepare the minister for, or perhaps dissuade him from, the gruelling trip ahead, told McCallum's staffer that going to Kandahar had been the most physically draining experience of his life. The message from a very fit and tough-minded career army officer got the attention that it deserved.

McCallum's journey into Kandahar from an undisclosed location in the Middle East began at four o'clock in the morning. After a quick breakfast, the minister and his group were "kitted out" with helmets, thirty-pound flak jackets, earplugs, box lunches, and bottled water—lots of bottled water. Around 5:00 A.M. they were taken outside and escorted to an airplane hangar for a security briefing. The sun was coming up, the temperature was already approaching forty degrees Celsius, and the humidity was far worse than the muggiest summer day in southern Ontario.

As the group entered the dark hangar, McCallum was approached by two men dressed in golf shirts, khaki pants, and wraparound sunglasses. They were in their mid- to late thirties, as fit and muscular as an NHL hockey player, sporting dark tans, beards, and hair much longer than would be tolerated in the army, navy, or air force. These men were members of Joint Task Force 2 (JTF2), Canada's elite special-forces unit. The activities of JTF2 are shrouded in secrecy and the Canadian public knows little about what it does. Despite its relative obscurity at home, JTF2 is well known in military circles abroad. It is one of the best-trained, most capable, and highly regarded special forces in the world.

These two soft-spoken, disarmingly calm, intelligent, and articulate JTF2 operatives were responsible for the safety of Canada's minister of national defence during his visit to Afghanistan.

Two and a half hours later, McCallum's Herc was flying a few hundred feet above the Kandahar desert. Through the aircraft's small, dirty portholes the minister and his party could see the terrain of one of the most godforsaken places on Earth. The desert looked like a moonscape—flat topography with sand and rock crevices as far as the eye could see, and no signs of human, animal, or plant life.

About an hour later the minister's Herc climbed to a higher altitude as it approached the airfield at Kandahar, known as KAF. The passengers were told to brace themselves. The airplane careened downward suddenly like an out-of-control roller coaster, dropping several thousand feet in a matter of seconds to the runway surface. This kind of "corkscrew landing" is an evasive manoeuvre to prevent the aircraft from being targeted by shoulder-held rockets or other types of anti-aircraft fire from the ground. The landing reminded the passengers—if they needed any reminding—that they had just entered a war zone.

McCallum and his party disembarked from the Herc and stepped out into the relentless sun and onto the ubiquitous dust—not sand, but dust—of Kandahar. It felt as though they had walked into a blast furnace. The oppressive humidity of the early morning had been replaced by a parched desert climate, with a mid-morning temperature of fifty degrees Celsius. By early afternoon the temperature had risen to nearly fifty-five degrees, normal July weather in Kandahar. As McCallum said, "The heat was oppressive, but you didn't notice it that much because the real discomfort was the dust in your face."

The airfield evoked scenes from the movie *Apocalypse Now*, only in a desert rather than a jungle. Dozens, if not hundreds, of American Black Hawk, Apache, and Chinook helicopters; F-14, F-15, F-16, and F-111 fighter aircraft; and Hercs and C-17 transport planes filled the sky and ground. The dust-choked air was acrid with the smell of gasoline, and traces of black smoke seemed to be everywhere. The terminal building of the old Kandahar airport, the headquarters for coalition military operations in the south, was a burnt-out shell. Strangely, behind this shell of the terminal was an empty in-ground swimming pool. Later that day, Canadians would see this bizarre sight when a CBC reporter interviewed McCallum poolside.

The minister, with his JTF2 bodyguards in tow, approached the terminal wearing a flak jacket and army helmet, and proceeded to inspect a small contingent of Canadian soldiers. Lieutenant General Daniel K. McNeill, the American three-star officer in charge of all U.S. forces in this theatre of operations, then greeted McCallum. McNeill thanked the minister for Canada's contribution to the war against the Taliban and al-Qaeda and told him that the eight hundred Canadian troops at KAF were among the best he had seen anywhere; they were better trained than their American counterparts. And McNeill, a one-time commander of the famous 82nd Airborne, knew something about well-trained troops.

After a briefing by senior officers on the situation in Kandahar, McCallum met and mingled with the members of the PPCLI. The soldiers looked impossibly young, all in their late teens and early twenties, with bleached hair and skin darkened from their constant exposure to the blistering Kandahar sun. They had been living in the dirt for six months. Their living conditions were starkly different from those of their colleagues in the air force, who left Kandahar each day on the Hercs and returned to the comfort of their base outside

Afghanistan, which was furnished with air-conditioned rooms, clean showers, and an excellent mess hall.

McCallum and his party could not help but be impressed with the internal fortitude, physical strength, and mental toughness of the PPCLI soldiers. They were Canada's finest. These men lived in tents in the dirt, ate outside with the dust in their faces and on their food, and used outhouses in fifty-degree temperatures. Sandstorms, so fierce that they precluded all work outside at the airfield, were a common occurrence.

Yet the minister heard no complaints from these young men thrust into this strange and inhospitable environment. This is what they had signed up and trained to do. They had but one complaint: They were disappointed that they had seen so little combat in their half year in Kandahar.

By the time the Canadians arrived in early 2002, their American counterparts had killed, cleared out, or driven the Taliban and al-Qaeda underground or back across the porous Pakistani border. The PPCLI generally patrolled outside and around the airfield complex to secure the airport. Canada's soldiers fired few shots during their first combat mission since the Korean War. They suffered four fatalities in six months, the tragic result of friendly fire when a U.S. F-16 fighter aircraft mistakenly bombed a Canadian training exercise.

The relatively uneventful nature of Canada's first deployment might sound ideal to many Canadians. But most soldiers see things differently. They train long and hard for war, and most of them badly want to put that training to work in difficult situations and prove their worth. Canada's soldiers want to fight and win.

They would have their chance to fight before too long. By mid-2007 (when this book went to press), the Canadian Forces (CF) would suffer sixty-six fatalities and several hundred wounded, almost all after February 2006. During the spring, summer, and early fall of 2006, Canada's new Governor General, Michaëlle Jean, the commander-in-chief of the Canadian Forces, would go to Trenton airfield almost weekly for the sad final repatriation ceremony of fallen Canadian soldiers.

After he had had lunch with the troops, McCallum was taken "on patrol" to get a better sense of the territory around the airfield. The Canadian Forces' state-of-the-art (LAV III) vehicles had already been sent back to Canada, so the minister and his party were loaded into 1960s vintage Warsaw Pact armoured personnel carriers (APC), owned and operated by the Romanians, who were replacing the departing Canadians.

The sun shining on the metal was so intense that the armour plating of the APCs would burn the skin of anyone who touched it. The guests from Canada were given frozen bottles of water that quickly melted and heated to forty degrees Celsius. The minister and his party needed two to three bottles an hour to fend off dehydration. None had the urge to urinate; the water simply came right out of their pores.

The Romanian vehicles, spewing black smoke from their antiquated diesel engines, slowly and loudly exited the airfield onto a dusty road that ran along its perimeter. On the way out they passed a cinder-block compound that was one of the detention facilities for captured Taliban and al-Qaeda prisoners, the "detainees." Carcasses of abandoned and destroyed military vehicles littered the road. Some were Soviet in origin and had been sitting there since the Soviet occupation of Afghanistan from 1979 to 1989. This region had been embroiled in bitter conflict for decades.

As the convoy moved down the road, Afghan locals, mostly young people, came out onto the roadside and waved at the passing vehicles. Thirty minutes later, McCallum and his party arrived in a village.

It was like going back in time a millennium—or even two. The Afghans lived in low mud-brick buildings with flat roofs. There was no running water or electricity; there never had been. It was hard to imagine how these people survived. Nothing, apart from the ubiquitous Afghan poppy, grew in the Kandahar dust, and there wasn't much livestock visible.

As part of their effort to win Afghans' hearts and minds, the Canadian Forces had built a wood schoolhouse with glass windows. The villagers were happy to have this state-of-the-art building, even if they didn't use it as a school. The most important technological innovation, however, was a simple hand-powered water pump, not unlike the pumps on any farm in rural Canada. Residents enthusiastically demonstrated to McCallum how this pump drew water to the surface from a hole deep in the ground, with an up-and-down motion of its wooden handle. The excitement was visible.

A wizened, ancient-looking man with a massive beard emerged from the small crowd of villagers and came forward to meet the minister. Beaming, he greeted McCallum with a warm embrace. He was the elder, the Afghan equivalent of the mayor. Through a translator, he thanked the minister for what Canada's military had done for his community, and invited him to his house for tea. Unfortunately, time and concern about security made the visit impossible, so McCallum shook the old man's hand, thanked him for his kind words, and returned to his armoured vehicle to be driven back to KAF.

Two hours later, Canada's minister of national defence boarded the old Herc and departed Kandahar for the Middle East. As Michel Gauthier had predicted, McCallum and his party were physically exhausted. Eight hours in southern Afghanistan seemed like eight days anywhere else. The Canadians welcomed the cramped, deafening, vibrating surroundings of the old Herc. As the aircraft took off, they left the dust of Kandahar behind. But each one was changed by that day in Kandahar.

None of the visitors had seen a place like this before. None had been put to a physical test like this before. Yet they felt lucky to have the opportunity to see first-hand this remote, rugged, desolate, ancient part of the world. They felt privileged to have seen the Canadian Forces in an operational theatre before they departed. No one expected to return to Afghanistan. Canada's mission was over, and there were no plans for a follow-on operation.

But they were mistaken. John McCallum would remain Canada's minister of defence for another year and a half. During that time he would return to Afghanistan twice more. And his successors would need to visit time and again over the next four years.

ONE

EARLY IN, EARLY OUT

Canada has soldiers that are buried all over Europe because we fought in defence of liberty and we're not about to back away from a challenge now because we think somebody might get hurt.
—JOHN MANLEY, MINISTER OF FOREIGN AFFAIRS, SEPTEMBER 12, 2001

I think we will play a major role, a front-line role. We will make sure the Canadian Forces get the resources they need to do the job. We'll stand with our allies in weeding out the perpetrators, in destroying the organizations, wherever they may be.
—ART EGGLETON, MINISTER OF NATIONAL DEFENCE, SEPTEMBER 18, 2001

I have made clear in the days since September 11 that the struggle to defeat the forces of terrorism will be a long one. We must remain strong and vigilant. We must insist on living on our terms according to our values, not on terms dictated from the shadows. I cannot promise that the campaign against terrorism will be painless, but I can promise that it will be won.
—PRIME MINISTER JEAN CHRÉTIEN, OCTOBER 8, 2001

The principal role that we hope they [the Canadian Forces] will have if, whenever and if they go there [Afghanistan]—because there is no final conclusion—will be to make sure aid gets to the people who need it. Of course, we don't want to have a big fight there. We want to bring peace and happiness as much as possible.
—PRIME MINISTER JEAN CHRÉTIEN, NOVEMBER 20, 2001

arly in, early out. That phrase captures the mindset of Canada's military and political leadership in late 2001 as they prepared to send the Canadian Forces to Afghanistan. In the wake of the 9-11 attacks on the United States, Art Eggleton, the defence minister at the time, summed up the dominant thinking in the government. Any Canadian military deployment to Afghanistan, he said, "may well be similar to a situation in Eritrea and Ethiopia where we went in on the first wave, we helped to establish the stabilization, the basis for ongoing peace support operations that would come after ... but then turned it over to somebody else."[1] Eritrea and Ethiopia were low-risk, low-fatality post–Cold War operations that the Canadian public barely noticed at the time and would not remember today. A very small number of Canadian forces were deployed. Yet that was the defence minister's reference point when he thought about the impending Afghan mission.

Six years later, after the deaths of sixty-six Canadian soldiers, and several redefinitions of the mission in Afghanistan, the Canadian Forces are more deeply involved than ever and are committed to stay until February 2009. So much for early in, early out and no big fights.

Members of the Chrétien government in the days and weeks following 9-11 had no idea what role Canada's military should, could, or would play in Afghanistan. In fact, Ottawa struggled for months to devise an Afghanistan policy that would satisfy the core political objectives of the government and, at the same time, be acceptable to the Canadian public.

The dilemmas surrounding the Afghan mission were obvious from the start. Right after 9-11, some in Ottawa wanted the Canadian Forces in Afghanistan fighting alongside the Americans in Kandahar, the birthplace of the Taliban and the stronghold of al-Qaeda. Others favoured Canadian participation in the International Security Assistance Force (ISAF), the European-led mission in the Afghan capital, Kabul. This appeared to be a safer mission, less directly tied to the Americans, and more akin to peacekeeping, the allegedly "traditional" role of Canada's military since the end of the Second World War.² There were some minimalists in the Canadian Forces who were so concerned about the overstretching of the military that they wanted to limit Canada's commitment to a token navy presence in the Arabian Sea to assist the international military effort in Afghanistan—a landlocked country.

The debate within the Chrétien government about Canada's military contribution to Afghanistan continued throughout the fall of 2001. Former foreign minister John Manley recalls a discussion he had with U.S. Secretary of State Colin Powell at a G-8 foreign minister's meeting that fall. "We'll be part of it [the coalition]," John Manley told Powell, "but we believe in the Powell doctrine, and if we were going to send forces to Afghanistan we wanted to make sure they were adequate to the task."²

In the end, Canada opted for an incremental buildup of forces through the fall and winter of 2001 to 2002. In the second week of October, Eggleton announced that a naval contingent would be sent to the region. He subsequently committed a handful of surveillance aircraft to "interdict" fleeing al-Qaeda and Taliban from Afghanistan. Only in early 2002 was a decision made to commit, for a short term, ground troops to Kandahar. Canada's political leaders believed that the commitment was low-risk and for a short period of time.

It was low-risk because the Canadians arrived too late to make a difference on the ground. American forces had cleared the Taliban and al-Qaeda from southern Afghanistan weeks before the Canadian Forces arrived on the scene.

However, as one former senior government official conceded, Canada's military contribution to the American effort in Kandahar in the first half of 2002 did have "cosmetic value." Canadian leaders used these cosmetics largely for Washington's eyes.

9-11: A Shock to Ottawa

The Government of Canada was rocked to its foundations on September 11, 2001. Some of Canada's top military and political leaders were not in Ottawa when the planes hit the World Trade Center. Chief of the Defence Staff Ray Henault and his NATO colleagues were on a tour of Europe and had just departed Italy for Hungary on that fateful morning in New York. Years later Henault reflected on the chaos of the day:

> At 1600 we landed in Budapest. Just as we landed, all the aides' cell phones went off. A plane had hit the World Trade Center; the messages were confused. There was an honour guard to meet us. The parade finished about 20 minutes later, and the cell phones began to go off again. I remember this vividly. By the time we got on the bus, it had been confirmed that a second aircraft had struck. There were twenty-six Chiefs of Defence Staff on that bus that afternoon, virtually the whole military leadership of NATO. The US Chairman of the Joint Chiefs was on his way to Budapest and turned around in the air. By the time we got to the hotel, I had determined that I had to get back to Canada ... Shortly after our arrival at the hotel, we called a special meeting and the US military representative confirmed that the towers had come down.[3]

Henault's boss, Art Eggleton, the minister of national defence, was in Sofia, Bulgaria. "We contacted him [Eggleton] and briefed him," said Henault. He continued:

> I spoke to the Prime Minister and assured Chrétien that we stood ready. Deputy Chief Greg Maddison was acting on my behalf, making recommendations to the PMO [Prime Minister's Office] and the PCO [Privy Council Office], and interacting with

NORAD. Eggleton agreed to come to Budapest to pick me up, as well as Jim King (our military representative in Brussels). I went to the NATO Council meeting on September 12th, where we discussed Article 5 [the provision of the *Washington Treaty* requiring member states to come to the defence of members when attacked]. The Council invoked Article 5 on the condition that the strike was perpetrated from the outside.[4]

The two men most responsible for Canada's defence and national security then headed home. "It was eerie, flying home," Henault recalled. "There was no air traffic. The crew said, 'There is no radio traffic. This must have been what it felt like before Lindbergh.' As we approached the North Atlantic coastline, American controllers told the pilot that if we overflew Maine, they would have to shoot us down."[5]

Within a very short time—hours and days—Canada's leaders made a series of fundamental and far-reaching decisions. On September 13, the prime minister quickly established an informal Cabinet committee to deal with the immediate crisis. Another ad hoc Cabinet committee on anti-terrorism was created on October 2. The government moved with unprecedented speed to draft anti-terrorism legislation and bring it before Parliament. The new legislation was rushed through Parliament and it received royal assent before Christmas of 2001.[6] Government ministries and agencies that had long been on the margins of power—the Department of the Solicitor General, the Canadian Security Intelligence Service, the RCMP, and Transport Canada—were suddenly central to the federal agenda.

The government was also getting ready to present its budget. Its theme was to be post-secondary education, and a great deal of work had already been done before 9-11. Now, at least as far as some ministers were concerned, all bets were off. The world had changed and Canada needed to respond to the new security challenges. The debate was intense. John Manley recalls disagreements in Cabinet about

whether or not this budget should be changed to recognize the post–
9-11 reality. "I was saying, 'Excuse me, it has to be a Security Budget,
have you been reading the papers lately?' while some other Ministers
were saying 'Let's not be sucked in by the Americans, let's show we're
still on our agenda.' I thought these people were nuts and I still do."[7]

Manley's view carried the day. The 2001 Budget, Paul Martin's last
as finance minister, was fast-tracked, its focus shifted almost exclusively
to national security. Delivered three months early, in December, it allo-
cated nearly eight billion dollars to departments and agencies responsible for Canada's national security. Canadians had not seen a budget like
this from their federal government in generations.

Meanwhile, in Parliament much of the conversation centred on how
to keep goods and people moving freely across the border with the
United States. Manley recalls telling his Cabinet colleagues at the time,
"The number one priority for Canada at this moment is to keep the
border open."[8] The foreign minister felt that the most effective way to
deal with the challenge of the border was to allay American worries
about continental security. In question period in the House of
Commons, ministers were asked again and again about the need for a
common security perimeter with the United States. There were very
few questions about Canada's military response to 9-11. Attention was
focused at home, not abroad. Stockwell Day, then the leader of the
Opposition, asked Jean Chrétien in question period in Parliament on
September 17 whether or not the government was considering anti-
terror legislation. He followed up within a few minutes with a broader
question: "Will the Prime Minister assure the House today that if the
United States correctly identifies the sponsors of terrorism and engages
in armed conflict, Canada will stand with the United States and our
NATO allies and provide, if necessary, Canadian military forces?"[9] This
was one of only a handful of questions in the House of Commons
about a potential deployment of the Canadian Forces that fall.

Meanwhile in the United States, the Congress was appropriating
billions of dollars to the Defence Department and the U.S. military for

the invasion of Afghanistan. Yet by contrast, Canada's military was virtually shut out of the "Security Budget" of 2001. Manley reflected on this: "The priority in December 2001 was how do we make sure we are not seen as the source of weakness and threat to the Americans."[10] That meant focusing on the border. It was not the Canadian Forces that would secure the border and so they got very little attention as officials juggled financial priorities.

Although there were good reasons in the wake of 9-11 to increase spending on intelligence and border security, the neglect of the Canadian Forces was not unusual in the Prime Minister's Office, in the Finance Department, and within the Liberal caucus.[11] The deputy minister of finance at the time, Kevin Lynch, a powerful Ottawa mandarin who enjoyed the respect of Paul Martin and the Prime Minister's Office, was a well-known opponent of the Defence Department. "Kevin hates defence, he hates foreign affairs," said Manley.[12] Lynch had worked for Manley when he was minister of industry and would work for him again when Manley would replace Martin as finance minister in 2002. Years earlier, when he was a senior Finance official working for the government of Prime Minister Brian Mulroney, Lynch had successfully urged draconian cuts to the defence budget. And in the mid-1990s under the Liberals, Finance Minister Paul Martin had cut the budget of the Canadian Forces by nearly a third to help eliminate the deficit. Now that there were urgent priorities in the aftermath of 9-11, priorities directly related to Canada's economy, Lynch and Martin were not about to put scarce dollars into the black hole of defence.

Although not all ministers shared this almost instinctive opposition to an increase in defence spending, many believed that the Canadian Forces were not particularly important or relevant to Canada's response to 9-11. "We were not anticipating long-term troop engagements on foreign shores," Manley explained. To be sure, the prime minister would be sending Canada's military to the Afghanistan region in some configuration for some period of time, but judging by the financial outlays to the forces in the wake of 9-11, any mission was to be modest, low cost, and short term. Early in, early out.

Scrambling at 101 Colonel By Drive

One of the blights on the landscape of downtown Ottawa is the grey, drab, 1970s-era twin tower structure at 101 Colonel By Drive on the Rideau Canal. This is National Defence Headquarters—NDHQ—as the several thousand military and civilian officials who work there know it.

NDHQ has North and South towers. The North Tower is filled almost entirely with civilian public servants. The South Tower is exclusively the domain of the Canadian Forces leadership. In the concourse between the two towers lies the National Defence Command Centre, locked behind vault-like doors. The Centre itself is on two floors and resembles, in its dramatic lighting, computer terminals, and coloured phones with direct links to other decision makers, the operations rooms that the movies have made familiar. This is the room where big operational decisions are made.

Personnel in the Department of National Defence (DND) and its associated agencies, a small fraction of whom actually work at NDHQ, make up the largest organization, public or private, in Canada—roughly one hundred thousand people spread throughout the country and around the world. It is the ultimate organizational paradox. DND is highly centralized, with all major strategic issues handled by an extraordinarily complex and labyrinthine civilian and military bureaucracy in Ottawa. At the same time it is remarkably decentralized; commanders at military bases spread across the country and on missions abroad make many seemingly less-important decisions that ultimately have great impact on individual Canadians and communities.

National Defence is the only department of the federal government that has two "deputy heads"—a civilian deputy minister, who is the chief policy adviser to the minister and financial manager of the department, as well as a chief of the defence staff (CDS), who is the head of the Canadian Forces—both of whom report to the minister of national defence. The separation of the civilian and military in this organization is pronounced and often acrimonious. This is a place where military and civilian perspectives clash, where disagreements can be as vicious and protracted as any military campaign, stifling and often grinding decision-making to a halt. The comments of one former senior DND official to an incoming minister reflected the deep internal divisions: "Civilians can never trust the military leadership, not because they are not trustworthy, but because they have a fundamentally different world view." What is important to military leaders is often irrelevant to civilians, and what is vital to civilians is frequently of no importance whatsoever to the military. This divergence in world views would play out many times, in many ways, over Canada's ongoing involvement in Afghanistan.

The sclerotic nature of the decision-making process in this complex behemoth of an organization is difficult to believe. One story tells the tale. The Pentagon, the American analog to NDHQ, was hit by one of the airplanes that was used as a guided missile on September 11, destroying a significant portion of the building and killing scores of people. Following those attacks, Canadian security personnel made clear what was obvious: Government buildings in Ottawa were at risk, and security was increased at many of the obvious targets around town. Yet it took the officials in NDHQ three years to decide that a public roadway, which passed underneath the twin towers of the building, should be closed. A decision to make that closure permanent did not occur until 2006. And to this day, NDHQ remains attached to a shopping centre through an underground passageway that is used by thousands of people each day. The pace at which military and civilian leaders protected their own building from threats was wildly at variance with the rhetoric of Canadian politicians and senior military leaders after 9-11. Both claimed again and again, in the bluntest possible language, that Canada was threatened by the same international terrorists—"detestable murderers and scumbags" to use the Chief of the Defence Staff Rick Hillier's famous phrase—that attacked the World Trade Center and the Pentagon.

In the fall of 2001 this unwieldy, slow-moving bureaucratic organization was charged with making recommendations to the minister of national defence, and ultimately to the prime minister, on what, if anything, Canada should contribute militarily to the international coalition that would ultimately topple the Taliban from power in Afghanistan.

ON OCTOBER 4, 2001, George Robertson, the Secretary-General of the North Atlantic Treaty Organization (NATO), issued an unprecedented statement. He announced that, in response to the 9-11 attacks, NATO was invoking Article 5 of the *Treaty of Washington.* This article states that any attack on a NATO member shall be interpreted as an attack on all; member states are then obligated to come to the defence of their ally. This was an historic moment for NATO—the first time in the fifty-year history of the alliance that Article 5 had been invoked. Canada, as a founding member of the alliance, was now legally committed and obligated. Ottawa could not sit this one out.

Three days later, U.S. Ambassador to Canada Paul Cellucci stated publicly that he expected the United States to ask Canada for military assistance at a forthcoming meeting of President Bush and Prime Minister Chrétien. Ottawa had been put on notice and began scrambling to cobble together a military commitment to what George Bush labelled the "War on Terror." The military leadership at NDHQ were ahead of their political leaders and had already been considering options for just such an operation.

The following day, Eggleton announced Operation Apollo, the moniker of the first American moon landing, and one obviously chosen to express solidarity with the United States in its moment of tragedy. Almost immediately, HMCS *Halifax* received orders to leave the NATO Standing Naval Force Atlantic and sail to the Arabian Sea to join the coalition fleet under Operation Enduring Freedom, the

U.S. mission to overthrow the Taliban regime in Afghanistan. A little more than a week later the *Halifax*'s sister ships, HMCS *Preserver* and HMCS *Charlottetown*, with a total complement of about 850 sailors, departed Canada to join Operation Apollo. And finally, on November 12, a fourth ship, HMCS *Vancouver*, departed San Diego, California, for southwest Asia via Pearl Harbor as part of the USS *John C. Stennis* Carrier Battle Group. *Sent out the navy first*

By early December 2001, Ottawa had secretly deployed elements of Joint Task Force 2 (JTF2), Canada's elite special forces, into southern Afghanistan.[13] This was the first time the unit had been sent abroad on a combat mission. Canada had dipped its toe into Afghanistan, even if most people didn't know it at the time.

This appeared to be the likely extent of Canada's military engagement in response to the 9-11 attacks—a relatively low-cost and low-risk, yet arguably substantive, deployment of naval assets that would be interdicting fleeing Taliban and al-Qaeda. Canada's navy would not be engaging in open warfare on the high seas. No sensibilities would be offended and it would not be politically controversial at home or abroad. And the Canadian public was unaware that ground troops, the JTF2, were on Afghan soil. Only on December 20 did Eggleton admit publicly that Canada had about forty commandos on the ground in Afghanistan.[14]

This limited response appeared to be entirely in keeping with the risk-averse managerial style of Prime Minister Chrétien. Even immediately after 9-11, when Canadians' public sympathy for their American neighbours was at an all-time high, the prime minister seemed reluctant to become—and to be seen to be—too close to George Bush. Prime Minister Tony Blair was the first to go to Washington, where he expressed Britain's sympathy and his willingness to stand in solidarity with the United States. Usually, a Canadian prime minister would have been the first, reflecting Canada's special friendship with its neighbour. In the aftermath of 9-11, it was Britain that claimed the mantle of America's best friend and it was Tony Blair who claimed a special relationship.

But appearances were deceiving. A great deal was happening behind the scenes in Ottawa in late October.

ART EGGLETON, career politician, former long-serving mayor of Toronto, holder of several senior positions in the Chrétien government, unexpectedly had become minister of defence after his predecessor, Doug Young, was defeated in the 1997 general election. Eggleton quickly settled into the difficult job, a job that politicians do not normally covet and that many view as a political graveyard.[15] He became minister just after the military had come through a thirty percent cut to its budget and the meat grinder of the infamous Somalia Inquiry. Canadian soldiers deployed in the early 1990s to Somalia had broken military discipline, torturing and killing a Somali youth. The Canadian public reacted with disbelief and then outrage, and the government empowered a commission of inquiry. The inquiry reached to the highest levels of the military command and faulted senior officers for the failure of leadership and a cover-up. The stench of Somalia was still in the air when Eggleton became minister. Morale within the defence department and military establishment was at an all-time low, as was public trust in the Canadian Forces.

Despite the political, financial, and military challenges and the low morale within the Canadian Forces, Eggleton seemed to relish the job. He travelled widely in his official capacity and even seemed to enjoy the endless ceremonies that he was required to attend.

Shortly after the Bush administration was inaugurated in January 2001, Eggleton had his first meeting with his new U.S. counterpart, the controversial secretary of defence, Donald Rumsfeld, a political veteran who had served in the same capacity in the administration of former president Gerald Ford twenty-five years before. One topic that came up for discussion was whether or not Canada would sign on to Washington's Ballistic Missile Defence (BMD) program. The BMD program had begun under the Clinton administration but when George Bush became president, he pushed hard to move the program forward.[16]

After his meeting with Rumsfeld, Eggleton joined his colleague, Foreign Minister John Manley, generally known to be among the most supportive members of the Chrétien Cabinet of the United States and the most "continentalist" in his thinking, on a visit to North American Aerospace Defence (NORAD) headquarters in Cheyenne Mountain, Colorado Springs, Colorado. NORAD, the celebrated binational aerospace defence arrangement between Canada and the United States, established in 1958, was undergoing its required periodic review. And at the time of Eggleton's and Manley's visit, BMD was being discussed as a possible add-on to the existing arrangement, an idea that was strongly supported within NDHQ.[17]

Even before the shock of 9-11, deepening Canada's role in continental security was on the agenda. And both Canada's foreign and defence ministers were predisposed to shore up their country's credentials with Washington on defence and security generally—credentials that were very shaky because of the deep cuts to the defence budget during the mid-1990s. As a result of the cost-cutting on defence in Canada, many in the Pentagon saw Canada as a "free rider" when it came to continental security. And to a significant degree that allegation was correct.

Improving Canada's stature in Washington on defence and security became an urgent political priority for the Chrétien government after 9-11. As a consequence, after NATO invoked Article 5, those members of the Cabinet who were closely attuned to the United States felt that Canada had to do more. Canada had to do better than its minimalist performance of the last decade. The United States, still reeling from the shock of the attacks, would expect nothing less from its loyal neighbour.

This new dynamic after 9-11 provided an opening for the military leadership. The occupants of the South Tower of NDHQ have always been preoccupied, almost obsessed, with their relationship with the U.S. military. The Canadian military has had a privileged position in NORAD, where it has worked closely with its American counterpart for nearly fifty years. The Canadian Forces were also increasingly dependent on their colleagues south of the border for everything from equipment to training, doctrine, and intelligence as a result of the reductions in Canadian defence spending over two decades. It is hard to exaggerate the almost seamless integration at the senior levels of the two forces, reinforced by personal networks and long-standing friend-ships. Indeed, Canada's generals and admirals tend to be more concerned about their relationships with their American counterparts than they are with their own political masters in Ottawa, a preoccupa-tion that would play out over the next few years on a variety of issues.[18]

In the autumn of 2001, the Canadian military leadership was a highly conservative, bureaucratic lot, especially when it came to recom-mending foreign deployments. The generals were deeply worried about the harmful effects of "operational tempo"—a term used in military circles to describe how the Canadian Forces were overstretched during the 1990s on various deployments to far-flung places like the former Yugoslavia, Somalia, East Timor, and Ethiopia-Eritrea. In other words, the dominant thinking held that the military, and particularly the army, needed a break, an "operational pause," a period of regeneration.

Yet the conservative military leadership recognized that the strate-gic environment had changed radically in the aftermath of the attacks against the World Trade Center and the Pentagon. Worries about overstretch faded into the background, at least for the moment. The leadership at NDHQ felt that Canada had to do more. A naval deployment and a handful of special forces were not enough to show the Americans that we were with them in their moment of crisis. Chief of the Defence Staff Ray Henault and his deputy, Vice Admiral Greg Maddison, certainly didn't think Canada could sustain a significant army presence in Afghanistan for the long term, particularly in a combat role. But they were more than prepared to recommend and even advocate a short-term ground commitment—early in, early out.[19]

For both the military planners and some of the key politicians in Ottawa, through the fall of 2001, the issue became not so much whether, but what type of army deployment—boots on the ground, in the vernacular—Canada would send to Afghanistan. And the day after Remembrance Day, November 12, Eggleton began preparing the public. He told the press that Canadian ground troops would be going to Afghanistan, but for a maximum of six months. The minister indicated that one thousand soldiers from the Princess Patricia's Canadian Light Infantry had been put on forty-eight hours' notice to join with four thousand of their British counterparts on a mission to Afghanistan. In fact, the Canadian army had been told as far back as early October to prepare for a deployment to Afghanistan.

The mission that Eggleton had in mind was known as the International Security Assistance Force (ISAF), a UN-mandated operation that fell somewhere between combat and peacekeeping. The minister described ISAF as "not an offensive mission, not a front-line mission. This is a stabilization mission to assist in opening corridors for humanitarian assistance."[20] He went on to say: "These people are not intended to go in under a full-conflict situation. And if it ever came to full conflict, they'd probably be taken out."[21] Eggleton thought of Canada's contribution to this force as an application of the "early in, early out" doctrine that had shaped recent deployments in Macedonia, Eritrea, and East Timor.[22]

For the politicians in Ottawa, ISAF was a comfortable political resting place. It was shaping up as a European-dominated mission, confined to the relative calm and stability of Kabul, the capital city of Afghanistan in the northeast of the country. It was to be humanitarian in its initial focus. Over time, it would evolve to provide security for the Afghan Transitional Authority that was being set up by the international community, after the signing of the Bonn Accords in December 2001 that laid out a framework for a post-Taliban Afghanistan. Canada had participated in the Bonn Conference and had pledged to help Afghanistan after the Taliban was overthrown. ISAF was not a combat mission. The war-fighting would remain in the hands of the American military hundreds of miles away, in the south of the country, which was trying to eliminate the last redoubts of the Taliban and al-Qaeda.

Yet Canada would get credit for having a significant number of boots on the ground. And these boots on the ground would be in the more "traditional" Canadian role of providing humanitarian relief to a war-weary population. It would be a dangerous assignment, to be sure, but the casualties would be limited. And there would be no awkward pictures on television of Canadian troops fighting and dying alongside the Americans. It seemed like a mission that was tailor-made for Canada and for a risk-averse Liberal government that wanted the appearance of independence and some distance from Washington, even while it showed solidarity with the Americans after 9-11. The military and political leadership were, this time, in agreement.

Then the ground shifted underneath Eggleton. Word started to come from the British, who were pulling the ISAF mission together, that this was really a European operation and that Canadian participation was not overly welcome. *The Globe and Mail* editorial of January 2, 2002, summed up the frustration of Eggleton and his generals:

> Meanwhile, Canada continues to wait by the phone for its invitation to participate, even as soldiers from Germany, France, Spain, Italy, the Netherlands, Denmark, Austria, Greece, Sweden, Norway, Finland and Romania arrive in Afghanistan to prepare for the 4,500-troop [ISAF] deployment.[23]

Two days later, the *National Post* reported that senior officials in Ottawa were privately furious with Opposition critics and military analysts who claimed Canada's allies were poised to reject Canadian troops because the country's military was ill equipped and could not sustain a long-term presence in Afghanistan.[24] Such talk would have embarrassed the military leadership. But more important to both the generals and the politicians was the emerging prospect that Canada might be shut out of a ground role in Afghanistan altogether. Canada wanted in. What were a government and a military to do that wanted to impress Washington with their commitment to the War on Terror?

The British finally asked Canada for an immediate deployment of two hundred engineers and three hundred infantry troops in three months' time. The request was treated with equal parts derision and offence at NDHQ, confirming their worst fears that the international community—or at least the Europeans—didn't see Canada as up to the task militarily. And as one former senior defence official pointed out, the Canadian Forces didn't even have two hundred engineers to spare for ISAF.[25] Eggleton finally conceded in early January that there was no acceptable role for Canada in ISAF. "A number of European countries said, 'Well, this is a European-led mission; this is a European kind of mission,'" Eggleton explained. "So I think quite clearly, European politics became a part of this decision-making process.[26]

Canada's troops would not be heading to Kabul in a humanitarian and stabilization role. But there was another route to Afghanistan—this one via Tampa, Florida—that now came to the fore.

From Tampa to Kandahar

During the protracted discussions about Canada's possible involvement in ISAF, a handful of Canadian Forces officers set up shop at U.S. Central Command Headquarters in Tampa, Florida. This was the command centre for all American military operations in the Afghanistan theatre. The Canadians were invited by the Pentagon, which was seeking to build support among friends for a military contribution to the American-led effort in Afghanistan—and ultimately Iraq.

At about the time negotiations for a Canadian contribution to ISAF collapsed, Canadian officers in Tampa began to report to Ottawa that the Americans wanted Canadian ground forces in southern Afghanistan with the United States military. This was new. Up to this point there had been no such indications from Washington. Neither Rumsfeld nor Secretary of State Colin Powell had called Eggleton or Manley to request Canadian troops. As Manley recounted, "We were getting messages from our guys in Tampa saying the Americans were

asking countries to 'Put your hands up, are you with us or not?'" Given
these unexpected reports from Tampa, Manley decided to take the
initiative to find out what precisely the U.S. wanted:

> I remember phoning Colin Powell from the Empress Hotel in
> Victoria to say, "What are you asking us to do exactly?" He
> [Powell] said, "Well, what do you mean?" And I said, "I'm told
> we are being asked to put forces on the ground and we want to
> know how many, what's the mission etc.?" He said, "I'm not
> aware of any of that." Then he [Powell] circled back to me a few
> days later and said, "This is just outrageous, I've told them [the
> Pentagon] 'I don't want our allies to be asked to do something
> without me in the loop.'"[27]

It wasn't the first or the last time that Rumsfeld and the White
House would keep Colin Powell out of the loop.

Despite the confusion in Washington, the message back to Ottawa
from Tampa was clear. The Pentagon wanted the Canadian army
alongside the Americans in Kandahar even if the secretary of state was
unaware of the request. And Canada wanted in. Former U.S. ambassador to Canada Paul Cellucci recalled Art Eggleton's speaking to him
about this. "I got a call on my cellphone from Art Eggleton during the
build up in Afghanistan. The message was 'We want to be part of this.'
It was not quite begging, but …"[28]

As a result, a proposal for Canada to send a battle group of eight
hundred soldiers to Kandahar to fight the Taliban and al-Qaeda with
the Americans went from the military chain of command to Eggleton,
who in turn recommended it to the prime minister and the Cabinet.
The proposal was immediately accepted, especially since participation
in ISAF was no longer an option. The military insisted that the United
States wanted Canadian troops on the ground and the government
continued to think that Canada needed to show greater support for
the American effort in Afghanistan. The choice the Cabinet made

was neither the best option nor the least offensive option; it was the only remaining option on the table.

The Kandahar deployment signalled a major shift in political and military thinking in Ottawa. It would be the first combat mission for the Canadian Forces since the Korean War, fifty years earlier. The chief of the defence staff made the change explicit: "We're not there to do traditional peacekeeping. We're there to bring security and stability to the region."[29] From the perspective of senior military officers, this was a long-awaited opportunity. The mission would allow the Canadian Forces to show the public that they were a well-trained fighting force, and not just blue beret–wearing peacekeepers. This image of peacekeepers was not only deeply ingrained in the public, but it was also wildly popular. That it did not fit well with Canada's history did not much matter to public opinion. More to the point, the mantle of peacekeeper grated on many in the military who saw themselves first and foremost as a combat-capable fighting force. This was the chance they had been waiting for.

Ottawa promised Washington that the battle group, along with a handful of transport aircraft to support them from a base in the Arabian Gulf, would be in theatre by February, and would remain in place for six months. Clearly this was not "early in," but it was certainly "early out." And true to their word, the Canadian Forces managed to meet this commitment by February 22, 2002.

The first Canadian combat mission in fifty years proved largely uneventful, with one notable and tragic exception. On April 18, 2002, a group of Canadian soldiers were engaged in a live-fire night training exercise at Tarnak Farms, the former home of Osama bin Laden, when an American F-16 fighter aircraft mistakenly dropped a bomb on the troops, killing four Canadians and wounding several others.[30]

There were a few combat engagements as well, notably operations Anaconda, Harpoon, and Torii, but by and large it was a relatively routine mission for the Canadian Forces. By the time they arrived in Kandahar four months after the American invasion, southern

Afghanistan had been largely pacified—at least for the time being. And when Eggleton's replacement, John McCallum, visited the battle group at the end of their six-month mission in July, the soldiers were clearly tired and ready to go home, but also somewhat disappointed that they hadn't seen more action.

So ended Canada's troop presence in Afghanistan. Or so most people thought. The naval assets would continue their efforts in the region for a while, and the air force would continue a maritime surveillance and coalition troop supply role in the region, but there were no plans for the Canadian army to remain engaged in Afghanistan. Canada in fact had no Afghanistan policy or plan beyond the summer of 2002, at least not with respect to the involvement of the Canadian army.[31] It was as if the decision makers in Ottawa thought Afghanistan—a country in the throes of war for three decades, devastated by waves of fighting and civil war, ripped apart by factional feuding, its roads and infrastructure devastated, its schools closed, its health services compromised, and its women sequestered for five years—would somehow put itself back together again without a major international troop presence to provide ongoing security and assistance in the lengthy reconstruction process. Or perhaps they felt that Canada had done its part and could sit the rest out, having satisfied the overriding priority of showing support for the Americans in their hour of need.

As the fall of 2002 approached, the period of operational pause and regeneration for the Canadian army that the leadership at NDHQ had repeatedly demanded seemed to be on the horizon. But a trip to Washington in January 2003 by Canada's new defence minister would upset those plans—and would ultimately draw the Canadian Forces even more deeply into Afghanistan.

TWO

"WE DON'T KNOW ANYTHING ABOUT THIS COUNTRY"

When officials in Ottawa made the decision in the winter of 2002 to send Canadian ground forces to Kandahar, the heartland of the Taliban in Afghanistan, they did so with their eyes on Washington. Afghanistan, distant and remote, could have been anywhere. What was the country like? How did its history matter to the challenges Canadian forces would face as they went "early in, early out"? As Ken Calder, then the assistant deputy minister of policy in the Department of Defence, would say in an unguarded moment in 2003, "We don't know anything about this country."

Afghanistan may have been remote and largely unknown to Canadian officials, but at one time, it was at the crossroads of the world. For millennia, armies marched across Afghanistan on their way to somewhere else, occasionally stopping and staying, bringing with them their cultures, their languages, and their traditions. If there were a guestbook in Kabul and Kandahar that had survived the centuries, it would show the mark of almost every great military leader in recorded history. Afghanistan attracted Alexander the Great, the Persians, the Arabs, Genghis Khan, the Moguls, Marco Polo, the British, the Russians, and now, the United States and NATO, with its partners. The Canadian Forces stand in a very long line.

The Afghans whom Canadian soldiers would meet are the descendants of people who have lived in this region for thousands of years.

Most tribes, although not all, come from one of seven major ethnic groups: the Pashtun, Tajik, Uzbek, Turkmen, Baluchi, Nuristani, and Hazara.[1] The Pashtun, who live largely in the south and east, are the largest group—constituting more than forty percent of the population—and many identify themselves primarily by their tribe or their clan within this broad grouping. Kandahar, where Canadian soldiers were going, is heavily Pashtun and the heart of modern Afghanistan.

Until the world's sea passages were discovered, Afghanistan was an essential highway from central Asia to the Indian subcontinent. It was only after the great powers began to circle the globe by sea that Afghanistan changed from a critical pathway to a buffer zone at the outer limits of imperial ambition.[2] Even today, it continues to be one of the fault lines of global politics.

The name "Afghanistan" emerged about seven hundred years ago, but it was used largely to describe the Pashtun tribes in the south. It was not until Ahmed Shah, a Pashtun from the Durrani tribal network, forcefully unified the tribes of Afghanistan into a single political entity in 1747 and established his capital in Kandahar that the Afghanistan that we know today was created. Modern Afghanistan was born in Kandahar; the capital moved to Kabul much later. From 1747 to 1978, with one brief exception, all of Afghanistan's rulers were Durrani Pashtuns, and from 1818 to 1978, all were members of the Mohammedzai clan within the Durrani tribe. Even under the leadership of the Durranis, the writ of the central government in Kabul never ran far, and it never superseded the tribal structure in the south of Afghanistan. The tribes and clans remain the sinews that bind Afghan society together.

The Afghanistan of today began fewer than a hundred years ago, in 1919, with the accession to power of a reformist ruler, King Amanullah, whose ruined palace still stands in Kabul. Dragging Afghans with him, he slashed at tradition and convention. He unveiled women, permitted women to travel abroad for higher education, ended the right of parents to betroth children against their will, introduced a secular code of law, and, in the ultimate insult to the tribal elders, dismissed government employees who had more than one wife. The rebellion was not long in coming; within a decade, Amanullah was gone and reform slowed to a snail's pace when it was not reversed altogether. Change was concentrated in Afghanistan's cities, particularly in Kabul, while the Pashtun south remained largely untouched and resistant, embedded in its rural, peasant agricultural traditions.

In the twentieth century, change came slowly to Afghanistan. The first school for girls opened in 1921, when Amanullah was on the throne. And seven years later, the first group of Afghan women left to study in Turkey, then in the throes of its own revolution. Only in 1959 did purdah, the screening of women behind walls, become optional and, in the next few years, women enrolled in university and entered the workforce and government. Women graduated from medical school at Kabul University and two women became senators.

The changes in Kabul and other large cities barely touched the rural south, where life continued as it had for generations. Kandahar, the urban centre of the south, lagged badly behind Kabul. Today, many of the villages of Kandahar province look exactly as they did hundreds of years ago, with their low mud-brick buildings and no electricity or clean well water. Villagers make bricks from a mould, the way their ancestors did, and struggle to eke out a living in a countryside that has been laid waste by thirty years of war. The lush pomegranates, the juicy grapes, and the glistening dates that Kandahar once exported are now harder to grow in the agricultural fields that have been devastated by a five-year drought and harder to export on the cratered and insecure roads.

In the Pashtun south, where the Canadian Forces were going, tribal leadership remains important. Although thirty years of fighting has weakened the tribal elders, they remain a defining characteristic of social and economic life among the Pashtun. The elders have always understood the importance of an Afghan state as an ally against competing tribes. It was not until late in the nineteenth century that Afghan rulers began to consolidate the power of the central government and extend its reach. Even as the state grew, it left tribal elders in positions of singular influence and intervened very little except to mediate disputes. State and tribe lived alongside each other, in uneasy cohabitation. "Tribes, however rebellious they may be, need a state but not too strong a state, to act as referee, to maintain intramural conflicts at a low level, to avoid the creation of a vacuum that could pit them against each other outside their 'solidarity space,' and simply to protect business," argues Olivier Roy, an experienced interpreter of Afghanistan. "Smugglers need borders, thieves need trade, highway robbers need highways—tribes need states."[3]

Afghan Fighters and the Soviet Invader

Afghan tribes have always been able to put aside their rivalries and join together to fight a foreign interloper that invades their country. On December 28, 1979, the Soviet army rolled into Kabul, six years after the Afghan Communist Party had overthrown the king of Afghanistan and the country had become a republic. After a second coup and the execution of the president, Soviet forces moved into Afghanistan—as they had moved into Prague and into Budapest decades earlier—to preserve a client regime. But Kabul was not Prague and it was not Budapest. The Russian forces in Afghanistan, almost from the moment they arrived, met with fierce resistance from the mujahideen, a force of tribal leaders who came together from across their usually deep divisions to rid themselves of the foreigner who was suddenly among them.

How did the mujahideen prevail against the overwhelming conventional superiority, against the well-oiled armour and infantry of the Soviet army?[4] How did they defeat a superpower?

The flexibility and suppleness of the mujahideen were an important part of their success. Afghan fighters were not organized in a centralized or hierarchical structure. Their loose, decentralized structure that gave autonomy to local leaders in their own areas would look bizarre to a "modern" Western military mind but, paradoxically, very familiar to a European general in nineteenth-century Europe. Traditional tribal leaders think of war as ongoing, semi-permanent activity that is, however, strictly limited in time and space. Warfare respects privacy, women and children in the villages, and the harvest season, when fighting ceases altogether. Negotiation and fighting go hand in hand, since war is not total, but a principal form of competition, a struggle for status and standing, for position, for pride and honour.[5] It is a strictly limited activity, with rules and purposes that are well understood. In this context, warfare and negotiation are handmaidens one to the other.

These principles of warfare are only put aside when a foreigner invades and tribal leaders come together to fight in jihad against the infidels. Afghans fight in jihad not to defend the state but to defend the faithful, and they fight to the death. Even in the midst of jihad, however, their operational principles of tribal warfare stood them in good stead when they faced Soviet forces.

The Soviet invasion was swift and successful, but invading Afghanistan has always been easy. Many have come, but few have stayed very long. The Soviet army fared no better than its predecessors. Tribal leaders collaborated to use tactics of traditional tribal warfare to cut Soviet supply lines, harass and terrorize Soviet troops, and break their will and spirit. Afghan fighters generally fought in their own territory, on terrain that they knew best. Local commanders had complete autonomy to make decisions and the flexibility to move with lightning speed. The mujahideen had no central command structure, no chain of command, and almost no division of labour. Each clan leader, each tribal leader, attacked Soviet supply lines and installations, and generally most were able to sustain the fighting over a long period using their own resources and those of the local population.[6]

Afghan fighters regularly used ambushes to pick off Soviet supply convoys and troops. The mujahideen led more than ten thousand ambushes of Soviet forces between 1985 and 1987, attacking at night to achieve maximum impact, using only machine guns, grenades, and sniper fire, and then retreating under the cover of darkness back to rocky and mountainous terrain that they knew intimately. These fighters were formidable.

Despite their far more sophisticated weaponry, Soviet forces were never able to stop this hit-and-run insurgent warfare.

Afghan fighters had an enormous local advantage. They knew the terrain and the mountains that provided safe haven. They had limited objectives: They needed only to harass, terrorize, and kill enough Soviet forces to break their morale. Afghan fighters were also fiercely motivated, far more so than their adversary. "We intended to fight to the last man," one mujahideen explained, "and they didn't."[7] And finally, they were fighting against a foreign occupier that broke the unwritten rules of war in Afghanistan. The tide turned for the mujahideen when Soviet forces began to use close air strikes to repel attacks, and killed women and children and devastated villages.[8] The killing of women and children in the villages violated the most important norms of the Pashtun code of honour and infuriated tribal leaders.

Once Soviet forces broke these taboos, it was much easier for local tribal leaders to overcome long-standing rivalries and collaborate in warfare against the hated foreigner. Soviet attacks that incidentally— not deliberately, but accidentally—killed women and children in their villages galvanized the Afghan opposition. The Soviet experience should tell a cautionary tale to Canada and its NATO allies.

It was not only what mujahideen fighters did inside Afghanistan that mattered. They were extraordinarily successful in internationalizing their struggle against the Soviet Union. Outsiders all around Afghanistan poked their fingers into the struggle and supported one or several tribal leaders.

Interference came most easily from Pakistan, home to more than sixty Pashtun tribes and four hundred clans and subclans. The arbitrary line—the Durand Line—that the British drew in 1893 to create Afghanistan split the Pashtuns. Today, fifteen million Pashtun live in Afghanistan and almost twice as many—about twenty-eight million— live in Pakistan, mostly in the border areas, where they make up about fifteen percent of the population. The literacy rate is about ten percent, there is little opportunity other than subsistence farming, and the region is the centre of smuggling across a border where thousands cross both ways every day.[9]

The frontier between the two countries has little meaning. Pakistan considers the Durand Line its internationally recognized border, but it has never been recognized by Afghanistan. It is clan and tribal loyalties that take pride of place for the Pashtun, not lines drawn by imperial powers. As early as the 1950s, Kabul insisted that the Pashtun tribal belt just inside Pakistan's border should be given the choice of independence, joining Afghanistan, or remaining within Pakistan. Afghanistan has more than once supported "greater Pashtunistan," an idea that Pakistan considers traitorous. Supporting the mujahideen and then the Taliban, Pakistan's leaders thought, would end these claims by ensuring a friendly and grateful government in Kabul. They would be sadly disappointed.

The Pakistan Intelligence Services (ISI), drawing on the close linkages among the Pashtun tribes on both sides of the border, began to provide funds, weapons, and training on their side of the border, just behind the Afghanistan frontier. This support grew as the insurgency deepened and thousands and thousands of fighters were trained in camps just inside the Pakistani border and then sent back to fight the Soviet invader.

Pakistan was not the only neighbour that provided money, training, and fighters. Iran provided financial support and allegedly some training to the Hazaras in the north, who are Shi'a Muslims. Tajikistan provided some funding for the Tajiks in the central and northeast regions of Afghanistan. Saudi Arabia provided extensive funding and support to those mujahideen who were militant Sunni Muslims, sympathetic to Wahhabi teachings. Egypt gave assistance as well to support Muslim fighters struggling against the infidels. Afghanistan was a very busy neighbourhood.

Help also came from outside the immediate region. Following the age-old maxim that "the enemy of my enemy is my friend," or at least my temporary friend, the United States, working directly through the CIA and indirectly through Pakistan, provided extensive financial assistance and supplied weapons to those who were fighting the Soviet Union. This assistance was important in strengthening the capacity of the mujahideen to train, to recruit, and to learn how to use new equipment. Although it is a matter of intense controversy, some experts insist that it was when the United States began to supply large quantities of shoulder-held Stinger missiles in 1986 that the tide of the war turned. The Stingers could hit Soviet aircraft, and they were so effective that they forced the Soviets to halt their helicopter flights during the day, flights that were essential to supply beleaguered troops. It was only a matter of time until the Soviet Union decided to withdraw its forces. The humiliating retreat home in 1989 through Uzbekistan, with nothing to show for almost a decade of spent blood and treasure, was the first nail in the coffin of the Soviet Union.

The Taliban: Rent-a-Space

Once Soviet forces had withdrawn from Afghanistan, Afghan warlords descended into a vicious, brutal civil war that ended only when the Taliban swept out of Kandahar to conquer most of Afghanistan in 1996. Outsiders were puzzled by the rapid eruption of fighting among Afghan leaders once the hated "foreigner" was gone. That was in part because they misread the capacity and resilience of Afghan fighters against the Soviet presence as a desire to reorder society, to change the fundamentals. This it certainly was not.

The mujahideen had fought the way they always fought. They had kept their camps outside their villages and towns to protect their families, their women and children. The central institutions in Kabul were not really in their sightlines during the war; they were focused on Soviet forces. Even during the war, they never levied taxes to pay soldiers or buy arms, and they did not see themselves as a government-in-waiting.[10] State-building was never their project, especially among the ethnic leaders who were not Pashtun and always distrusted the central government. The central government was separate, distant, and in a deep way, peripheral to the lives of many of the Afghan fighters. It is not surprising that Kabul, the capital of Afghanistan, was almost completely destroyed, first in the civil war among the warlords and the mujahideen, and then again in the fighting between the Taliban and the warlords from the north and the west; neither cared very much about the capital city. Afghan society has always been radically decentralized, with strong ethnic groups and tribes in different parts of the country. At best, ethnic leaders who were not Pashtun took senior positions in the military and the bureaucracy and tolerated the centralizing tendencies of Afghan kings as a necessary evil to constrain continual violence.[11]

The civil war that followed the Soviet withdrawal was relentless, fuelled by a booming and very profitable illegal trade in opium. The war engulfed Kabul in fierce and bloody house-to-house fighting that inflicted thousands of casualties on despairing civilians and reduced whole neighbourhoods to rubble.

Out of this chaos came the Taliban from the south, originally a small group of students, or *talib*, followers of Mullah Omar who taught at a *madrassa*, a religious school, in a small village near Kandahar. Gangs were then terrorizing the population in the city, and some inhabitants turned to the small group of *talib* for help after a woman was raped by local bandits. The Taliban restored order and quickly took control of Kandahar with the support of a population grateful for the order that they imposed.

The Taliban were militant Islamists who wanted to purify Afghanistan of its corruption and violence. They wanted to change Afghan society. Very quickly they imposed order and an intense observance of Islamic law in Kandahar, and then looked beyond their base to the rest of Afghanistan.

Many Taliban leaders had close contacts with senior officials in Pakistani intelligence who provided funding, weapons, and training.

The Taliban had a steady stream of recruits through the *madrassas* that trained their students and the village mullahs who taught and preached on the western frontier of Pakistan. When the Taliban needed fighters, the *madrassas* in Peshawar shut down for a few days and students streamed across the border.[12] The Taliban were also connected personally to the Saudi intelligence services; some had been students in a vocational school run by the chief of staff to Prince Turki bin Faisal, the head of Saudi intelligence. To supplement those sources of funding, the Taliban collected taxes from the poppy growers in exchange for keeping the roads open for export. In the next two years the Taliban took Herat and Jalalabad, and in September 1996, the Taliban finally captured Kabul and consolidated their power everywhere but the north and the west.

Afghanistan had a new government with its seat of power not in Kabul, but in Kandahar, as it had been long ago. Mullah Omar rarely left his compound; the Taliban were largely uninterested in the business of governing. Their overwhelming preoccupation was theology, not state-building in Kabul. "The Taliban," argued Ahmed Rashid, "are essentially caught between a tribal society which they try to ignore and the need for a state structure which they refuse to establish."[13] They made their decisions in small closed councils around Mullah Omar while the state structure in Kabul decayed. Ministries stood half empty, with little staff, buildings in ruins, pale shadows of what they had once been.

The Taliban brought with them a streak of puritanical and militant Islam, a militancy that was unfamiliar and uncomfortable to most Afghans.[14] In the eastern part of Afghanistan, militant Islamists had attempted to suppress *Pashtunwali*, the Pashtun tribal code, but they met with passive resistance from Pashtuns, who saw no conflict between the Islam they practised and their code of honour. Islamic courts had always accommodated tribal codes in the south, understanding well the deep attachment to Pashtun traditions and practices. When the Taliban first appeared in the heartland of Pashtun society, they were welcomed as leaders who would end the all-out fighting, provide order and protection, and end the violence in the cities. It was not their Islam that was attractive, but their capacity to police the streets. But with that ability came one of the most militant forms of Islam anywhere in the Muslim world. "The Taliban," Rashid concluded, "are poorly tutored in Islamic and Afghan history, knowledge of the Shari'a and the Koran and the political and theoretical developments in the Muslim world during the twentieth century ... They have given Islam ... a new face and a new identity ... one that refuses to accept any compromise or political system except their own."[15]

For the women of Afghanistan, a long, dark night had begun. Laws were passed forcing women to wear burqas in public, and they were beaten if they dressed "immodestly," if an ankle showed beneath a skirt. They were denied education, and were forbidden to work outside the home. Some women were stoned to death for alleged sexual misconduct. Women in the cities were especially hard hit, as they were more likely to be educated and to work outside their home. Families were reduced to starvation because women were forced to stay at home, and many neighbourhood clinics and schools closed. Forty percent of the doctors, about half the civil service, and approximately seventy percent of teachers were women. Children were forbidden to sing and to play music, and were not allowed to do what Afghans have done for as long as they can remember: They were not allowed to fly their kites.[16]

Dr. Sima Simar, the first minister of Women's Affairs after the Taliban were overthrown, remembered this black period as a catastrophe, redeemed only by the astonishing courage of Afghan women who educated girls in home schools, often risking their lives, and who cared for the sick secretly.[17] Afghan women, she recalled, were left largely to their own devices. Now that the streets were quiet, the world largely lost interest. Few took note of the ruthless oppression of women, and even fewer stayed to help. Most of the world's governments turned their attention elsewhere now that the Soviets were gone and the fighting had largely died down. International organizations that were providing assistance negotiated long and hard with the Taliban, trying to get the edicts that excluded women from participating in their programs reversed. The Taliban were implacable. Most UN agencies and non-governmental organizations left, unwilling to compromise on women's participation but deeply worried about how the widows and orphans—there were thousands in Afghanistan after years of fighting—would survive. By 1998, almost all "outsiders" were gone.

Under this cover of inattention and indifference from most of the world, Osama bin Laden strengthened his ties with the Taliban's leadership. Pressed by both the United States and Saudi Arabia, Sudan expelled bin Laden, who then came back to Afghanistan, first to Jalalabad and then to the Tarnak Farms just outside Kandahar. Bin Laden had been deeply involved with the mujahideen as they fought to expel the godless Soviet foreigner, and seeking refuge a decade later, he returned, not surprisingly, to Afghanistan.

From a cave in Tora Bora, bin Laden first declared war on the United States in August 1996.[18] Mullah Omar, who did not know bin Laden and had no quarrel with the United States or with Saudi Arabia—he received financial support from the Saudi royal family— was alarmed by the declaration of war and sent a delegation to Tora Bora. Bin Laden's attacks on the Saudi royal family put Mullah Omar in a very difficult position. He had promised Prince Turki bin Faisal of Saudi Arabia that bin Laden would cause no trouble.

The Taliban hoped that bin Laden would help to rebuild the shattered infrastructure in Afghanistan and finance construction. In a fateful decision, they offered bin Laden their protection if he would refrain from attacking Arab governments. Bin Laden agreed. This was the beginning of a complex mutually beneficial relationship between the Taliban and al-Qaeda. After the attack on the USS *Cole* in October 2000, recruits and funds from the Gulf flowed to al-Qaeda, and bin Laden was able to keep a constant stream of funding flowing to the Taliban.

Mullah Omar consistently refused to hand over bin Laden to the Saudis or the United States. Again and again, he referred to the Pashtun tribal code that forbade the betrayal of guests.[19] In effect, the Taliban rented space in Afghanistan to al-Qaeda and provided protection in exchange for financial support. It proved to be a Faustian bargain.

There is irony here. Mullah Omar could not have understood that the ascetic and pious bin Laden was working to provoke an invasion of Afghanistan. Bin Laden had declared war on the United States, had attacked its embassies in Africa, had blown up a U.S. warship, all in the hope of provoking an American invasion of Afghanistan that he thought would suck the lifeblood of the United States as it had of the Soviet Union. He thought that the United States would break apart, as had the Soviet Union when its forces were defeated by Afghan fighters. Washington did not respond, and so bin Laden concluded that he would have to perpetrate an outrage to get the reaction that he wanted.[20] The planning for the attacks on the World Trade Center and the Pentagon began soon after.

Bin Laden achieved his objective but not the outcome that he wanted. After 9-11, Washington decided that it would fight a proxy war. It sent U.S. special forces to work with the Northern Alliance, a loose coalition of tribal leaders in the north and the west of Afghanistan, the traditional rivals of the Pashtun. The special forces did try to find Pashtun who opposed the Taliban. Many Pashtun were appalled by the brutality of the Taliban, by its puritanical interpretation of Islam, and by its strict code and its militancy, and there were signs of revolt against the Taliban in the Pashtun heartland as early as 1997. They were nevertheless deeply suspicious of the Northern Alliance and few came forward. After weeks of bombing from the air, the Northern Alliance, working closely with U.S. special forces, defeated the Taliban forces. Within two months, the Taliban were gone and Osama bin Laden and what remained of al-Qaeda fled to the mountains for sanctuary.

What seemed an easy victory fought with local allies would come back to haunt the United States and Afghanistan. "Great historical transformations are always bought dearly," wrote Jacob Burckhardt, the distinguished historian of the nineteenth century, "often after one has already thought that one got them at a bargain price."[21] This victory was deceptively easy. The United States had routed the Taliban and now faced "only" the stabilization and reconstruction of Afghanistan. Ignorance and arrogance were both at play in this judgment. The invasion was the easy part, as the Soviet experience had shown. Overthrowing governments was not difficult work. The Taliban had been deeply unpopular outside the southern provinces—and even in the south—because of their rigidity, repression, and the violence that they inflicted on their own citizens. Few mourned when they were defeated. "The Taliban had promised peace," insisted a village elder, "instead they have given us nothing but war."[22] Sustaining a successor government was an entirely different matter, as was reducing the violence and starting the process of economic, physical, social, and political reconstruction. The United States and its partners had no plans for the transition. Their focus was squarely on al-Qaeda and bin Laden. Yet in the wake of the deceptively easy victory, coalition forces now found themselves responsible for Afghanistan, its governance, its economy, and its security. It was at this moment in Afghanistan's history that the Canadian Forces would first come to Kandahar.

THREE

STAY THE COURSE

"It's Defence," uttered an incredulous John McCallum over the phone to his chief of staff just minutes after being told that he would be made Canada's thirty-fifth minister of national defence. At the time, McCallum was the junior minister responsible for regulating Canada's banks. Twenty-four hours later, on May 26, 2002, McCallum was sworn in as the new civilian head of the armed forces at the most crucial period for the defence and security of Canada in fifty years. Eight months after 9-11, for the first time in decades, Canada's leaders were worrying about security at home. Concurrently, the Canadian military had eight hundred troops in a combat mission in Afghanistan and several ships in the waters in the surrounding region.

Prime Minister Chrétien had dismissed Defence Minister Art Eggleton to punish him for giving an untendered consulting contract to a former girlfriend. That same day, Sunday, May 26, 2002, McCallum received a mysterious phone call from Chrétien's chief of staff, Percy Downe, asking him to come to Ottawa, to bring a dark suit, and to wait in his apartment for further instructions. Under no circumstances was McCallum to tell anyone why he was in the nation's capital.

That the fifty-two-year-old former economics professor was in line for a senior ministerial portfolio was no surprise. Already a national figure in his own right, McCallum was recruited as a star candidate for the Liberals in the election of 2000. After seven years in power, the

Liberal government needed some new thinking or at least some new faces. McCallum would bring new life and spruce up the increasingly tired and shopworn Chrétien administration.

McCallum had been a professor, then a dean, and then the chief economist at the Royal Bank of Canada. He was a frequent economic commentator in newspapers, on television, and on radio. A senior Cabinet post made sense, with perhaps the finance portfolio as the most obvious fit. But the position of Minister of Defence made no sense to anyone, including McCallum. Not to mention that there were many other more logical choices for the job.

Trade Minister Pierre Pettigrew had been in government for six years, had held two international portfolios, and once worked at NATO. John Manley, now the deputy prime minister and de facto head of Canada–U.S. relations, a long-serving minister and Chrétien favourite, was considered a steady hand within government circles and was as attuned to the United States as anyone in Liberal ranks. Health Minister Anne McLellan was known to be a strong voice on national security and sympathetic to the military, in part because she had a large army base in her riding in Alberta. Finally, there was the tough-minded David Collenette, another Toronto-area minister and Chrétien confidant. Collenette had been the prime minister's first defence minister.

There was, however, a problem with moving any of these people to NDHQ. Each was a powerful, competent politician in an important portfolio, managing delicate domestic files. Shifting one of them meant backfilling that vacancy with someone from another senior slot—in short, a full-scale Cabinet shuffle.

Chrétien wanted to avoid the political fallout that came from a large-scale Cabinet shuffle. At the time, maintaining the appearance of a stable, well-functioning government was paramount. In the spring of 2002, Chrétien's hold on the prime minister's chair was under daily assault from Finance Minister Paul Martin's supporters, who were lobbying hard for a transition. The prime minister wanted a quick fix for his government's latest problem, one that gave no openings to his opponents.

McCallum, on paper the most impressive and well known of the junior ministers, was the logical candidate to move to the front benches, regardless of his lack of political experience, not to mention the absence of credentials in defence or international policy. The plan was surgical—pull out Eggleton and drop in McCallum—a clean move with limited intra-governmental fallout. And another simmering problem in Chrétien's Cabinet could be dealt with simultaneously. Don Boudria, the minister of public works, was also in the middle of an ethics scandal.[1] The same quick, surgical approach was used with Boudria; he was demoted in a one-to-one switch with House Leader Ralph Goodale.

Defence and foreign policy considerations were not at all on Chrétien's mind when he made his decision to replace Eggleton. That became clear when, just prior to the swearing in at Rideau Hall, the prime minister asked McCallum if he had any military background. McCallum replied, "Well, I served as a cadet for two years when I was in high school." To which Chrétien replied enthusiastically, "That is why I make you my minister of defence." And off they went to the Governor General's residence to consummate the appointment.

The Friendly Professors

The first phone call John McCallum received on his first day on the job at NDHQ was from Bill Graham, the foreign minister. Graham had replaced John Manley a few months earlier. A sudden resignation by Industry Minister Brian Tobin had triggered the last major Cabinet shuffle of Chrétien's prime ministership and led to Manley's appointment as deputy prime minister.

That day, Graham was calling from abroad to congratulate the defence minister on his appointment and to express his desire to meet soon. The call marked the beginning of an excellent professional relationship between the two men most responsible for Canada's role in the world. As Graham would later tell McCallum, "You [the Canadian

Forces] are the principal instrument of my policy, yet our departments are often at odds on the big issues, so you and I and our staffs have to work together closely and get along if we want to get anything done around here." It wasn't long before McCallum, ever the economist, would deferentially reiterate the point to Graham in meetings: "Yes, Bill, we are derivative of you."

McCallum's attitude toward Graham was anathema to some of the senior military officials. They felt that his deference undermined their standing with their opposite numbers in the Foreign Ministry. But McCallum wanted to build and maintain a strong relationship with Graham, since he expected that they would have to work together to manage the very tough issues that were likely coming down the track.[2]

It was not always the case that the defence and foreign ministers got on well. For instance, Lloyd Axworthy, Chrétien's foreign minister in the late 1990s, and Art Eggleton had quite different backgrounds, agendas, and perspectives on the world. The relationship between the two men was known to be strained. On Ballistic Missile Defence, for example, Eggleton was a strong proponent of Canadian participation while Axworthy was a passionate critic of the system.

Graham and McCallum were far more alike. They were able to build a strong and healthy partnership in part because they had shared educational experiences. They were both former academics at two of Canada's top universities—Graham a professor of law at the University of Toronto, McCallum an economics professor at McGill. Both were educated in elite private schools—Upper Canada College and Trinity College School, respectively. Both studied in the 1960s at Old World universities—Graham at the University of Paris, McCallum at Cambridge.

Each was brought up both in the ivory tower and in the world. Both men are pragmatists, not given to government by theory. They are both fiscal conservatives yet social progressives. And, perhaps most important, they are both largely devoid of the ego, arrogance, and self-importance that are a common affliction of men at the apex of power. Both are convivial and congenial men who enjoy dining out with friends, staff, and colleagues, and like good conversation. Both are open-minded and good listeners. Even though they held two of the most demanding and stressful portfolios in the Government of Canada, they both liked having fun. As a result, they were popular with their colleagues, the press, their officials, and staffers in Ottawa.

One fundamental difference did exist. McCallum was more of a risk-taker, more willing to challenge his department's views, advice, and agenda, and ready to chart his own course. Graham, on the other hand, was more conservative, more reluctant to challenge the bureaucracy in Foreign Affairs. He was more tolerant of their orthodoxies, perhaps because he shared them. This was a man with a deep and sophisticated understanding of foreign policy in all its dimensions, gleaned from years as an international lawyer and a respected chairman of the House of Commons Standing Committee on Foreign Affairs.

This difference in willingness to take risks might also have reflected the differing ways they had come to the Cabinet table. Graham, twice defeated in elections before becoming a Member of Parliament in 1993,[3] had sat on the backbenches for a decade before being invited to join the Cabinet, even though many senior Liberal Party leaders, including former deputy prime minister Herb Gray, regarded him as the best-qualified foreign minister since Lester Pearson.[4] Graham was disinclined to put at risk all his hard work and patience by alienating the professional foreign policy establishment in Ottawa unless it was absolutely essential. He knew well how angry civil servants could sabotage a minister.

McCallum had a much easier time. In the 2000 election he was "parachuted" as a star candidate into a riding he had never lived in and had rarely visited. He was elected in a landslide, and within eighteen months was appointed defence minister. To this neophyte politician, taking risks and driving an agenda seemed to be a perfectly reasonable course of action, especially in light of the obvious need for leadership in the portfolio at that time. He did not fully understand how easily the Defence Ministry could become a political graveyard.

Welcome to the Machine

During McCallum's first few weeks in his new job, he heard hardly anything from his military advisers about Afghanistan (apart from briefings for the upcoming release of a Board of Inquiry report on the friendly fire incident of April 18, 2002). NDHQ officials were preoccupied with getting their new minister up to speed on what they regarded as more pressing priorities: the perennial need for more money for the military;[5] the need finally to get moving on the acquisition of a new maritime helicopter;[6] the need to acquire large transport aircraft, Boeing C-17 Globemasters;[7] and the need for Canada to agree to participate in the U.S. Ballistic Missile Defence system.[8]

The Canadian Forces were making plans to withdraw from Kandahar when McCallum was appointed, and there were no plans for a renewed troop commitment. Afghanistan was therefore well down the priority list of officials at NDHQ.

It wasn't until June 28, fully one month after McCallum had taken over from Eggleton, that he got his first substantive briefing on Afghanistan. Ray Henault, the chief of the defence staff (CDS), told his minister that the Canadian navy would continue its interdiction function in the Indian Ocean and North Arabian Sea, but its role would diminish over the coming months. And the air force was scheduled to cease its surveillance operations in the fall.

The minister was then forewarned that, in six to eight weeks' time, Canada would get a formal request—a so-called diplomatic note, or "dipnote," from the U.S. State Department to the Canadian Foreign Ministry—asking for a renewed troop presence. Perhaps the United States was concerned that the Europeans were losing interest in Afghanistan and would try to reduce their presence. Canada's military leadership was suggesting a positive response to the American request;

Ottawa could send another battle group to Kandahar early in 2003. The long-standing desire for an operational pause to regenerate the troops had mysteriously dissipated.

Henault and his deputy, Vice Admiral Greg Maddison, made one further point to their minister that day, and they made it forcefully. They argued that under no circumstances should Canada agree to be part of the ISAF mission in Kabul. The general and the admiral were reading the political tea leaves; they knew that the Europeans were now not only willing to have Canada in ISAF, but also that they might actively solicit Canadian involvement. The two senior military leaders likely assumed, based on past experience and what they knew of the Chrétien government, that ISAF would be an attractive mission for the prime minister, the foreign minister, and perhaps the new defence minister.

The military leadership argued that the ISAF mission was too dangerous, with no obvious end point or way to measure success. It would become a quagmire for the Canadian Forces. The objectives of the mission, they argued, were unclear. The rules of engagement were vague, making it difficult for the Canadian Forces to defend themselves adequately against the violent extremists and terrorists that operated in the labyrinthine warrens of the city. And, most important, they argued that Canada's military forces would be unable to extricate themselves from Kabul because no country would be willing to replace them in the losing proposition that was ISAF.[9] John McCallum reflected on this advice years later:

> I remember them telling me that ISAF was a mess, that we couldn't get out once we got in. They told me it was more dangerous, but I never quite understood how a security force in Kabul was more dangerous than a combat force in Kandahar. To be fair to them, there were a lot of gaps in the ISAF mission, such as medical and the airport, and countries hadn't firmly committed and some of those gaps we didn't have the resources

to fill, so if other countries didn't come forward to fill those gaps it would have been dangerous.[10]

That was the official advice and rationale for the military's opposition to the mission. But the fact that the Europeans had embarrassed the Canadian Forces months before as they waited in vain on the doorstep of ISAF was likely also a factor. In addition, the Canadian Forces have always preferred working with the Americans over any others, and are often quite dismissive of some European militaries, particularly the Germans (who were leading ISAF at this time), the French, and the Italians. "They [the military leadership] were very cosy with the Americans and liked the idea of us being in combat, rather than peacekeeping. ISAF wasn't exactly peacekeeping but it was more the traditional peacekeeping model rather than combat. There was also always this thing about interoperability with the Americans. They generally looked closely to their American peers. Those were the people they wanted to impress. They felt more comfortable with the Americans partly for psychological and cultural reasons," stated McCallum.[11] The advice, in a nutshell, was to go back to Kandahar with the Americans, and stay well clear of Kabul and the Europeans.

In the normal course of events, a recommendation from the military to redeploy eight hundred ground troops to Afghanistan within a few months would have been the first item a new minister was briefed on upon assuming office. It would have been brought to his attention on his first day in office, not after a month. Why did that not happen in this instance? Since 9-11 the military leadership had consistently advised the politicians to limit a ground force contribution to Afghanistan to six months and then to withdraw so as to regenerate the troops from the relentless operational tempo of the previous few years. Why did these same people suddenly do a 180-degree turn in the face of this impending request from Washington?

In all likelihood, neither NDHQ nor the Foreign Ministry expected a request from the Americans to renew Canada's military commitment in Afghanistan when McCallum became minister of defence in late May 2002. If they had, Bill Graham would have mentioned it to him right away. It would have been a top item in the new minister's transition material from his officials. The only plausible explanation is that NDHQ heard about the request from somewhere in the Pentagon, through their networks, in late June, before anyone else in Ottawa. McCallum's officials could not advise him on the Foreign Ministry position on the forthcoming request; few in Ottawa had seen this one on the horizon.[12]

After this sobering briefing, McCallum, who had been given some very difficult tasks to pursue in the first month of his new job, and who was already working on a strategy to secure more funding for the Canadian Forces in the upcoming budget, was now being asked to sell the prime minister on a further deployment of ground forces to Kandahar in a few months' time.[13] The raison d'être for the deployment was to support Washington. The operational challenges of Kandahar were not discussed.

At this point, the new defence minister had no idea what challenges Afghanistan would pose. He had not yet been there, and he had had very little discussion with his officials. And he had not yet had a single substantive conversation on the subject with either the foreign minister or the prime minister.[14]

John McCallum now had a lot more to think about. And he decided fairly quickly that he had better go to Afghanistan that summer.

MCCALLUM WAS enormously impressed with the professionalism of the Canadian Forces he had encountered during his visit to Kandahar in July. In September, McCallum met with the senior officials at NDHQ to discuss once again Canada's role in Afghanistan. He was now told that the Americans would be asking the Canadian army to return to Afghanistan in mid-2003, and that Washington would want Canada in Kandahar, not in Kabul. This was an important point, because at the same time the Foreign Ministry was starting to hear that ISAF might be expanded and that the Europeans were indeed looking for countries like Canada to contribute.

Two days later the defence minister, accompanied by his most senior civilian and military officials, had his first bilateral meeting with Bill Graham at the Lester B. Pearson Building, the headquarters of the Foreign Ministry. Afghanistan was discussed—it was the fourth item on a four-item agenda. Afghanistan was not a high priority in the Pearson Building. As Bill Graham reflected, during his time as foreign minister from early 2002 to mid-2004, "it [Afghanistan] was a non issue; if you will, at Foreign Affairs, it was seen as more of a defence issue."[15]

Nonetheless, senior officials in Foreign Affairs suggested that Canada should look carefully at ISAF. The request from the Americans to go back to Kandahar had still not arrived at the Pearson Building. As Graham and McCallum became more interested in ISAF as an option, the military leadership became increasingly anxious, waiting for the request they thought was coming.

The Colonel Comes a-Calling

On Halloween day 2002, McCallum's chief of staff received an unannounced visit at his office from Colonel Richard Boyd, senior military attaché to the U.S. ambassador to Canada, Paul Cellucci. It was unannounced because Colonel Boyd had full, unfettered access to the Department of National Defence and even to the minister's office, a highly unusual privilege that no other foreign diplomat in Ottawa enjoyed. Boyd could literally walk the halls of NDHQ as he saw fit and drop in on people working there.

A highly likeable fellow, Boyd knew all the senior players in Canada's military on a first-name basis, and liked to entertain them over a game of golf at the exclusive Royal Ottawa Golf Club. His total access was illustrative of the depth and closeness of the relationship between the Canadian and American militaries.

On this day, Boyd, or Rick, as he asked people to call him, proposed that McCallum visit his counterpart, Secretary of Defence Donald Rumsfeld—known in the Pentagon as the "sec def"—in Washington in December. Boyd suggested that it would be important for McCallum to see the sec def prior to any U.S. decision on Iraq. He implied that the choices on Iraq would likely come to a head early in the new year.

Normally, organizing a meeting with Donald Rumsfeld on two months' notice would be next to impossible, but Boyd was certain the sec def would rearrange his schedule to accommodate his new Canadian counterpart. And so he did, although the meeting occurred in early January, not December.

For this critical first meeting with Rumsfeld, McCallum took with him his two most trusted and senior civilian advisers—his deputy minister, Margaret Bloodworth, and his assistant deputy minister for policy, Ken Calder.

Almost everyone at NDHQ referred to Ken Calder as Dr. Calder, although this formality did not reflect his personality. He is a mild-mannered, soft-spoken, and likeable person who exhibits little ego or pretence. Calder had earned a doctorate in military history from the London School of Economics, and at this point was nearing the end of a more than thirty-year career at NDHQ. He commanded great loyalty among his staff. Calder, an expert on NATO, NORAD, and the Pentagon, had written the last two White Papers on defence. He was also one of the few senior leaders in the Defence Department to emerge unscathed from the trauma of the Somalia Inquiry.

Calder held steady throughout the dark days. By 2003 he had been the senior civilian policy adviser in NDHQ for a dozen years. He knew the history—and the secrets—of NDHQ better than anyone else. And he understood the military "mind" in all its subtleties. He knew all the players in the military and foreign policy establishment personally and had worked with most. He was well connected in the Pentagon. Calder's reputation preceded him: You didn't go to him for a visionary, original agenda. He had seen too much and was too realistic and cautious for that. But if you wanted to know what not to do, how to stay out of trouble, Calder was your man. And from almost day one, Calder and John McCallum got on famously.

The other official at NDHQ that McCallum respected equally was Bloodworth. She had been appointed to her job two weeks prior to McCallum's taking over, and she too was new to the Department of National Defence. Yet Bloodworth was far from new to the senior ranks of the federal public service. A lawyer by training, she had held at this point in her long career some of the most senior positions in departments dealing broadly with national security.[16] On 9-11 she was the deputy minister of transport, and, working quickly with little ministerial guidance, she orchestrated the safe landing in Canada of hundreds of airplanes from the United States. It was an extraordinary achievement, reflective of her superb judgment.

Her reputation was impeccable; she was seen as a steady hand, an expert on government process and the rights and wrongs of how to get things done in the system. She commanded almost universal respect among her colleagues and the many Cabinet ministers she had served.

There were no senior military officials on this vitally important trip to Washington. McCallum and his officials expected a civilian-only meeting, with no senior U.S. officers present. As a result, officials in the South Tower showed little interest in attending. The military were secure in the knowledge that their eyes and ears would be in the room during the Rumsfeld meeting. Rear Admiral Ian Mack, military attaché to Michael Kergin, the Canadian ambassador in Washington, would sit in on the meeting with McCallum, Rumsfeld, and their senior civilian advisers.

The Pentagon Outmanoeuvres the South Tower

McCallum and his team flew by Challenger jet into Washington on an unseasonably warm day on January 8, 2003. They were to meet Rumsfeld the following day. A few hours prior to the meeting, the minister received a final preparatory briefing from Michael Kergin and Admiral Mack. The briefing was designed to round out McCallum's general knowledge and provide some broader political context for the upcoming meeting. Kergin advised the minister to reaffirm to Rumsfeld how important this bilateral relationship was to Canada. He told McCallum to reassure the secretary of defence that Canada was a secure and reliable ally, a message that most Western nations were reiterating to the Americans after 9-11. McCallum was told that $435 billion of a $2.1 trillion U.S. federal budget for 2002 to 2003 was earmarked for defence and homeland security, and fully sixty percent of discretionary spending fell into this same category. This drove the point home, if it needed doing, that Washington was focused on one issue—the security of the United States of America.

Before leaving the impressive Canadian embassy building for the Pentagon, McCallum asked Kergin about the relationship between George Bush and Prime Minister Chrétien. The conventional wisdom in Ottawa was that, at best, the relationship was strained. Kergin, who had sat in on meetings between the two, replied that in some ways the chemistry between Bush and Chrétien was better than it had been between President Clinton and Chrétien. The assessment was somewhat surprising, since the relationship between the prime minister and Clinton had been very good. Kergin explained that both Bush and Chrétien had a businesslike approach to issues, whereas Clinton was a policy wonk.

Donald Rumsfeld greeted John McCallum with a handshake on the steps of the Pentagon and escorted him into the sec def's boardroom. Rumsfeld was accompanied by Ian Brzezinski, deputy assistant secretary for NATO and Europe and the son of Zbigniew Brzezinski, President Carter's national security adviser. And to the great surprise of the Canadians, also present for the meeting was General Richard (Dick) Myers, chairman of the Joint Chiefs of Staff, the highest-ranking officer in the U.S. military. Myers was not expected to be at this meeting, at least not as far as NDHQ and the Canadian embassy knew. If his presence had been anticipated, Canada's chief of the defence staff would certainly have been part of the delegation.

McCallum's party began to realize that this was no ordinary "bilateral" with the Americans. For both the sec def and the chairman of the joint chiefs to give a Canadian defence minister an hour of their time was highly unusual—and especially so when the Americans were in the final planning stages for the invasion of Iraq, which would occur in a matter of weeks.

Afghanistan might not have been at the top of the agenda when Bill Graham and John McCallum met in September, but it was Rumsfeld's priority that day, even though the Canadians were led to believe that Iraq would be foremost on the sec def's priority list with Canada. The briefing material that McCallum's officials gave him for the meeting reflected this view. Afghanistan was to be the seventh item on a nine-point agenda, and the minister was advised to respond only to what the Americans said rather than to initiate a discussion.[17]

Afghanistan was high on Rumsfeld's agenda because he badly wanted to reduce the U.S. troop presence there—to free up needed American military resources for the impending war in Iraq. He could free American forces by bringing more allies into what he thought was a stabilization, reconstruction, and nation-building operation in Afghanistan. Stabilization, peacekeeping and nation-building were never the Pentagon's preferred operations, and especially now that major combat action was in the offing, Rumsfeld wanted to hand off Afghanistan.

Rumsfeld began by telling McCallum that the future of ISAF would come up at NATO in June. He was concerned about who would follow the Germans and the Dutch once they had completed their six-month rotation in ISAF in the summer. McCallum replied that he thought that the United States and Canada should work together to bring ISAF under NATO, in part to help resolve the issue of finding replacement forces. If ISAF were under NATO, it would then become a collective responsibility. McCallum's German counterpart, Peter Struck, first put this idea to him in November, when they met in Berlin. Struck, a career social-democratic politician deeply wedded to multilateralism, made a strong argument to McCallum that NATO should lead ISAF, and asked for Canada's support. Struck also told McCallum that Rumsfeld supported this proposal. McCallum, at that time already thinking about a possible Canadian role in ISAF, embraced the notion, on the advice of Calder, and told Struck that he had Canada's full support. McCallum also promised that he would raise the issue with Geoff Hoon (the British defence minister), whom he was to meet the following day in London.

In response to McCallum's suggestion, Rumsfeld replied that making ISAF a NATO responsibility had some appeal, but that the mission would still need one country to take command and provide the bulk of the troops. Then Rumsfeld dropped the other shoe. He made it very clear that, as far as he was concerned, few if any countries in the world were better suited to lead ISAF than Canada. Reflecting on that exchange years later, McCallum recounted, "Rumsfeld, without saying the word *Canada*, described a country that was so obviously Canada that I laughed."[18] But Rumsfeld's request was no laughing matter, especially for Canada's military, which had been telling its minister for months that it wanted no part of ISAF. "He [Rumsfeld] was flattering Canada, that we had the right kind of experience, and the right kind of culture to lead such a mission. That we had a closer affinity to the US than 'Old Europe'—closer in spirit, mentality and procedures than European countries. There was great enthusiasm for Canada on Rumsfeld's part. I was quite taken aback," said McCallum.[19]

McCallum replied that ISAF was an option for Canada, but he pointed out that Canada's military were less than keen on this mission, that they were concerned about a quagmire. Rumsfeld indicated that the United States was open to the possibility of a Canadian battle group returning to Kandahar because he thought the mission was about to begin concentrating on humanitarian work and the training of the Afghan army, tasks Rumsfeld felt were well suited to the

Canadian army. But the formal request from Washington for the Canadian army to return to Kandahar, the request that McCallum's generals had been telling him to expect, never came up. McCallum summed up the meeting with Rumsfeld years later: "He [Rumsfeld] totally pulled the rug out from underneath our military."[20] Rumsfeld wanted Canada in Kabul, not Kandahar. And so did Dick Myers, despite the wishes of his Canadian counterparts in Ottawa. The chairman of the Joint Chiefs of Staff backed up Rumsfeld and indicated that leadership in ISAF was key to the Kabul region and Canada was the preferred country to lead the force.

Before the meeting moved on to other issues, McCallum made one final point to Rumsfeld. While he made no commitment on ISAF, he told the Americans bluntly that "If we did this we won't have anything left for Iraq."[21] McCallum recalled Rumsfeld's reply: "He said 'Yeah, I know that,' and then we moved on."[22] As the meeting moved to a discussion on Iraq, it became quite clear that, while the sec def wanted Canada's political support for the invasion, he was not at all interested in a Canadian military contribution to the Iraq War.

SO ENDED John McCallum's first meeting with Donald Rumsfeld, a man who would soon become synonymous with arrogance, intransigence, misguided policy, and abject military failure. In three years' time, under pressure from the escalating violence in Iraq, an unrepentant Rumsfeld would resign his post.

In that conversation between McCallum and Rumsfeld were the seeds of the difficult challenge that would confront Canadian soldiers three years later. The secretary of defence wanted to strip down American forces in Afghanistan so that they could be transferred to Iraq. The job was almost done in Afghanistan, he thought, and the challenges were stabilization, development, and nation-building. There was no sense that the Taliban had withdrawn to the safety of the mountains and were reorganizing and regrouping, preparing to fight another day. That Rumsfeld did not give much consideration to that option shows astonishing ignorance of counterinsurgency and of the strategies and tactics that the insurgents were likely to use. He should have known better, for this kind of strategic retreat is hardly new in the history of guerrilla warfare. Perhaps Rumsfeld was so preoccupied with the coming war against Iraq that he could spare very little time to think seriously about Afghanistan. By January 2003, U.S. intentions in Iraq were clear, but far less clear were the negative consequences for Afghanistan. The United States was simply unprepared to finish what it had started and was handing off the responsibility. Canadian soldiers would ultimately pay the price.

Years later, McCallum vividly recalled his final exchange with Rumsfeld that day. "As we were walking out, he accompanied me to my car. And I said, 'I hear you're a squash player.' He said, 'Yeah, yeah' and he was getting all keen. 'Yeah, I just played last night against this thirty year old. Really good player. Top of his group or whatever.' And Rumsfeld is a lot older than thirty. And he said, 'But you know what? I beat him.' And I said, 'Oh, that's good.' And then he said, 'Do you know what was even more fun than beating this guy? Watching him lose.'"[23] Creepy

FOUR

WALKING A TIGHTROPE

B efore McCallum left Washington, he met with Canadian journalists, both those who were based there and those who had
followed him to cover his meeting with Rumsfeld. They were
not at all interested in Afghanistan. They were interested only in the
discussions Rumsfeld and McCallum had had about Iraq. Iraq had
pushed Afghanistan off the public agenda.

Even though the UN Security Council was locked in debate and the
United States would not launch its invasion of Iraq until March, it had
been clear since the fall of 2002 that the Bush administration was
determined to topple Saddam Hussein—a regime that Washington
claimed concealed weapons of mass destruction (WMD) and
harboured al-Qaeda terrorists. What position Canada would take on
the impending war had dominated the national debate in Ottawa for
weeks.

Through the late fall, Bill Graham and Prime Minister Chrétien
walked a tightrope when they answered questions. Chrétien had said,
"We were among the first countries to tell the Americans that you
cannot go there [Iraq] without the support of a resolution of the UN
Security Council."[1] But both he and his foreign minister were also
careful to leave the door open for Canadian participation in an Iraq
invasion even if the United Nations failed to approve military action.
"It may be that diplomacy will not in the end succeed," explained
Graham, "but we must exhaust every conceivable effort to operate

within the mandate of the UN. It is possible that circumstances might develop such as those that occurred in the case of Kosovo, where a UN mandate would not be feasible ... Those circumstances don't exist today."[2]

Chrétien went even further, at one point suggesting that a UN mandate for military action against Iraq already existed. "If the Americans or the Brits have great evidence that Saddam Hussein—who is no friend of mine—is not following the instructions of the UN ... if the proof is made of that," said the prime minister, "of course Canada will support an activity in there ... We have a resolution ... that calls for action if Saddam Hussein is not following these instructions of the United Nations. It is mentioned in that resolution that action can be taken against them if they don't accept and conform with that resolution."[3] A second UN resolution, while desirable, was not essential, the prime minister argued, if the Americans provided evidence that Iraq had concealed weapons of mass destruction.

It fell to Colin Powell, the respected U.S. secretary of state and former chairman of the Joint Chiefs of Staff, as well as the most moderate member of the Bush foreign policy team, to convince skeptical leaders like Chrétien. In a riveting speech to the UN Security Council on February 5, 2003, Powell laid out detailed intelligence confirming that Hussein had weapons of mass destruction. Despite extensive preparation by the secretary of state and repeated questioning of intelligence agencies before he delivered his speech, the evidence he cited was either wrong or misleading.

Just after the final UN Security Council debate on Iraq but before the invasion, Donald Rumsfeld spoke to European allies at the Munich Security Conference. He forcefully told the assembled defence and security officials and experts that Powell's speech "presented not opinions, not conjecture, but facts." And he went on to say, "It is difficult to believe there could still be questions in the minds of reasonable people open to the facts before them." The foreign minister of Germany, Josckha Fischer, de facto host of the gathering, retorted with as much force, "Excuse me, I am not convinced."[4] As it turned out, neither was Chrétien.

IT WAS DIFFICULT for the Canadian public to figure out exactly where its government was going. Journalists peppered Graham and Chrétien with questions wherever they went. Canada's position on an issue that was so clearly important to the United States was no small matter. If the government's position was opaque to the public, the underlying message seemed clear enough to the experts: Ottawa had not yet made up its mind. The government preferred another UN resolution author- izing intervention, but, if the Security Council remained deadlocked, Canada might consider supporting the United States, depending on the circumstances at the time. The prime minister, a pragmatist, was keeping Canada's options open for as long as possible.

But the media were uncomfortable with the ambiguity. Frustrated by what the less charitable journalists saw as duplicity and the more gener- ous saw as lack of clarity on the part of the government, the Canadian media desperately wanted McCallum to disclose information from his discussion with Rumsfeld on Iraq. Up to this point, the prime minister and the foreign minister had been the government's spokesmen on Iraq. Experienced with the media, both knew how to say a great deal but reveal almost nothing. McCallum was a neophyte politician and less familiar with the government's messaging on Iraq. And he was less skilled in dealing with the press than his more experienced colleagues.

Shortly after his meeting with the secretary of defence, McCallum held a "scrum" in the Canadian embassy with about twenty journalists present. They questioned him aggressively, demanding to know what he had told Rumsfeld about Canada's position on the impending war. When asked in the press scrum in Washington about the government's position and what he had said to Rumsfeld, McCallum bluntly stated, "We reserve our right to make that decision [even if there is no Security Council resolution] … many, many countries are in a position where they are offering contingency co-operation. Some may say 'We're only doing it with a UN mandate.' We're saying we much prefer that, but we may do it otherwise."[5]

No one in the government had articulated the Canadian position quite this clearly before, or so it seemed to the press and Members of Parliament back in Ottawa. And the fact that McCallum had made this statement in Washington, just after a meeting with Rumsfeld, left some journalists with the impression that, for the benefit of a Washington audience, he was expressing a clearer position there than Graham or Chrétien had expressed in Ottawa. Nothing could be further from the truth. As far as McCallum was concerned, he was articulating Canada's position, with no change. He did not regard his comments in Washington as different in any way from what Chrétien and Graham had been saying in Ottawa.[6]

Nonetheless, McCallum's comments touched off a firestorm at home. Some of the chattering classes in Ottawa insisted that the government had changed its position on Iraq and that the new position was no longer fully supportive of the United Nations. For many of the Opposition Members of Parliament, and not a few Liberals, this position was unacceptable, inconsistent with Canada's long-standing support of the UN and multilateral institutions more generally. The Liberal chairman of the House of Commons Standing Committee on Foreign Affairs, Bernard Patry, said McCallum "went too far" and should have conducted broader consultations at home and with European countries before announcing a shift in Canada's policy toward Iraq.[7] For people like Patry, and there were many like him in Parliament, Canada could never support an American intervention in Iraq without UN authorization. For some, even UN approval wouldn't be enough to justify Canadian military involvement in such a "Republican" adventure. Meanwhile, David Pratt, Patry's colleague, Liberal chair of the House Defence Committee and a well-known "hawk," supported McCallum, insisting, "He struck the right tone, he kept his options open."[8]

The controversy fed on itself for days. Chrétien's caucus became increasingly unsure of the government's position and whether or not it had changed. A rift began to open within the caucus on a fundamental issue. To make matters worse, at that time Chrétien was always looking in his rear-view mirror at Paul Martin; he assumed that the former finance minister, now a backbench MP openly campaigning to replace the prime minister, would move to unseat him prematurely by orchestrating a caucus revolt at the first available opportunity. Iraq could become that opportunity if not managed carefully.

A few days into the crisis, McCallum received one of the few phone calls that he would ever receive from Prime Minister Chrétien during the two years he served in his Cabinet. The call lasted only a minute or two. The prime minister simply informed his defence minister that he would be going on national television to lance this boil. The prime minister was preparing McCallum for what the media would perceive as a serious slap in the face, regardless of how delicately Chrétien handled the issue.

Within hours, the prime minister was on live television from the National Press Theatre, stating that the Government of Canada's position was to work through the UN: "The Canadian position is that on matters of peace and security, the international community must speak and act through the UN Security Council." When asked about McCallum's equivocal comment in Washington, Chrétien simply stated that his minister had answered a hypothetical question, which was not appropriate: "He replied to a hypothetical question that he has reflected upon and corrected ... since that time," Chrétien said. The prime minister implied, without saying so directly, that he had an inexperienced minister on his hands and that was all there was to this controversy. Chrétien had managed to put the Iraq genie back in the bottle, for at least a short time.

The South Tower Pushes Back

Soon after returning to Ottawa, McCallum and Bloodworth sat down with the senior military leadership to debrief them on the meeting with

Chrétien canadian position

Donald Rumsfeld. The debriefing was only a formality; immediately following the meeting with Rumsfeld, Admiral Mack, Canada's military attaché in Washington, had fully informed the chief of the defence staff of the discussions that day at the Pentagon. The real purpose of this meeting was for McCallum to tell his military advisers that they needed to start looking not just at an ISAF contribution but also at the feasibility of Canada's leading the mission. This marked the beginning of a regular series of meetings over the next eight weeks among McCallum, Bloodworth, Calder, Henault, and Maddison on ISAF, Iraq, and the relationship between the two issues.

RAY HENAULT, a former helicopter pilot in the Canadian air force, had become chief of the defence staff in June 2001, after he impressed Prime Minister Chrétien with his performance during the Kosovo War in 1999. Canada had contributed fighter aircraft to NATO operations, and these aircraft had participated in the bombing of Serb targets in Kosovo. Henault, then the deputy chief of the defence staff—the general in charge of all Canadian Forces operations—went on television regularly during the Kosovo air campaign to brief journalists and update the public on Canada's involvement in the war. A fluently bilingual Franco-Manitoban, Henault was economical with language and delivered lucid press briefings. He satisfied the demands of the media with basic information. He was "feeding the beast," as the saying goes, without giving too much away. And he seemed to know instinctively the boundary between generals and politicians. He was exactly what a cautious prime minister who was no particular fan of the military wanted in a top general.

Henault was an incrementalist—a bureaucrat—primarily concerned with managing an organization that had gone through years of painful downsizing, scandal, and debilitating morale problems. It is difficult to exaggerate the impact of the Somalia scandal on the morale of the forces, and the prolonged inquiry stretched the punishment over years. When Henault became CDS, the Canadian Forces were in disrepute and disrepair. The new chief of the defence staff was not interested in charting a bold new course for the Canadian Forces, but rather in holding this fragile organization together. One of his top priorities was managing inter-service politics and keeping all of his generals and admirals relatively happy—or equally unhappy. Logrolling, as it were.

His deputy, Vice Admiral Greg Maddison, had previously served as head of the navy. He was ambitious, experienced, and hoped to succeed Henault as chief of the defence staff. The normal requirement of "service rotation" for the position of CDS among the three services gave Maddison a distinct advantage: After Henault, an air force man, had served, it would be the navy's turn, as Maurice Baril, an army general, had held the post before Henault.

Maddison achieved his fifteen minutes of fame in the winter of 2002 when he appeared before the Commons Standing Committee on Procedure and House Affairs. He had been summoned to the committee to address the claim made by the Opposition that Art Eggleton had misled Parliament. It was known that the minister had failed to brief the prime minister about a JTF2 operation in Afghanistan that resulted in the capturing of al-Qaeda "detainees." *The Globe and Mail* had prominently displayed pictures of the operation on the front page. What was still unclear was how much the minister knew about the operation when it was reported in the press.

When asked whether Eggleton had been briefed on this operation in advance, Maddison answered "yes," but he then suggested the minister did not fully understand what he had been told. Only at a subsequent briefing, "there was a click and [Eggleton] said, 'Right, you're right, it did happen that way.'"[9] The light went on. Maddison's statement seriously wounded Eggleton politically, a wound from which he would never really recover. It was also career limiting for Greg Maddison. Politicians are generally unforgiving of senior officers or officials who humiliate their kind in public.

IN MID-JANUARY Henault and Maddison met with McCallum and Bloodworth again, this time to discuss a meeting at U.S. Central

Command (CENTCOMM) headquarters in Tampa that would occur within the next twenty-four hours. It was described as a "planning meeting" on the Iraq operation, and would be at the rank of mid-level officers. A large number of countries would be present. Canada was invited.

Both Henault and Maddison believed strongly that the Canadian Forces should be present at this planning meeting, and that the Americans would not perceive their participation as a commitment to support or contribute militarily to the Iraq War. In fact, the South Tower had already indicated to the Pentagon that Canada would be at the meeting. The military leadership were now testing the waters with their minister. "I remember having arguments with them [Henault and Maddison]. They wanted to be more heavily engaged than I wanted them to be engaged. They were implicitly assuming we would be going with the Americans [to Iraq]," stated John McCallum.[10]

The CDS claimed that the value of what Canada was doing in the North Arabian Sea was diminishing. By implication, Canada needed to do more to support the Americans. Henault then said that the army wanted to put forces on a higher state of readiness so that they would be ready to deploy to Iraq, if required. In his comments, the CDS put a number of military options on the table as possible contributions to a Canadian mission to Iraq, including CF-18 fighter aircraft, a destroyer and other naval assets in the Persian Gulf, and a mechanized battle group as part of the invasion force.[11] These were consistent with the options that had been leaked to the *National Post* and appeared in the press on January 10, when McCallum was in Washington:

Canadian Forces planners are putting everything on the table for a contribution to any war in Iraq, military sources say, including a brigade group of up to 3,000 mechanized infantry, armour and artillery troops that would fight alongside US and British soldiers. One source, who spoke on condition of anonymity, said the navy, air force and army are pushing to make the maximum effort possible despite well-publicized shortages of equipment, funding and personnel.[12]

The source and motivation for these untimely leaks remain unclear, but it appears to have been a ham-fisted strategy by military officials to pressure the government to support the United States in its military operations in Iraq.

McCallum reflected on these conversations with his officials: "I remember being presented with options for Iraq, not at my request. They had a favourable gloss, whereas options for Afghanistan [ISAF] were presented with an unfavourable spin. Afghanistan was last as a choice of options for them [Henault and Maddison]. It was quite clear in my mind that they would have much preferred to go to Iraq."[13]

Henault has a somewhat different recollection of events. "I always brought forward to the Minister and to the government a range of military options and an analysis of their impact on the Canadian Forces," he said. He continued:

I never gave advice about the political consequences since that was beyond my scope. I did speak about resource constraints within the CF, what we were capable of and what we were not capable of doing. I never gave the government a single option. They always had a range of options. We had a large number of people and partnerships at coalition headquarters. We had built confidence, serious confidence, in counter-terrorism action since 2001, we had built very high confidence in the United States and elsewhere. We did have a large role to play. It was important to maintain credibility and to support our allies operationally. We made no connections between Iraq, BMD, and Afghanistan. We always presented options to the government. It is important that we make a contribution to the military community of which we are a part.[14]

The minister read his advisers correctly. NDHQ favoured a Canadian military role in Iraq over an ongoing one in Afghanistan. In January, Maddison had received advice from his staff indicating that there "were no substantive military objectives remaining in Op Apollo [Afghanistan]. Therefore, main effort should be towards Iraq."[15]

The tone of Henault and Maddison's advice to McCallum reflected this view.[16] While the general and the vice admiral were not pushing hard for the government to send ground troops to Iraq, they did make the point that, in their opinion, the war would be very short, lasting no more than six weeks, with an air campaign of perhaps as little as five days. Their analysis led them to believe that the Americans would overwhelm the Iraqi military with greater numbers and far superior technological force, defeating them quickly, as they had done in the first Iraq War in 1991. Therefore, it followed logically, if Canada was in at the front end of this operation, we would limit our exposure—early in, early out. This analysis proved correct but took no account of what would happen in Iraq after the regime had been toppled and the Iraqi military defeated. Bill Graham foresaw this danger. "I told Colin Powell," Graham said, "that it would be just like the Israelis in the West Bank, and what are you gonna do then?"[17]

This six-week war scenario, with no plan for consolidation after the regime had been removed, was consistent with what McCallum had been told in Washington in early January. After the meeting with Rumsfeld, he visited the Center for Strategic and International Studies (CSIS), a respected Washington think-tank. It was populated with refugees from the senior ranks of the Clinton administration, and was run by John Hamre, a highly respected defence and security expert and former deputy defence secretary during the Clinton years. Hamre and his colleagues at CSIS still had strong and active links with the Defence Department, the State Department, the National Security Council, and the CIA. Officials on the inside had told them that the Bush administration had absolutely no plans for Iraq beyond a six-week military campaign that would remove the regime, destroy the Iraqi army, and take control of the country. It was as if the administration thought that once the odious regime of Saddam Hussein was removed, a new, popular, and stable democratic government would somehow naturally emerge. The new government would bring peace and democracy to a religiously and ethnically divided society, a society that Saddam had tyrannized for decades, that had been brutalized and stripped of its civil society, and one that had no democratic history.

This scenario was staggeringly naive, deeply ideological, and breathtakingly irresponsible, but it was the basis of American policy.[18] Senior Canadian military leaders, when they suggested that Canada should commit forces to the toppling of Saddam's regime, also had little to say about the morning after the "war" ended. There was good advice, both in the United States and in Canada, that warned of the violence that would erupt in Iraq after the government had been overthrown, but it did not reach the highest levels of the military in either country—or if it did, it was ignored. In the United States, the secretary of defence and his close coterie of civilian advisers ignored expert advice. They simply shut down and closed out the work of civilian advisers, especially those in the Department of State, who were warning of violence and disintegration once Saddam had been removed. In Canada, the military was simply not well connected enough to those experts outside government who could provide the warning. They, like their counterparts south of the border, focused only on the battlefield and on what they expected would be a short battle that they would win through overwhelming military advantage and technological superiority. Both in Iraq and in Afghanistan, Canada's senior military leaders did not think about the war that would ensue after the battle was over.

The Minister Takes Charge

McCallum listened intently to what his generals were saying that day about Iraq. He ended the meeting with a surprising instruction. He told his senior military officers to advise the Pentagon that Canada would not be attending the planning meeting to prepare for the invasion of Iraq.[19]

The minister felt strongly that Canada's presence at the Tampa meeting would leak, and would be understood as a signal of active engagement in planning with the Americans for the invasion of Iraq, even though Ottawa had not yet made a decision about whether it would participate. He also felt that if the Canadian Forces were present at this meeting, "we would get deeper into it, get drawn in."[20] McCallum had been burned once on Iraq a few days previously, and he was not about to be singed again over a low-level planning meeting. The defence minister then told his senior advisers that if, in the final analysis, the Canadian government decided to support the Iraq War, which he felt was increasingly unlikely at this point, sending ground troops was the least likely option. McCallum knew that neither the prime minister nor Graham was likely to support sending Canadian troops to Iraq, even if the government supported the invasion. He also knew that doing so would consume too many scarce troops, making it impossible for Canada to lead ISAF, an option that he was increasingly weighing in his mind.[21]

A few days later McCallum sat down with Bloodworth and Henault again. The CDS reported that Canada's withdrawal from the planning meeting on January 15 had confused the U.S. staff in Tampa. Henault also stated that the Americans were ready to commence military action against Iraq in one month. Again, Henault claimed that a Canadian naval contribution, perhaps consisting of both frigates and destroyers, would be welcome in Washington. If Canada sent ships, it could support both Operation Enduring Freedom (OEF) and Operation Iraqi Freedom (OIF)—what the military calls a "double-hatted task force." The general and his deputy felt that a naval commitment was the most valued contribution that Canada could make.

Then Henault added something new to this increasingly complex mix. He pointed out that CENTCOMM was moving the bulk of its operations out of Tampa beginning the next day, and would be setting up shop in the Persian Gulf state of Qatar. If Canada wanted to remain in CENTCOMM and continue to have its eyes and ears on what the Americans were planning in both Afghanistan and Iraq, a memorandum of understanding would need to be signed with the Government of Qatar right away, and Canada's officers in Tampa would need to move to the U.S. headquarters in Qatar. Bill Graham was opposed to sending the Canadian Forces to Qatar, for the same reason that McCallum opposed having them attend the planning meeting in Tampa.[22] But military leaders in the South Tower desperately wanted some of their officers in Qatar; they argued that if Canada was not in CENTCOMM, all the vital information and intelligence the Canadian Forces had been receiving about Afghanistan and Iraq would end. The military insisted that such a loss of intelligence was dangerous for the Canadian Forces in theatre. It was unacceptable.

McCallum agreed that since the Canadian navy still had ships in the region under Operation Enduring Freedom, Canada needed to have at least a handful of liaison officers in Qatar.[23] But he reiterated that even if the prime minister supported the American invasion of Iraq, he could not conceive that Chrétien would agree to deploy ground troops in the early stages of the war. And he reminded his advisers that Rumsfeld's priority for Canada was ISAF, not Iraq. Maybe, the minister concluded, we should concentrate our planning on Afghanistan.

In the third week of January, the CDS introduced another thread into the tapestry. He told McCallum that Canada had one hundred officers on exchange with the American and British militaries, and that up to thirty of these officers could be indirectly involved in operations against Iraq, either on the ground, in the air, or at sea. McCallum was advised to remind the prime minister of this fact.

This seemingly esoteric issue of exchange officers was vitally important to the military leadership. They were adamant that, regardless of the Government of Canada's ultimate decision on the Iraq War, these officers should remain in place. They claimed that pulling them out would be devastating to Canadian–American and Canadian–British military-to-military relations. They argued that Canada had made a commitment to its allies with these officers, and had to honour it; we would expect nothing less of our allies if the shoe were on the other foot. As Bill Graham reflected, "The advice we got from the military was pulling them out would cause irreparable damage [to the Canada–U.S. relationship] at the military level."[24] Ultimately, McCallum, Graham, and the prime minister were persuaded by the logic of the argument, but it didn't make their decision any less controversial when it became public knowledge.

Finally, at the end of January, the CDS advised McCallum that a memorandum of understanding had been presented to the Government of Qatar and could be signed that day. The Canadian Forces would be on their way to the Gulf within seventy-two hours.

Yes to Kabul

Right after returning from Washington, McCallum debriefed Graham and the prime minister on Rumsfeld's desire to have Canada lead ISAF. A consensus began to form at the political level and in the Foreign Ministry in Ottawa that Canada should take on the leadership, especially if we were not going to Iraq. Some inside the government even began to refer to this as "the Afghanistan solution." "There was no question, every time we talked about the Afghan mission, it gave us cover for not going to Iraq," said Graham.[25]

But McCallum had another problem to resolve first. His military leadership adamantly opposed going to Kabul. He knew where they stood from a policy perspective. But what he needed now from his generals was advice as to whether the undertaking was militarily feasible. McCallum could not recommend this mission to the prime minister without such advice.

In late January McCallum met with his senior officials to discuss ISAF. He was told that it totalled about 4,700 troops, including 500 personnel in the headquarters. NDHQ estimated that, to replace the

Germans as leaders of the mission, Canada would need to deploy 2,655 troops. This was no small undertaking for the Canadian army, which totalled about 19,000 regular force troops at the time, 1,300 of whom were in Bosnia.

Henault insisted that Canada could not even consider taking on the leadership of ISAF unless a number of preconditions were met. We would need an embassy in Kabul and an ambassador with real clout. Canada would need a commitment from the Americans that they would leave in place the assets they had contributed to ISAF, mainly headquarters elements. And Canada would need assurances that another country would take over from Germany the responsibility of running the Kabul airport, the main supply link and exit from the city if conditions deteriorated badly. Most important, Canada needed to find a partner country—in effect, the second-largest troop contributor to the mission.

Henault also began to embrace the notion that putting a NATO flag on the ISAF mission was vital to Canada's becoming the lead nation. Here the minister and his generals agreed. Putting NATO in charge of ISAF was the best way to ensure an exit strategy for the Canadian Forces. The argument was that Canada could take the lead for twelve months—two six-month rotations of troops—and during that time it would become NATO's responsibility to find a replacement lead once Canada's tour had ended.

Senior defence officials—military and civilian—were also worried that the Foreign Ministry underestimated the degree of effort and difficulty in mounting this mission. So they agreed that Canada needed a very senior official from Foreign Affairs who would be dedicated to this file; that a committee of Defence Department and Foreign Ministry officials would need to be established immediately and meet daily; and that a team of diplomats and military staff officers needed to go to Kabul right away to assess the situation on the ground, ascertain what assets Canada would need, and meet with President Karzai.

Henault committed to call Dick Myers to ensure that, if Canada took on this assignment, the American assets would remain in place.

And he told McCallum that regardless of mounting political pressure, all the minister could commit to publicly at this point was that Canada was exploring the possibility of contributing to ISAF.

Later that same day McCallum hastily reconvened his senior officials and told them that he had just been advised that the prime minister had decided in favour of the ISAF mission, subject to military advice confirming that the Canadian Forces had the capacity to assume the lead. An announcement would be made the following week, and there could be absolutely no leaks. Ominously, the Prime Minister's Office (PMO) had warned the minister that if there were a leak, his efforts to obtain increased funding for the military in the upcoming budget could be compromised. And finally, McCallum communicated to his officials that this decision had no bearing on the possibility of deploying ships or even special forces in support of an Iraq operation if the government decided to support that war.

To help reassure the CDS, who was planning to phone his American counterpart, McCallum promised that he would call Rumsfeld immediately to ensure that the United States committed its assets, as well as support, in the effort to obtain a partner nation. Spain, Norway, Denmark, and France were considered possible partners. But then NDHQ got word that the Germans might be thinking about staying in Kabul for another six months, with a reduced footprint. NDHQ and McCallum agreed that Germany, because of its experience in ISAF, was the preferred partner nation for a Canadian lead. Thus, the prime minister was advised to call Chancellor Gerhard Schroeder right away to get German agreement.

A few days later, on February 4, 2003, the ISAF proposal was discussed in Cabinet and was well received. Former heritage minister Sheila Copps later talked about that Cabinet meeting:

I was at the table when the decision was made, and there were two theatres playing out. One was in Iraq and the other was in Afghanistan and we deliberately made a decision to go to

Afghanistan because we knew very shortly down the road we would be asked to participate in a US–led invasion of Iraq which we did not want to do and this was a neat political way of squaring the problem ... of Canada–US relations.[26]

Copps's erstwhile opponent and one-time leadership rival John Manley agreed with her interpretation of events. "Well, I don't disagree with her on that, it's maybe one of the few things I don't ... that was very much in contemplation of the issue we would have on Iraq ... Sheila is right that it was anticipated and commented upon [in Cabinet] that our commitment in Afghanistan was enough for us to say to the U.S., don't ask us to do more."[27]

In fact, the decision was not really made at the Cabinet meeting. It had effectively been made just prior to the meeting. But this discussion of ministers—a focus group of sorts—gave the prime minister all the comfort he needed to follow through once he had received Henault's military advice through McCallum.

The following day McCallum was told that Chrétien would be calling Schroeder within twenty-four hours. But he was also informed that the prime minister was not keen on partnering with Germany. Chrétien was evidently concerned that Washington would bundle Canada together with France and Germany, the two countries that most openly and vigorously opposed the Bush administration's foreign policy in general and particularly opposed the use of force in Iraq.

Twenty-four hours later McCallum made his phone call to Rumsfeld. He told the secretary of defence that Canada wanted to lead ISAF in partnership with Germany, but that the government could not commit until a few issues were settled. He asked for Rumsfeld's commitment that U.S. assets would remain in place. And he asked for Washington's support for putting ISAF under the broad umbrella of NATO. Rumsfeld committed to both, and also to provide quick reaction support in case of an emergency—in other words, the military capability to extract troops if they needed to be withdrawn urgently from Kabul. McCallum reiterated the point he had made in Washington: If Canada took on this mission, we would have no remaining capacity to deploy ground troops to Iraq.[28] Rumsfeld said that he understood and that it was fine with him. The two agreed that NDHQ and the Pentagon should begin the process of developing a memorandum of understanding on the U.S. assets. Finally, on the advice of his officials, McCallum pointed out that Canada would not commit to expanding the ISAF mandate beyond the city of Kabul. Rumsfeld had been pressing ISAF to begin moving out beyond Kabul, but he accepted McCallum's position.

Right after McCallum hung up with Rumsfeld, he called Peter Struck in Germany. Unable to get through to his counterpart, he spoke with Struck's military assistant, Colonel Buehler. They agreed that McCallum and Struck would meet to discuss ISAF at the Munich Security Conference in a few days' time. Buehler said Struck still favoured NATO's taking over ISAF, although he conceded that the French were opposed and had claimed that Afghan president Karzai was as well. Canadian officials saw this as rather typical and predictable French obstructionism on NATO issues, so they did not take French objections too seriously at NDHQ. Importantly, Buehler confirmed that Germany was considering staying in Kabul for another six months, and he liked McCallum's idea of a Canada–Germany partnership. Buehler said that he would raise the matter with Struck immediately.

After these two calls, it appeared that the pieces of the puzzle were now falling into place for Canada to take the leadership of ISAF. The only remaining issue was Henault's final advice on the military feasibility of the Canadian Forces' assuming this responsibility. That came the following day when he advised McCallum that the Canadian Forces could commit a battle group and brigade headquarters (slightly more than two thousand soldiers) to ISAF for one year, assuming all the other preconditions were met. With this advice in hand, McCallum then told his senior team, "The goal is now to get a deal in Munich [with Struck] and announce early next week." The senior team also

decided that McCallum would meet in Munich with his Italian counterpart and with Lord Robertson, the NATO Secretary-General, to
begin the process of finding a partner for the second six-month period
of Canada's lead, should Germany end its partnership after the first
six months.

A Deal in Munich

On February 10, McCallum met in Ottawa with his top military and
civilian advisers to brief them on the meetings he and Ken Calder had
had in Munich in the last few days. He informed his officials that they
needed to be ready to announce that week a commitment to lead the
mission in Kabul for twelve months. Struck had told him it was likely
that Germany would stay on with Canada for the first six months of
the Canadian deployment. But the Germans would not be in a position to announce this formally for one month. "I got along very well
with Struck, we saw eye to eye ... wanting a role for NATO and thinking we could work well together [in ISAF]," said McCallum.[29] And
Rumsfeld told McCallum in Munich that he had extracted a commitment from the Italians to stay in Kabul for twelve months after that.

McCallum had met with his Italian counterpart, Antonio Martino,
in Munich. They had met before and got along well. Martino spoke
fluent English, and both men were smokers and economists who had
studied under giants in the field. Martino was trained at the University
of Chicago under Milton Friedman, and McCallum at Cambridge
under the last surviving disciples of John Maynard Keynes. Despite
their warm and collegial relationship, McCallum did not get the kind
of ironclad commitment from Martino that Rumsfeld had claimed to
extract.[30] Nevertheless, it was clear in Munich that everyone but the
French wanted NATO in Kabul.

After listening to the minister, Henault then gave McCallum the
final green light he needed. Canada could lead ISAF—it was work-
able—but the commitment would preclude Canada from any ground

operation in Iraq. McCallum then told his advisers he would try to speak to the prime minister that day—before question period—to obtain his approval for an announcement immediately.

The defence minister was able to arrange a meeting with the prime minister that day. Fifteen minutes before question period, McCallum was summoned to the prime minister's office, Room 309-S in the Centre Block in the House of Commons. He quickly briefed the prime minister on the new developments and told him that the CDS advised him that the mission was feasible militarily and that our allies wanted Canada to take on the role. This was a real opportunity for Canada to show international leadership, and it would help get Canada off the hook on Iraq. The Canadian Forces hadn't taken on a task this signifi-cant in decades. McCallum felt strongly that an announcement should be made immediately, before a leak occurred. Chrétien agreed. McCallum briefly left the meeting and asked his legislative assistant, who was waiting outside the prime minister's office, to find a Liberal Member of Parliament to ask the question. Anita Neville, a Liberal member of the House Standing Committee on National Defence and Veterans Affairs, happened to be in the government lobby at the time. She agreed to ask the minister of national defence a question in the House to give him the opportunity to announce the ISAF decision to the Canadian public in the full glare of the national news media.

More than satisfied with his rare meeting with the prime minister, McCallum took his leave of 309-S. On the way out he said to the prime minister, "Well, that was easy." To which Chrétien replied, "Yes, but don't come around here too often."[31]

McCallum then descended the stairs and went into the Chamber. At 2:45 P.M., thirty minutes into the daily question period, the question was put to him. "Mr. Speaker, we have recently read reports that Canada could be considering a return to Afghanistan. Could the minister of national defence please tell the House if this is true?" McCallum answered, "Mr. Speaker, Canada has been approached by the international community for assistance in maintaining peace and security in Afghanistan for the UN–mandated mission in Kabul. Canada is willing to serve with a battle group and a brigade headquarters for a period of one year, starting late this summer. We are currently in discussion with a number of potential partners."[32]

Canada's leadership of ISAF was to be short-term, only one year in duration. The exit strategy for this mission—finding a replacement nation for Canada—began in earnest before a single Canadian troop had set foot in Kabul. But few in Ottawa realized at the time that the assignment to Kabul, and Canada's efforts to bring NATO into Afghanistan, would draw Canada into a long-term military operation in a country where security was deteriorating. This was the first step down a long road.

FIVE

HALF PREGNANT

I t was clear by the winter of 2003 that Ottawa's decision to send two thousand troops back to Afghanistan on the eve of the Iraq War was, as Sheila Copps has since confirmed, "a neat political way of squaring the problem." The political problem, of course, was how to support Washington in its "War on Terror" without supporting the war in Iraq. The answer to the problem was the so-called "Afghanistan solution."

In September 2002, fifty-five percent of the public opposed Canadian participation in military action against Iraq. Opposition to the war continued to deepen over the next six months, especially in Quebec and British Columbia. The Chrétien government always paid disproportionate attention to opinion polls in Quebec. Historically, French Canadians have bristled at Canada's involvement in Anglo-American military operations that they saw as "imperial adventures," and the invasion of Iraq in 2003 clearly fell into that category.

The Liberal caucus expressed little enthusiasm for Canadian participation in a second American war halfway around the world. Ottawa was skeptical of Washington's claims that Saddam had weapons of mass destruction that posed an imminent threat to global peace and security. Some in Ottawa felt that the war was largely a grudge match by George W. Bush against Saddam, who had tried to assassinate Bush's father. George Bush, they argued, was now getting ready to rectify the error of his father, who had failed to overthrow Saddam when he had the opportunity in 1991. Others argued that this was a blatant attempt to gain control of Iraq's oil resources by exploiting the pretext of weapons of mass destruction—the UN inspectors had come to no final conclusion—and the highly questionable assertion that Saddam harboured terrorists.

By February 2003, even though Ottawa had kept its options open publicly, it was increasingly clear that Chrétien would not join Britain's Tony Blair in support of the Iraq War. Chrétien tipped his hand when he publicly contradicted John McCallum for hinting it was possible that Canada might support the Americans should the UN fail to authorize the use of force. And on February 13 the government's position became even clearer when Chrétien delivered a speech to the Chicago Council on Foreign Relations. This speech, carefully crafted in Ottawa and at the Canadian embassy in Washington, was designed for an American audience and was intended to clarify Canada's thinking and, as gently as possible, to warn Washington of the long-term consequences. One line in particular, written by John McCallum, foreshadowed Canada's ultimate decision: "Therefore it is imperative to avoid the perception of a clash of civilizations. Maximum use of the United Nations will minimize that risk."[1]

The UN was deadlocked, and it appeared increasingly unlikely that the Security Council would pass a resolution authorizing the use of force. Canada's senior diplomat at the UN, Paul Heinbecker, nevertheless made one last valiant effort to broker an acceptable compromise. Canada proposed that UN weapons inspectors be given an additional month to do their work, in exchange for agreement from France and Germany to accept military intervention if the inspectors found that Iraq was in violation of UN resolutions. The prime minister worked the phones from Ottawa with world leaders, urging them to support the Canadian proposal as a way out of the immediate crisis.[2]

Not only was there insufficient support for the Canadian proposal from other members of the UN Security Council, but Canada's initiative also infuriated the United States. A month later, Ambassador Paul Cellucci blasted McCallum, bluntly telling him that Washington did not appreciate the Canadian initiative. Moreover, the Americans were especially angry that Colin Powell got no forewarning that Canada would present this last-minute proposal at the UN. As Cellucci explained, "The French said they would use their veto, so more time wouldn't have changed anything."[3]

On March 17, Prime Minister Chrétien announced in the House of Commons his decision not to participate in military operations against Iraq. Canada had been forced, finally, to clarify its position after London asked Ottawa, on behalf of Washington, for an answer that day on whether Canada would participate in the Iraq War.[4] In response to a question from Leader of the Opposition Stephen Harper, the prime minister read a prepared statement that explained the Canadian decision:

> Mr. Speaker, I want to set out the position of the Government of Canada. We believe that Iraq must fully abide by the resolution of the United Nations Security Council. We have always made clear that Canada would require the approval of the Security Council if we were to participate in a military campaign.
>
> Over the last few weeks the Security Council has been unable to agree on a new resolution authorizing military action. Canada worked very hard to find a compromise to bridge the gap in the Security Council. Unfortunately, we were not successful. If military action proceeds without a new resolution of the Security Council, Canada will not participate.[5]

In light of the failure at the UN, this statement was tantamount to announcing Canada's refusal to participate in military action. Reflecting on the gravity of the moment, Eddie Goldenberg, Chrétien's senior policy adviser, would later write: "For Canada to say no to the United States—the world's only superpower, our next-door neighbour, our very close ally and friend, and the destination of 87% of our exports—was not a decision to be taken lightly."[6]

The announcement of Canada's decision on Iraq unfolded in a similar way to that of the ISAF mission a month earlier. Just prior to question period on March 17, Bill Graham and John McCallum were summoned to the prime minister's office in Room 309-S in the Centre Block. The prime minister, Goldenberg, and a few other officials and PMO staff were in the room. A page containing the statement that the prime minister would give in the House in a few minutes' time was distributed. Then Goldenberg read it aloud to those in the room. Graham and McCallum were asked for their views.[7] It was clear to both men that the question was rhetorical and did not invite a serious discussion about the merits or content of the statement. Rather, the prime minister was merely extending them a courtesy.

Both Graham and McCallum agreed with the statement. But the foreign minister did suggest that perhaps he should give Washington a warning about what was coming.[8] Graham, who had an excellent relationship with Colin Powell, could try to contact his counterpart immediately. Failing that, he could call Paul Cellucci, the U.S. ambassador in Ottawa. It was a simple courtesy that the Americans would appreciate, even though they would be disappointed in Canada's decision. And it was a reasonable-enough suggestion that might in some small way help to limit the damage in Washington.

But Goldenberg wasn't having it. He asked Graham if he thought it appropriate to inform the American government before informing the Canadian people.[9] That intervention ended the discussion. Within a few minutes, Chrétien stood up in Parliament and announced Canada's position to the world.

Despite Goldenberg's desire to keep the decision secret until the prime minister had made his announcement, the American television network CNN got wind that something important was coming out of Ottawa. They chose to carry question period live that day, something they had never done before and have never done since. Another day in Ottawa, another leak.

The Americans were more than a little surprised both at Canada's decision and at the way it was communicated. Paul Cellucci reflected: "We thought Canada would support the war in Iraq. After the announcement [that Canada would not support the Iraq War] my staff were called to a meeting at Foreign Affairs and were told three things. One, Canada will say good things about the President and bad things about Saddam Hussein. Two, Canada will keep its ships in the Persian Gulf in the War on Terror. Three, Canada will keep its exchange officers in place."[10] But Ottawa then badly mishandled the ongoing communications on the Iraq issue, Cellucci insisted, causing further damage in Washington. "Then the Prime Minister called it an unjust war, contrary to what the Department of Foreign Affairs told us," said Cellucci.[11]

Bill Graham saw it differently. "Cellucci had clearly misled Washington. He was listening too much to the hawks in our military. He seriously believed we were going to Iraq. He never talked to me. I would have been very cautionary had he. He came to see me after the decision, and he just tore a strip off me."[12] Not all Americans agreed that Canada had mishandled the communications. A group of senior American businessmen in Chicago told Graham that Canada didn't suffer in the United States the way the French did because "we didn't rub the Americans' noses in it."[13] Chrétien had apparently told Graham at the time, "Thank God we are not on the UN Security Council; our diplomats work all their careers to get us on the Security Council but there are times like this when you don't want to be on it."[14] Canada was well advised, the prime minister clearly felt, to keep a low profile.

Condoleezza Rice, the U.S. national security adviser, fairly represented Ottawa's thinking. The day after Canada's announcement on Iraq, at a White House senior staff meeting, she reported that she had spoken with her counterpart in Canada, who said, "Sorry, they can't be part of this, but [they] promised to keep their rhetoric at a low boil— just enough to satisfy Canadian public opinion but without being belligerent or provocative."[15]

The Legacy

Today, Canada's decision not to participate in the Iraq War is widely considered to be one of Prime Minister Chrétien's three most important achievements of his decade in office. Along with the *Clarity Act,* which sets out the process for a referendum on Quebec sovereignty, and his work with Finance Minister Paul Martin to eliminate thirty years of federal deficits, Chrétien's refusal to commit Canada's troops to the invasion of Iraq stands as a measure of the prime minister's foresight and wisdom.

Some criticize the way Chrétien made his decision on Iraq, delegating Canadian decision-making to the UN Security Council—effectively to France, Russia, and China, the powers likely to exercise a veto against the draft resolution—while limiting debate and discussion within Parliament. There is justification to this criticism; Canada has a very shallow and closed process of debate and discussion on issues of national security.

Some also question the motives for the decision. The prime minister was preoccupied by a forthcoming election in Quebec and did not want to give ammunition to the Parti Québécois, the *indépendantiste* party in Quebec, and he did not want to split his caucus. Both were certainly important considerations and played a significant role in the final decision. The day after the bombing in Iraq began, the *Toronto Star* reported on its front page that seventy-one percent of Canadians supported the prime minister and that support for his position was highest in Quebec.

Yet there is another story to be told about Canada's decision not to participate in the invasion of Iraq. This story is much less flattering. In the days and weeks preceding the announcement in the House of Commons, a series of discussions took place behind closed doors among Canada's military leadership, civilian officials, and politicians. These conversations led to decisions that, at the very least, undermined the integrity and coherence of Canada's position on Iraq and, at the worst, made a mockery of it. They also revealed deep-seated problems in Canada's foreign and defence policy-making, and in the management of Canadian–American relations and civil–military relations. In short, serious problems exist in some of the country's important structures, institutions, and policies.

Task Force 151

In early February, Chief of the Defence Staff Ray Henault and his deputy, Greg Maddison, told McCallum that the Canadian navy had an opportunity to lead a multinational naval task force, which included American ships and those of other countries not yet committed to an invasion of Iraq. The task force, known as TF 151, would support Operation Enduring Freedom (OEF), but would require a change in the area of operations for Canada's navy; the navy would move farther up into the Persian Gulf, very close to Iraq's territorial waters and a long way from Afghanistan. To lead this task force, Canada would have to deploy a destroyer—the thirty-year-old *Iroquois*—that had command and control capability. This would mean a net gain for Canada of one ship in the region—two frigates and one destroyer—for a six-month assignment. And the CDS indicated he wanted to sail the *Iroquois* from Halifax on February 17.

Years later, when asked about why he recommended Canada take on the command of TF 151, Henault responded: "My recommendation was linked to operational performance. Our Navy has been doing business there from the very beginning. We had a very strong operational involvement. It made sense that Canada continue, even though we were not going to be involved in the Iraq War. The Dutch, the French, the Greeks were in the same position that we were in. We had been heavily involved since 2001 and I did not want to leave an operational hole."[16] Henault made an operational and political argument for why the Canadian navy should have remained part of the task force, but did not address why Canada should have sought command responsibility, a vitally important detail.

After McCallum had had one or two more discussions with Henault and Maddison, it became apparent that TF 151 would be de facto, if not de jure, "double-hatted." It would support OEF but would also probably provide some as yet undefined support to Operation Iraqi Freedom (OIF) once hostilities had commenced against Iraq.

The multilateralists in Foreign Affairs, who were so deeply committed to the UN process on Iraq and were strongly opposed to Canadian involvement in the war without another UN resolution, might have been expected to dismiss the idea of leading the naval force. But surprisingly, Canada's senior diplomats held a much more pragmatic, Washington-centric view. Canada's ambassador to NATO, David Wright, on a visit to Ottawa, urged McCallum to take on the leadership of the task force. Wright warned the minister that Canada would pay a price if it didn't double-hat its ships in the region. The senior mandarins in the Pearson Building were also generally supportive of leading TF 151. They saw it as a demonstration of tangible support for the United States in the region and argued that this support was especially important given the likelihood that Canada would refuse to participate in the war against Iraq.

Bill Graham reflected later on the advice he got from senior officials in Foreign Affairs:

The discussion centred around the problem, we're not involved in the Iraq campaign, what justification do we have to be involved in the naval operation [TF 151]. And our view was the naval operation dated from the original mission to restrain the Taliban and control al-Qaeda, and that therefore this was a legitimate presence in the Gulf for a different purpose. And for us to pull out at that time would have been highly aggravating to the Americans and our other allies ... One thing that certainly cinched it for me was there was a French vessel in the Task Force, so I said if the French can stay there—with all their Cartesian logic—we can do the same.[17]

Deputy Prime Minister John Manley subsequently made similar arguments. He thought that with the Iraq decision behind the government, "We've made our point with the Americans. A Canadian role in this naval task force," he said, "gives us something to point to with the Americans."[18] Ottawa decided that Canada would assume command of TF 151, and would worry later about how it would manage the problem of continuing to lead once the U.S. invasion of Iraq had begun.

Predictably, officials at the South Tower leaked the news. On February 11, *The Globe and Mail* reported that "Ottawa and Washington have agreed that a senior Canadian officer will command all allied naval warships, aside from the U.S. aircraft carrier and its close escorts, in the Persian Gulf south of Kuwait and extending through the Strait of Hormuz. Commodore Roger Girouard assumed command on Friday of the new Task Force 151, which will be responsible for escorting ships, intercepting and boarding suspect vessels and guarding against attacks on shipping."[19] The paper went on to point out that this initiative was part of a Canadian plan to increase preparations in anticipation of a war against Iraq and that twenty-five senior Canadian officers had been sent to an American base in the Persian Gulf state of Qatar to plan for that purpose in Iraq.[20]

Three days later, *The Globe* went further: "If war breaks out, the Canadian warships will, at the very least, start escorting civilian ships such as tankers in co-operation with other allied navies, which would be critical to the war effort. 'The region will be more dangerous,' Cmdre. Girouard said. 'We would be in a situation where we would have to co-ordinate some escorts, in particular in the strait, by offering protection to ships and oil tankers that don't have the means to defend themselves.'" The Canadian Commodore suggested that were Canada to participate in the war against Iraq, the warships would likely escort ships farther north, closer to Iraq.[21]

The scene had been set, publicly, for controversy.

[handwritten margin note: "no participation in Iraq, different reasons for why."]

The South Tower Gets Uncomfortable

It wasn't until the end of February that the military leadership fully realized where the prime minister was going in his thinking about Iraq. When they did, Henault and Maddison shifted gears. They told McCallum that Canada would have to pull out of the leadership of TF 151, which it had just assumed, if Ottawa was not going to participate in military operations against Iraq. Henault has since confirmed this advice to McCallum, but for an entirely different reason: "Yes, I did recommend that we resign the leadership of Task Force 151. The leadership had operational implications for our forces. We had provided a very high level of support for naval operations. We needed to give the Navy time to reconstitute. The Navy needed a break in the operational tempo," said Henault.[22] But at this point the navy had only been involved in TF 151 for a matter of days.

The lawyers were then brought in to help navigate these treacherous waters. International lawyers in both the Department of National Defence and in Foreign Affairs believed that if TF 151 were protecting ships involved in the invasion of Iraq, then Canada might legally become a belligerent or a party to the conflict. "The Judge Advocate General [the chief military lawyer] was not very popular with the CDS [Henault] when he gave these legal opinions," reflected McCallum.[23] Graham went further: "The tricky bit was we had some legal opinions intimating the fact that if we were there and were doing interdiction work, that we were at war with Iraq technically and legally, even though we were saying politically that we were not. This was very murky waters, there is no question about that."[24] Since Iraq interdiction work was likely to be part of the mandate of the naval task force, it seemed clear to officials in Defence that Canada would have to bow out. Or perhaps the Americans would save Canada the embarrassment and reassign the command of TF 151 to a nation that was part of the coalition.

Foreign Affairs thought differently on this issue from Defence. The diplomats were now deeply concerned about the Canada–United States relationship in the wake of the impending "No" on Iraq. They saw

Canada's leadership of this naval task force as a way to mitigate Washington's inevitable displeasure at Canada's refusal to participate in Operation Iraqi Freedom.

But the military leadership disagreed. What Foreign Affairs proposed was not feasible militarily and would be far too confusing operationally, they argued. A Canadian officer aboard a Canadian ship would be commanding the ships of other nations, including an American ship, involved in a coalition that was at war when Canada was not part of that coalition. To the military, such a position was untenable and, frankly, unimaginable. The senior military leadership also expected that Canada would be asked to leave Qatar once active coalition operational planning began, if Ottawa did not officially support the Iraq War. This would have made leading TF 151 impossible.

Clearly, the South Tower wanted the Canadian government to support the United States in its war against Iraq and to make a military contribution to the war effort. And initially, before Chrétien had made his decision on Iraq, Canada's generals and admirals probably thought that taking on TF 151 would "help" the politicians make the "right" decision. Surely Canada could not continue to lead this task force and not be part of the Iraq coalition. And surely Canada would not pull its navy out of the task force days after it had assumed command. There was a black and white choice to be made. Military leaders hoped to create the enabling conditions for the outcome they wanted. They did not, however, consider the domestic political factors that weighed so heavily with Chrétien.

Officials in Foreign Affairs, unlike their colleagues in the South Tower, wanted it both ways. They did not want Canada to support the Iraq War without another UN resolution, which they considered highly unlikely. Yet they wanted Canada's military to remain in the region to help manage the Ottawa–Washington relationship. In a sense, they wanted to be half pregnant, a position no senior leader in Defence could contemplate, much less accept.

The prime minister himself eventually resolved the internal debate about Canada's role in TF 151. While Chrétien understood the difficulties, he did not want Canada to be seen to be leaving the Persian Gulf at that critical time, even if the military leadership regarded the operation as unworkable. The prime minister was a pragmatist, and he wanted deft management of the highly charged issue of the role of Canada's navy in the region. Ottawa would need to put a little water in its wine, take some political risks at home, and move forward with a somewhat less-than-coherent policy on Iraq.

McCallum and Graham then decided that McCallum would call his French, Greek, and New Zealand counterparts immediately—they all had ships in TF 151 and their governments all seemed unlikely to support the Iraq War—to ascertain how they were planning to manage their participation in the task force.

The first call was to Mark Burton, minister of defence for the Government of New Zealand. Burton, facing the same legal dilemmas, was agonizing over the problem and indicated he planned to talk to his own prime minister shortly. Burton asked McCallum to call him back once Canada had reached a clear position.

The next call was to Paris, to Michèle Alliot-Marie, the fiery French defence minister who was best known internationally for doing battle with Donald Rumsfeld, both in public and at the NATO table. As far as Alliot-Marie was concerned, there was no international legal impediment. A communications problem existed, to be sure, but not a legal issue. In her view, France could continue to participate in TF 151 without legally being a belligerent in the war against Iraq. Or at least Paris had convinced itself of this argument. McCallum's Greek counterpart, Yannos Papantoniou, thought that Greece could stay in TF 151 as long as it remained exclusively engaged in Operation Enduring Freedom (OEF) tasks. It would not support operations against Iraq. On March 17, McCallum heard from Mark Burton that New Zealand would remain in TF 151.

In Ottawa, there was great angst among the military leadership that the prime minister's opposition to the Iraq invasion made it impossible

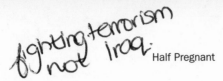

for Canada to retain the leadership of TF 151. But the prime minister thought otherwise. His statement in the House of Commons indirectly revealed his predisposition: "We have ships in the area as part of our participation in the struggle against terrorism. Our ships will continue to perform their important mission against terrorism." That was the distinction. Canada would remain leader of TF 151 but wear only one hat—the OEF hat—even though the military argued that separating the two would prove to be almost impossible operationally. It would be the navy's responsibility to make the policy work and to ensure that Canada limited its tasks to those that were legitimately part of OEF.

Now that the policy with respect to TF 151 was clear, NDHQ turned its attention to the challenging issues of implementation. Commodore Girouard was instructed that the Canadian navy was not to engage in activities associated with the invasion of Iraq. But the general instruction could not address myriad political and operational issues. Some Iraqis would flee once combat began. If a Canadian ship interdicted them, would they be returned to Canada or handed over to the Americans? Detainees from Iraq would have no legal status in Canada because Ottawa was officially not supporting the Iraq War. And were the Canadian navy to hand over an Iraqi national to the United States, Canada would appear to be—and legally might well be—supporting the war. There were no clear answers to those kinds of questions. Ultimately, it was decided that if a Canadian ship were to seize an Iraqi national, Commodore Girouard would call home for instructions.

These tortured scenarios illustrated Canada's extraordinarily awkward position once it had decided to retain command of TF 151. The contradictions were obvious and the wound was self-inflicted. At times the contortions of military leaders approached the comic. In April, after the war had started, Girouard was forced to make a bizarre public statement: "There's no doubt in my mind that if Saddam Hussein himself ... was found in a vessel that we stumbled upon for some reason, we would not knowingly let a member of that level of the regime go. We would relate back to National Defence headquarters [in Ottawa] for guidance."[25] In other words, the black hole on the Rideau would have to decide what to do with Saddam Hussein.

Clarity from the Allies—Contortions in Canada

The Dutch, the New Zealanders, and the French then clarified their positions. They ordered their naval commanders not to allow their ships in TF 151 to operate in the entrance to the Persian Gulf, so as not to provide support to the war. They were also instructed not to engage with Iraqi vessels or vessels under an Iraqi flag.

But Canada's naval commanders were not as lucky. In an effort to satisfy Ottawa's political objectives in Washington, they now found themselves in extraordinarily difficult circumstances. Girouard expressed publicly how difficult it was for him to do his job in TF 151:

> I've been given a box by the chief of defence staff. I've coloured an awful lot of that box and there's no doubt in my mind that there are times when I've come really, really, really close to the edge of the line, but I haven't gone over. It was explained to me very succinctly, as I represent Canada now, where I should not be going. That has had its challenges.
>
> I was asked to do something and I assessed what the situation was and I told them that I could not do that, that I felt it fell into the OIF, the Operation Iraqi Freedom rubric. They thought about that for a little bit and they agreed and at that point, an American asset took up a particular job.[26]

Canada's role in TF 151 as commander was unique. The United States and other countries clearly saw the task force as doubled-hatted, serving both OEF and OIF. As a result, some countries chose to work under one hat only, and were able to restrict their ships' operations geographically to ensure that they provided no direct support to the war. Since Canada had command of the task force, it had no such luxury. Whether or not Canada's ships in TF 151 actually carried out any duties directly related to the war in Iraq will probably never be known. Yet according to the official record, the Canadian navy somehow managed the seemingly impossible. It ran and participated in a double-hatted naval task force but did not get involved in command or operational responsibilities related to one of these hats. A very blurred line existed between OEF and OIF, a blurriness that the United States probably deliberately encouraged. Washington considered these operations as a single integrated mission, all part of the War on Terror.

Canadian activities undertaken in theatre were judgment calls by Girouard and other officers that were likely not cleared with NDHQ. On the record, Canada's ships in TF 151 never detained an Iraqi. Had they done so, the incoherence of this mission and of Canada's Iraq policy would have been fully exposed.

IT WAS NOT just the command of TF 151 that undermined the coherence and integrity of Canada's policy on the war in Iraq. There were also the exchange officers. Early on McCallum was told that Canada had a hundred or so low-level exchange officers who were employed largely in technical support roles with the American and British militaries. The military advice was unequivocal: These officers should remain in place at all costs, regardless of the government's ultimate decision on the Iraq War.[27] Pulling them out would do permanent and irreparable damage to Canada–U.S. and Canada–U.K. military-to-military relations. Canada would lose access to information and intelligence. And there would be an intangible loss of trust with our closest allies that might never be recovered. "I was very concerned about the operational aspects," stated Henault. "Our men had become key to operations, and to pull them out just when these units were moving into combat would have put large numbers of people at risk. It would have created a substantial hole in the decision making process."[28]

Kept soldiers there on the basis of relations. (exchange officers)

On the eve of the war, McCallum received new, more detailed information about these officers. "We had about 100 officers and non commissioned officers on exchange," reflected Henault.[29] These men and women were assigned to American, British, and Australian units. These positions had been described to McCallum as technical, located outside of Iraq, some in a U.S. headquarters in Kuwait. There were no shooters, no infantrymen, no fighter pilots. The military painted a picture for the minister of a benign, marginal group of people that should be of little concern to anyone.[30] What the minister did not know until later was that the most senior Canadian officer on exchange was a brigadier general, Walt Natynczuk, who was directly involved in planning the invasion of Iraq from the American headquarters in Kuwait.[31]

In McCallum's view, it was bad enough that a Canadian brigadier general was working at U.S. headquarters in Kuwait. Then Henault informed McCallum that the U.S. military HQ was mobile and was leaving Kuwait and entering Iraq with Natynczuk in tow. The one fig leaf—Kuwait, not Iraq—had been removed. McCallum reflected:

> One of the problems I had was a misconception of military terminology. They said we had people at the headquarters in Kuwait. And at that point I didn't understand—or maybe they deliberately didn't tell me—that headquarters move. One day Henault came in and said General Natynczuk has moved into Iraq with the headquarters. If I had known this was a possibility in advance maybe I would have pushed to pull them out. It was pretty untenable not to be part of the Iraq war but to have soldiers in Iraq … I remember discussions where we considered pulling them out and the military were hugely resistant to this, claiming that it would cause irreparable harm to their relationships with the Americans. This was probably an exaggeration.[32]

Graham felt much the same way. "That was a serious concern for us. General Natynczuk was there [in Iraq]. This was a very slender legal thread on which we hung."[33] Henault thought otherwise. "We had legal advice that our presence would not create the status of belligerent for us. This legal advice was shared with the Department of Foreign Affairs. Our legal people were adamant on this issue," stated Henault.[34]

After the decision not to participate in military operations against Iraq was announced, the government was excoriated daily in the House of Commons and by the media for keeping these exchange officers in place. Had Natynczuk's precise role become publicly known, there would have been even more intense criticism of the government in Parliament, in the press, and in the public. But the government managed to keep his presence out of the news. The prime minister himself took questions on the exchange officers, as did McCallum and Graham. The response to the Opposition attacks was simple: These officers would not be involved directly in the conflict; Canada had made these commitments to its allies; the commitments had to be respected; we would expect nothing less of our allies. Government leaders stuck to this line of argument, even though other countries that had chosen not to participate in the war quickly withdrew their exchange officers assigned to British and American forces in the region once hostilities broke out.

Yet the exchange officers who remained in place and Canada's command of a double-hatted task force gave the Opposition the ammunition it needed to claim that the government's policy was duplicitous. They characterized the Chrétien government as one that wanted to have its cake and eat it too. To some degree, it did.

This was a government that was so transfixed at all levels with managing relations with Washington—politician to politician, general to general, senior official to senior official—that the foundation of Ottawa's policy on the war in Iraq was put at risk. The decisions on exchange officers and the command of TF 151 needlessly exposed the government's policy to daily assault and even ridicule in the House of Commons. As McCallum recalled, "That's when [Stephen] Harper called me an idiot."[35] In an almost schizophrenic way, the government bragged publicly about its decision to stand aside from the war in Iraq because it violated core principles of multilateralism and support for the United Nations. At the same time, senior Canadian officials, military officers, and politicians were currying favour in Washington, privately telling anyone in the State Department or the Pentagon who would listen that, by some measures, Canada's indirect contribution to the American war effort in Iraq—three ships and one hundred exchange officers—exceeded that of all but three other countries that were actually part of the coalition. McCallum himself told Paul Cellucci, the U.S. ambassador in Ottawa, that Canada was "the opposite of Spain," a country that originally supported the invasion of Iraq but that contributed very little militarily to the war effort. The government then spent the next few weeks monitoring very closely what its allies were contributing to the American war effort in the region to ensure that Canada would not be left behind. Just in case, senior officials in Ottawa identified other assets—political and military—that the Americans might appreciate.

The events of that winter of 2003 reveal both a conflicted policy on the Iraq War and a clash of world views among civilian officials, politicians, and military leaders. The military leadership was so obsessed with its relationship with the Pentagon that it was willing to risk its own credibility with its political masters. Military leaders tried to drive foreign policy in the direction they wanted it to go, not normally an appropriate role for the military in a democracy. One senior official said "that DND gets the militaries of other countries to pressure and lobby Ottawa on its behalf."[36] There is, of course, an irony to this story. The South Tower created a trap for the government by urging that Canada lead the TF 151. Once the war had begun, however, they found to their discomfort and chagrin that the politicians and diplomats liked the final destination more than the generals did.

The story of Canada's policy on the war in Iraq is also a story of a political leadership that spoke with one "principled" voice to Canadians and another, quite different, "pragmatic" voice in Washington. Fortunately, few in the public could hear the two voices at the same time.

SIX

PULLING IT TOGETHER

Once the debate about Canada's participation in the war in Iraq was over, at NDHQ, minds turned to the next major task at hand—making Canada's ISAF commitment a reality. Time was of the essence. Canada had agreed to become the lead nation in Kabul beginning that summer. And there was much to do, much to plan, and much to resolve before then.

In mid-April 2003, McCallum met with his senior civilian and military advisers to discuss the challenges they would confront in ISAF, including the question of who would replace Canada as lead when its term ended. Rumsfeld had assured McCallum that Italy would replace Canada after a year in theatre, but word was now coming in to NDHQ that neither Italy nor Spain was interested in replacing Canada as ISAF lead in 2004. And while Germany planned to remain engaged at a significant level in Kabul until 2006, it did not want the ISAF lead for a second time. This was no small problem for Canada's military planners. If a replacement were not identified soon, would Canada be able to get out of Kabul or at least reduce its troop commitments in a year's time? Putting a NATO flag in Kabul therefore became even more urgent.

Other problems were emerging. The ISAF commanders were considering the western section of Kabul, the most topographically challenging part of the city, as Canada's area of operations. It is located on one side of a ridge with two passes leading into it and, therefore, Canadian forces could be cut off from the rest of the international forces. Canada would require a robust force to deal with that possibility. The Canadian army needed the capability to survive on its own for a time if necessary.

Western Kabul was also the most devastated part of the city, with very little functioning infrastructure. It had been on the front lines of the civil war between the Taliban and the Northern Alliance before the U.S.–led invasion. Seventy percent of the buildings in Kabul were destroyed, including seventy-one thousand houses, and a disproportionate amount of that destruction was in the western part of the city. The city was rife with disputes among residents about land ownership, and sewage was a problem. On a trip to Ottawa in late May, Nigel Fisher, a senior official with the UN Mission in Afghanistan, told Calder, Bloodworth, and McCallum's chief of staff that "western Kabul was still a mess" and that it was the "worst part of the city."

Attacks against international forces were also increasing. Germany had lost sixteen of its soldiers. And Canada's military leadership remained highly critical of the management of ISAF, pointing out that it consisted of a five thousand–person force, with only eight hundred troops on the ground and a very heavy headquarters contingent. But Canada was locked in at this point.

As the nation with the largest number of troops in Kabul, Canada would be entitled to the position of deputy commander at ISAF headquarters—an officer of the rank of major general, a two star. Henault recommended this position be given to Brigadier General Andrew Leslie, who would be promoted.

Leslie was a controversial figure inside the Canadian Forces. The grandson of former chief of the general staff and minister of national defence Andrew McNaughton and the seventh generation of his family to serve in the Canadian Forces, he is highly motivated, sophisticated, and intelligent. Forty-five years old at the time, he looked ten years younger. Leslie would put a good face on Canada in the international community and with the Karzai government. Inevitably, Leslie had his critics as well. Some of his colleagues considered him too ambitious, too "political"—meaning too cozy with the politicians—and too willing to take risks. Nevertheless, Henault recommended him, and McCallum accepted the recommendation enthusiastically. He had gotten to know Leslie recently and was a fan.

There was a bigger question to consider: Did Canada want the overall command of ISAF at some point during the deployment to Kabul? Canada would have the largest number of troops on the ground in Kabul—about two thousand—but this did not necessarily mean that a Canadian general would be given the command of all forces in the multinational mission. Did Ottawa want that prestigious and high-profile post to go to a Canadian? This was no small matter. A Canadian officer had not commanded a multinational force of this scale and importance since the Suez Crisis of 1956. If Canada did want this responsibility, Ottawa would have to fight for the command.

There was also worrying information. McCallum was told that the United States wanted to reduce its footprint in Afghanistan from ten thousand to three thousand troops. This was a major concern to the leadership of the Canadian Forces—and for good reason. The situation in Afghanistan, which military leaders had thought relatively stable just weeks before, was worsening. Incursions by armed groups from Pakistan were on the rise, and the level of combat in the spring of 2003 was higher than it had been in the winter. The risk to Canadians was growing, and the United States was the only country with the requisite firepower and capability to pull the forces out if things got really out of hand.

Unofficial reports suggested that things were even worse on the ground. In mid-April, Bloodworth and McCallum's chief of staff had met with Ross Reid, a former minister in the Mulroney government. He had been working in Afghanistan for the National Democratic Institute, an American organization that helps to create democratic institutions in developing countries. Reid's analysis of the situation was shockingly pessimistic. He painted a grimmer picture of Afghanistan than did the generals at NDHQ.

A ruthless thug and a former leader of the Northern Alliance, Marshal Mohammed Qasim Fahim, now led the Afghan Ministry of

Defence. During the Soviet occupation of Afghanistan, Fahim joined the Afghan mujahideen led by the legendary Ahmad Shah Masood. He became Masood's intelligence chief and eventually the de facto leader of the Northern Alliance after Masood's assassination in 2001. By 2003, with Fahim as defence minister in the Afghan Transitional Authority, many thought that he was more powerful than President Hamid Karzai, in large part because he commanded a militia several times larger than the nascent Afghan army.

Reid reported that Fahim was widely regarded as a corrupt and ruthless warlord. Karzai, Reid said, had failed to take advantage of the opportunity that the international community had given him. There was little visible change since he had become president—no movement on political reform. Afghans were becoming disillusioned with their new president.

Reid confirmed that the security situation in Kabul and across the country was deteriorating, largely as a consequence of incursions across the Afghan–Pakistan border, which he described as "unmanageable." He also pointed out that the Pakistan Intelligence Services—the ISI—as well as the Iranians, continued to meddle in Afghanistan's internal affairs. More ominously, many citizens saw the Afghan National Army (ANA)—the institution that the international community thought of as the key to the future stability of the country and central to the exit strategy of Western troops—as a source of insecurity and instability. Consequently, the Afghans wanted the international community to play a stronger role in their country. They especially wanted ISAF to extend its mandate and authority across the whole of Afghanistan to provide security to a war-weary population. Rumsfeld was also pushing for extension, primarily to free American forces for Iraq.

But Reid was somewhat more optimistic about western Kabul, the area where the Canadian Forces would be operating, than were the generals at NDHQ. While it was indeed tricky terrain—with one million inhabitants, no electricity, and little functioning infrastructure—

it had important strengths and assets. In this part of Kabul, community spirit was strong, local non-governmental organizations thrived,
and social cohesion was comparatively high. Western Kabul was also
the home of the University of Kabul.

Reid's assessment seems prescient today. His analysis of the impact
of insurgents crossing the border from Pakistan as "unmanageable,"
and his insistence that ISAF would have to increase its responsibilities
foreshadowed the critical challenges Canadian soldiers would face four
years later. Today, ISAF is in fact deployed throughout the country.
And it is now conventional wisdom that the Afghan–Pakistan frontier
is indeed unmanageable.

NATO Steps Up to the Plate

On April 16, 2003, at the urging of Germany, the Netherlands, and
Canada, the North Atlantic Treaty Organization decided to take
responsibility for the ISAF mission. NATO confirmed this publicly:

> NATO is taking on new operations which meet the common
> security interest of the Allies. We commend the participation of
> Allies in the International Security Assistance Force (ISAF) in
> Kabul, Afghanistan, and the present role of Germany and the
> Netherlands as lead nations in the mission. From August, NATO
> will take the lead role by assuming the strategic coordination,
> command and control of ISAF. ISAF will continue to operate
> under United Nations mandate.[1]

The NATO umbrella was important to Canada. Ottawa saw
NATO's involvement as key to the success of Canada's mission in
Kabul, especially since no replacement nation had yet emerged. The
presence of NATO gave the military leadership at NDHQ a measure
of comfort should the situation on the ground deteriorate badly. It
helped as well that, in theory at least, Brussels would have the primary

responsibility for finding a country to replace Canada after it had honoured its one-year commitment to ISAF.

ON MAY 5, German defence minister Peter Struck paid a brief visit to Canada on his way home from a meeting with Donald Rumsfeld. Upon his arrival in Ottawa, Struck and his advisers met with McCallum and his senior officials at the Ottawa International Airport. The two defence ministers had met several times before in Germany and at NATO meetings. They got along well and spoke frankly, even when their advisers were in the room. Struck, a soft-spoken man in his sixties, smoked a pipe and spoke through a translator. Yet occasionally he would respond to a question or punctuate a remark in fluent English.

As they sat down to begin their "bilateral," the conversation turned immediately to Iraq. There was at the time some discussion of NATO getting heavily involved in Iraq. Poland, which was part of the coalition in Iraq, was expected to formally ask NATO to assist around the city of Mosul. Struck stunned McCallum when he informed him that neither Germany nor France would block NATO's involvement in Iraq. McCallum was concerned: Surely NATO could not handle two "out-of-area" operations at the same time. If it were to deploy in Iraq, it followed logically that NATO would be less capable of managing the challenges in Kabul effectively.[2]

McCallum told Struck that Canada was not at all keen on NATO involvement in Iraq. He expected his German counterpart to agree. However, Struck was reserved now that Canada had agreed to take over from Germany. Struck said that he needed to see what the United States, the United Kingdom, and Poland wanted NATO to do in Iraq before he could make any commitments. Germany clearly didn't relish the thought of antagonizing the Americans again.

But McCallum did extract one important assurance from Struck that day. Germany would in all likelihood continue to operate the Kabul airport, the vital link to the outside world and the escape hatch for ISAF forces. Canada had no capability to run this airport.

Henault had advised the government that the Canadian Forces could not take on this mission unless some competent power took responsibility for the airport. McCallum was relieved to have Struck's assurance that Germany would secure the airport. Another box ticked off.

Next on their agenda was the issue of the command of ISAF. Struck told the Canadians that NATO—and by that he meant the Supreme Allied Commander, Europe (SACEUR), General Jones—would decide which country would get the command. Germany, he said, might well be asked to continue as commander even though it would be providing fewer troops than Canada. Or perhaps Italy would be approached to provide a senior officer to take command. The Germans evidently did not see Canada assuming this tough responsibility.

Struck also reported on his assessment of Rumsfeld's thinking about Afghanistan, having just met the secretary of defence in Washington. Struck thought that the United States was not anxious to reduce its forces in Afghanistan, contrary to the rumours that were swirling around. In addition, Struck described Washington's new concept, the Provincial Reconstruction Teams (PRTs).

Developed by the U.S. army, the Provincial Reconstruction Teams would include both military and civilian personnel working together in the Afghan provinces. The official role of the PRTs was to "conduct operations to strengthen the Interim Afghan Transitional Authority's influence through effective interaction with regional, political, military, and religious leaders, the UN Mission in Afghanistan, Security Sector coordinating bodies, international organizations and non-governmental organizations within the regions." The teams were to "encourage peace and stability within provinces/regions and monitor the supervision of developmental activities throughout Afghanistan."[3] Over time, PRTs were expected to engage directly in development and reconstruction work of their own. Each team would be tailored to the particular needs of a given region. In one province, the focus might be on supporting local government administration, in another it might be on training police, and in a third it might concentrate on infrastructure development.

PRTs were at the core of the post-war nation-building strategy the United States had developed for Afghanistan, a strategy that was totally absent in Iraq. It was Washington's intention to spread a network of PRTs throughout Afghanistan, ideally with at least one team from each coalition country. These teams would, in Pentagon planning, serve two vital purposes: The first was to help rebuild and extend security throughout Afghanistan, a country that had been at war consistently for thirty years and was devastated by the almost continuous fighting. The second was to permit the Americans to gradually reduce their footprint in Afghanistan by bringing in Europeans, Canadians, and other coalition partners to do the longer-term reconstruction work.

The Bush administration, when it had first come to office, had mocked "nation-building" as something the United States did not do. The American military was neither keen nor experienced in nation-building. It appears that the Pentagon developed the concept of PRTs as part of its exit strategy from Afghanistan. To encourage other nations to take responsibility for provincial teams, the Americans built a "demonstration" team early on in the region of Gardez.

When Struck and Rumsfeld met in May, both men agreed on the importance of the Provincial Reconstruction Teams. The Germans saw the PRTs as consistent with what they wanted to emphasize in Afghanistan—reconstruction rather than combat or counterinsurgency operations. Struck thought they would help to bring stability to the regions. He told McCallum that, notwithstanding Germany's heavy, ongoing commitment in Kabul, the country might send a PRT of thirty to fifty civilian experts and seventy to eighty soldiers elsewhere in Afghanistan. Before too long, Germany would indeed lead two PRTs north of Kabul, in Feyzabad and Konduz, with contributions from other European countries.

John Meets George

The following day, May 6, McCallum met with NATO Secretary-General George Robertson in Ottawa. George Islay MacNeill Robertson, Baron Robertson of Port Ellen, was Secretary-General of NATO from 1999 to 2004. He was a Scot and a Labour Party stalwart who was elected six times to the British House of Commons and who served as chairman of the Labour Party in Scotland. Robertson—articulate, tough-minded, with a dry sense of humour—was Tony Blair's first defence minister. And he was famous for his straight talking.

The Secretary-General was enthusiastic about a role for NATO in Afghanistan. He thanked McCallum for Canada's persistence in ensuring a role for the alliance in Kabul, telling him that the consistent pressure from Canada and Germany had helped break down French resistance. He told McCallum that ISAF—the first out-of-area operation for the alliance—completely changed the nature of NATO. For Robertson, this was change for the good.

Then the Secretary-General asked the question that McCallum had been waiting for. Why didn't Canada assume command of ISAF? Robertson indicated that no one would stand in Canada's way and that it was appropriate for Canada to assume the command. This was heartening to McCallum, especially since his meeting with Struck the day before had created the impression that the Europeans did not see Canada as capable of commanding this mission.

Robertson also confirmed Struck's view that the U.S. interest in Afghanistan was not waning. He pointed out that both Rumsfeld and his deputy, Paul Wolfowitz, had recently visited Afghanistan and subsequently told Robertson that Washington planned to honour its commitments to Afghanistan, whatever the demands of Iraq. But Robertson's next comment was worrying: He said that, in his opinion, a consensus was growing for NATO involvement in Iraq; even the French wanted NATO in Iraq. Nevertheless, Canada should not despair. Although there would inevitably be a competition for resources, ISAF would not suffer, or so McCallum was reassured.

Fortunately for the alliance, the Secretary-General was wrong in his prediction that NATO would go into Iraq. Since NATO has taken over ISAF, it has struggled to get the necessary commitments of troops from member states so that the mission can succeed. ISAF turned out to be a much bigger "burden" for NATO than its leaders had anticipated. The competition for resources that Robertson spoke about, in an almost glancing way, has been acute and potentially fatal for NATO's mission in Afghanistan, even with no NATO deployment in Iraq.

In time, Robertson would learn the hard way. Before the end of 2003 he would preside over a NATO ministerial meeting where he requested six helicopters for the mission in Kabul. The Secretary-General was stunned to find that no country in his twenty-six-member organization was willing to commit the six helicopters. No member state had the excess helicopter capacity, or so they all claimed. ISAF, at this point, was clearly not a high priority for most NATO members. It was "out of area," outside Europe, and European governments and their militaries were still preoccupied with Bosnia. There was little inclination to help in Afghanistan. Robertson was so exasperated by this recalcitrance that, during the NATO meeting, he decided to go public to put pressure on countries to make the contribution that he needed. He told the press that the greatest military alliance in the history of the world was incapable of finding half a dozen helicopters to ensure the success of its first out-of-area operation. Even this public pressure failed, and the Secretary-General didn't get his helicopters.

Making Mr. Afghanistan

Soon after the meeting with Robertson, McCallum and Henault agreed that Canada should make an aggressive push to seek command in Kabul. Henault was to call the NATO Supreme Allied Commander, Europe (SACEUR), General Jones, an American, the next day to explore the possibility of Canada's taking command. And Henault recommended to McCallum that if Canada were offered the post, General Rick Hillier should be nominated for the job.

Hillier had just been promoted to lieutenant general and put in charge of the Canadian army. He was at the top of Henault's list for the high-profile assignment because he was by far the most qualified of any of the senior officers in the Canadian Forces. His official biography tells the story: "Born in Newfoundland and Labrador, General Rick Hillier joined the Canadian Forces as soon as he could. Throughout his career, General Hillier has had the privilege and pleasure of command-ing troops from the platoon to multi-national formation level within Canada, Europe, Asia and the United States." In short, Hillier was a commander's commander.

Hillier's bio also illustrates how this highly decorated officer could be self-deprecating—a soldier's soldier, as it were. "General Hillier enjoys most recreational pursuits but, in particular, runs slowly, plays hockey poorly and golfs not well at all."

Like many officers of his generation, Hillier had spent the formative years of his career based in Germany at the end of the Cold War. But he was no "sausage general," the derogatory term used to describe offi-cers who spent long stretches of time in the comfortable confines of West Germany. In fact, Hillier had more experience on foreign opera-tions than just about any senior officer in the Canadian Forces. He had spent the 1990s on the front lines of conflicts that erupted as the Cold War ended, notably as commander of NATO's Stabilization Force, Multinational Division (Southwest), in Bosnia-Herzegovina. Hillier was well known and respected in Europe, and in NATO circles.

He also had unique experience in the United States. In 1998, as an exchange officer with the U.S. army, Hillier was appointed as the first Canadian deputy commanding general of III Corps, U.S. Army, in Fort Hood, Texas. In effect, Hillier was second-in-command to a force of approximately thirty thousand American troops. His command was a third larger than the entire Canadian army. This kind of experience, along with his affability and natural Newfoundland charm, made him well known, respected, and liked within the U.S. military and in the Pentagon.

Despite Hillier's impressive credentials, Canada had to work hard to press its case in Europe. Robertson had told McCallum that the command was Canada's for the taking, but his judgment proved overly optimistic. As time went on, it became apparent that Henault was making little or no progress in Brussels. Finally in mid-September, McCallum called Robertson to make it crystal clear that Canada wanted command of ISAF during the second half of its one-year lead-nation commitment.

Robertson was no longer unequivocal. He was now uncertain about whether Canada would get the command, given internal NATO bureaucratic rivalries and intra-alliance politics. McCallum, frustrated, reminded Robertson of their conversation in May. "We heard they were going to put the British in command, when we had the biggest force, so I thought that was a slap in the face. I used quite strong language with him [Robertson]" recalled McCallum.[4] He would be calling Rumsfeld to discuss the matter. Robertson then buckled, telling McCallum that he would urge SACEUR to give the command to the Canadian nominee. And he asked McCallum to delay calling Rumsfeld, and thanked McCallum for alerting him to Canadian sensitivities about the issue before it blew up in his face in Brussels.

McCallum's intervention worked. Word soon came from Brussels that Canada would eventually be given command of ISAF, at the beginning of the second half of its term in February 2004. And Hillier was the general who would become commander. His appointment virtually guaranteed that Rick Hillier would replace Ray Henault as Canada's top soldier—and so he did in less than two years. Hillier's command of ISAF would also ensure that the priority the Canadian military attached to Afghanistan would increase dramatically over time, and that Canada would become more and more deeply involved in the counterinsurgency that was brewing in Afghanistan.

Holiday at Camp Julien

In late June 2003, McCallum made his second of three trips to Afghanistan, this time to Kabul. He was to meet the Afghan political leadership to help ensure that the Canadian deployment was going smoothly.

When he arrived in theatre the Canadian Forces were in the middle of constructing their state-of-the-art thirty-million-dollar base, Camp Julien, which was designed to hold two thousand Canadian troops but would eventually have the capacity to hold many more. The camp was located between the palaces of the king and queen, two formerly opulent but now decrepit structures that sat high on hilltops at either end of the Canadian base. Camp Julien was not yet ready to receive guests, so McCallum and his party stayed on the other side of the city at ISAF headquarters.

On this trip McCallum would have three significant meetings: one with his Afghan counterpart, the notorious Marshal Fahim; one with the deputy interior minister; and one with the president of the Afghan Transitional Authority, Hamid Karzai.

Kabul was a stark contrast to what McCallum had seen the previous July at the Kandahar airfield and surrounding area. It was dry and dusty like Kandahar, but the temperature was a relatively comfortable thirty-five degrees Celsius. A pleasant breeze blew down from the Hindu Kush, mountains that ringed the city and penetrated the clear blue sky of the capital. At night it was cool.

As the minister and his party drove through the streets of the city, they saw destruction and devastation. Most of the buildings had been destroyed and the streets were sewers. Masses of people, almost all unemployed and young, were everywhere. The traffic was a choking, chaotic mix of old cars, horse-drawn carts, bikes, and motorcycles. While there were no reliable estimates of the population of Kabul, experts typically used a range of 1.5 to 3 million people. Refugees from all over Afghanistan were streaming into the city, looking for work, food, and shelter.

Major General Andrew Leslie, the incoming Canadian deputy commander of ISAF, accompanied McCallum on this trip. As they drove through one part of western Kabul, Leslie pointed out a network of warrens that stretched for kilometres. Leslie explained that many of the shanties within this labyrinth were the homes of Taliban and al-Qaeda extremists. The Germans did not go into this ghetto, for fear of being ambushed. But Leslie said that he intended to send in foot patrols to help secure the area.

On June 24, McCallum met with Marshal Mohammed Qasim Fahim at the Afghan Ministry of Defence. Known to the Canadian military as "Fahim Khan," he was allegedly worth hundreds of millions of dollars extorted through the opium trade during the war between the Taliban and the Northern Alliance. He commanded a personal militia of seventy thousand troops. The nascent Afghan army was only ten thousand strong at this point. The international forces in Kabul watched Fahim very closely; it was only ISAF that stood in his way and prevented him from overthrowing Karzai. At one point during the late summer of 2003, Fahim appeared to be on the verge of mounting a coup. It took several days and the positioning of thirty ISAF armoured vehicles between Fahim's tanks and the presidential palace to put the defence minister back in his box. Karzai eventually fired Fahim in 2004 due to intense political pressure from Western nations. In early 2006, however, President Karzai brought him back as an adviser to help manage the insurgency. Fahim had been one of the most effective commanders in the Northern Alliance when it fought the Taliban before the American invasion in 2001.

A stocky man in his mid-forties, the marshal sat behind his desk during the meeting, slumped in his chair. He grunted to McCallum through an interpreter, stating that Afghanistan was moving toward peace and prosperity and needed the international community. He thanked Canada for helping defeat the Taliban and al-Qaeda and for Canada's participation in ISAF. Fahim told McCallum that his country was ready to receive Canadian troops and to co-operate with them.

McCallum responded that Afghanistan was a major priority for Canada and that his government had committed an unprecedented six hundred million dollars in aid. He described Canada as "in between the U.S. and Europe"; Canada had a history of peacekeeping and humanitarian aid, and was neither an old colonial power nor a modern-day empire. He then asked Fahim how he thought Canada could help to make ISAF a success. "Afghanistan is in need of every aspect of life," replied Fahim, "especially education and health care." Fahim said he understood that Canada "knows the cultural aspects of different countries," implying that he expected a sensitivity from Canada toward Afghans that might not be forthcoming from other countries. His comments showed a sophisticated understanding of Afghanistan's problems that caught the Canadians off guard. They had not expected as much from a murderous fighter and criminal.

McCallum and his party then travelled a short distance through the streets of Kabul to the Interior Ministry. He was to meet with the minister, Ali Jalili. But after having been kept waiting in an outer office for half an hour or so, the Canadians were advised that Jalili had been called away to deal with an urgent matter and that his deputy would fill in. It was a brief and somewhat confusing meeting. But the deputy minister made clear how urgent it was that Canada help with police training—particularly with the border police—something the Germans had been doing. Assistance in training police was desperately needed in Afghanistan and remains a priority. McCallum promised that he would explore what Canada could do when he returned to Ottawa. And he did, with no success. The RCMP claimed it had neither the mandate nor the resources to undertake this kind of mission.

Then it was on to the Presidential Palace and the rose-filled grounds, where McCallum was to meet Karzai over tea. Karzai, an ethnic Pashtun, was born in Kandahar and came from a family that had been among the strongest supporters of King Zahir Shah. Perfectly fluent in English, Karzai had studied in India, and then returned to raise funds for the struggle against the Soviet occupation of Afghanistan during the

1980s. Urbane and sophisticated, he had also served as a deputy foreign minister in the government of Burhanuddin Rabbani. Initially Karzai had been a supporter of the Taliban but broke with them because of their close links to Pakistan. He subsequently left Afghanistan and lived in exile in Quetta, Pakistan, where he worked to reinstate the king. His father was assassinated in 1999, allegedly by Taliban agents, and from then on Karzai had worked to overthrow the Taliban regime.

The face of Afghanistan that the president presented could not have been more different from the one presented by the warlord Fahim. Karzai was soft-spoken and articulate. He had a commanding, regal presence and spoke with great authority. He pointed out that sixty thousand people of Afghan origin were living in Canada, one of four countries with large Afghan expatriate communities. He insisted on the need to hold elections in his country, regardless of how difficult that might be. There had been talk of postponing the elections, but Karzai was committed to meeting the original timetable. Why shouldn't they? The "constitutional process was going well," and discussions were even ongoing about a national anthem.

And then the president stated the obvious. What most Afghans wanted were the basic elements of a decent life: security and employment. Afghanistan needed jobs and roads. While the economy was doing better—the new currency was maintaining its value, surpassing the Pakistani rupee, and wages were rising—there was still a long way to go. Karzai argued that an innate and healthy streak of entrepreneurship already existed among Afghans and needed only encouragement and support. This entrepreneurial talent was evident in pockets of the capital city. Amid the rubble of central Kabul, McCallum and his party had driven past an internet café that would not have looked out of place in Toronto, Paris, or London.

And finally, Karzai echoed the view of his rival, Fahim, that while Afghans do not like or trust government very much, they desperately want the basic public services. Schools and health clinics matter to the public. Nonetheless, Karzai emphasized that security was the overriding concern of this war-weary population. As a result, the development of the Afghan army needed to move forward more quickly, and Afghanistan and Pakistan needed to manage much more effectively what Karzai called the "terroristic system." He welcomed NATO's role in ISAF and wanted it expanded throughout Afghanistan. And he thought Canada should consider deploying a Provincial Reconstruction Team (PRT).

Five months later, McCallum met again with Karzai on a return trip to Kabul to assess progress on the ground and to deepen his political relationships with key figures in the Afghan government. He also met a second time with Fahim, as well as with British and international officials. They discussed the importance of disarming the warlords and the vexing issue of poppy eradication. But his most significant visit on this trip was to the Americans.

The U.S. military had invited an enthusiastic McCallum to visit its PRT in Gardez, the first team that was established in Afghanistan. Gardez is located sixty kilometres south of Kabul, near the Tora Bora region. The Canadian delegation was picked up in two American Black Hawk helicopters, which were supported by two Apache helicopters and an F-16 fighter aircraft flying top cover. The trip was an hour long through the mountains surrounding Kabul, south to Gardez.

Upon arrival, the American commander of the PRT gave the Canadians a quick tour. The camp was a grouping of small flat-roofed houses that had been abandoned during the American invasion, and a central building designed to be a meeting room and dining hall. The Americans wanted to showcase the PRT and thereby encourage Canada to deploy one of its own.

American officials told McCallum how the Gardez PRT built schools and hospitals and how the U.S. military was working with civilian agencies such as USAID in an integrated approach to the reconstruction of Afghanistan. This integrated approach was very similar to the Canadian Three *D* approach—the integration of defence, diplomacy, and development—that had recently become the basis of

Canadian foreign policy in troubled countries. The American briefing was deliberately designed to appeal to Canadian political sensibilities and the Canadian delegation quickly saw it for what it was—a sales pitch.

Selling Canada on a PRT was unnecessary. Back at NDHQ, the military, civilian, and political officials had already reached an agreement. The Ministry of Defence had all but decided to create a Canadian PRT, subject to coordination with the Foreign Ministry and final approval from the prime minister. After the Canadian Forces had completed their one-year commitment in Kabul, the plan was for Canada to deploy a two hundred–person PRT somewhere in Afghanistan.

Both the American and Canadian militaries saw PRTs as their exit strategies. The Pentagon saw PRTs as a way to get the allies into Afghanistan and the United States out. The Canadian Forces leadership saw a PRT as a way to get Canada out of Kabul and into a smaller, safer mission in some other part of the country.

In 2003, as Canadian troops were about to deploy, officials thought that Canada would get out of Kabul by creating a PRT and thereby reduce its troop commitment from two thousand to two hundred by the fall of 2004. What no one realized at the time was that, far from being an exit strategy to a smaller, safer mission, the PRT would lead the Canadian Forces deeper and deeper into the most dangerous part of Afghanistan.

PRT made things worse not better.

SEVEN

TRANSITION

I n the spring of 2003, Paul Martin—Chrétien's finance minister and heir apparent for a decade—was sitting as a backbench Member of Parliament. A year before, in a moment of high drama on national television, Martin had informed Canadians that he was considering leaving the Cabinet to actively pursue his campaign to succeed—or unseat—the prime minister. Forty-eight hours after making that statement, Martin left the Cabinet.

He spent the next year raising large sums of money and organizing his leadership campaign. But he also engaged in a broad range of organized policy discussions and dialogues with leading experts from across the country. Martin was preparing to become prime minister and he and his staff were trolling the waters for new ideas that would define his government once he took over from Chrétien. He wanted to present a bold, ambitious agenda—"transformational" was the favoured word—that would sharply distinguish his government from the "managerialism" and "incrementalism" that had characterized the Chrétien government.

In May—about two months after Chrétien's decision not to participate in the invasion of Iraq and three months after the announcement that Canada would participate in ISAF—Martin convened a meeting of experts in his office on Parliament Hill to advise him on foreign policy. The future prime minister was particularly concerned about the state of the Canada–U.S. relationship in the wake of the decision on

Iraq. He had been hearing from his many contacts in the Canadian business community that relations with the Americans were deteriorating badly due to Canada's unwillingness to support the United States when the chips were down. Canadian businessmen selling into the U.S. market were, they claimed, feeling the chill. It was becoming clear that improving relations with Washington might now be the top priority for a Martin government, which was expected to take over from Chrétien in six months. Martin was also looking for big ideas on foreign policy, ideas that would signal a change to Canadians.

Most of the people who gathered either in Martin's office or on the phone that day were well-known "liberal" academics and policy experts. Tom Axworthy, former principal secretary to Prime Minister Trudeau, was present, as was John English, former Member of Parliament, respected Canadian historian, and official biographer of Pierre Trudeau. Alan Alexandroff, trade policy analyst and a long-time adviser to Martin, was patched in by phone from the University of Toronto. Gordon Smith, former deputy minister of foreign affairs and now director of the Centre for Global Studies at the University of Victoria, who had been involved in one way or another in every major Canadian foreign policy issue in the last thirty years, was also there. And rounding out the room was Martin's chief of staff, Tim Murphy; his director of policy, Paul Corriveau; and McCallum's chief of staff.

This kind of non-hierarchical, seminar-like discussion—Martin, with his feet propped up on the table, drinking cup after cup of coffee, and the rest gathered around and piped in by phone—was typical of Martin's style. He liked to engage in informal, wide-ranging, often lengthy debate before making any decisions. And he was not timid about asking basic, fundamental questions, even if in the process he revealed his lack of knowledge on a subject.

On the big questions, Martin's intellectual curiosity often led to interminable, almost philosophical, sometimes frustrating debate. His inquiring mind endeared him to officials and advisers—finally here was

a senior politician who didn't think he knew everything and really
wanted advice. But his inquisitiveness was also a fatal flaw. Heads of
governments make myriad decisions every day, often on gut instinct
and without hours of discussion and consultation. Unfortunately,
Martin was not an intuitive decision maker and didn't trust his political instincts. He relied on analysis, argument, debate, focus groups, and
polling to reach substantive conclusions on issues. After he had finally
decided on a position, he would then work out the political implications with his intensely loyal, fiercely partisan staff. When he became
prime minister, this style inevitably led to a sclerotic, constipated
decision-making process that is still the stuff of legend in Ottawa.

At this meeting Martin told the assembled group that he was
concerned about the state of the Canada–U.S. relationship. He agreed
with Chrétien's decision on Iraq, but he thought the prime minister
had badly mishandled its execution and communication and, consequently, Canada's relationship with Washington had been unnecessar-
ily damaged. He thought that the government had made mistake after
mistake. There was the failure to give anyone in Washington or in the
American embassy in Ottawa forewarning of the announcement about
Iraq. McCallum himself emphasized how the ham-fisted handling of
the announcement strained relations in Washington. "Our government
announced in a very undiplomatic way that we were not going to have
anything to do with Iraq, and basically my relationship with Rumsfeld
got a lot cooler after that."[1]

And there was the "Dhaliwal matter." On his way into a Liberal
caucus meeting, Herb Dhaliwal, Chrétien's minister of natural resources,
gratuitously remarked, "The public everywhere is saying 'Don't go to
war,' and I think the world expects someone who is the President of a
superpower to be a statesman. I think he [George Bush] has let, not only
Americans, but the world, down by not being a statesman."[2]

His comment caused a firestorm in Washington. Dhaliwal was not
a private person but a member of the Cabinet and it appeared as if he
were speaking for the government. His injudicious comment created a

perception that some in the Liberal caucus were keen to criticize George Bush. The *National Post* reported that:

> Mr. Dhaliwal's jab at Mr. Bush's leadership ability followed a series of sharp criticisms of the U.S. President by Liberals during a Commons debate on the Iraq crisis earlier this week.
>
> Anti-war Liberal MPs compared Mr. Bush to a criminal waging an illegal war, called him arrogant and said he was dangerous because he mixed his evangelical Christian beliefs with politics.
>
> There has been no repeat of the sweeping anti-American remarks made two weeks ago by Carolyn Parrish, the Ontario MP who was forced to apologize after saying she hated American "bastards."[3]

To add insult to injury, these comments came just a few months after Chrétien's director of communications, Francie Ducros, referred to Bush as a moron in a room full of reporters at the NATO summit in Prague. A Canadian reporter filed a story with Ms. Ducros's remarks and, within hours, the incendiary comment was broadcast all over the world on the BBC World Service. Four days later, after he initially rejected her proffered resignation, Chrétien accepted it, presumably placating, at least a little, the angry White House.

But the prime minister failed to discipline Dhaliwal. As John Manley recalled, "The White House was very upset about Dhaliwal ... I got it from Tom Ridge [Bush's Secretary for Homeland Security]. At that point in time Chrétien should have been on the phone to Bush."[4] In the wake of Dhaliwal's comments, Paul Cellucci mused about Canada's response to terrorism and the economic relationship in general. Mr. Cellucci said the disappointment with Canada was so strong that it could have an impact on diplomatic and economic relations, which had already suffered from years of trade disputes over softwood lumber and wheat exports. "There may be some short-term strains here," he said. Pressed for details, Cellucci said Canada would have to "wait and see." He added that Canada played down the threat of more attacks by al-Qaeda, which had destroyed the World Trade Center in 2001, and appeared to be more interested in keeping the border open to traffic than in keeping the border secure. "For Canada the priority is trade, for us the priority is security," Mr. Cellucci said. "Security trumps trade."[5]

But Martin wasn't terribly worried about Bush. He told the group gathered in his office that day in May 2003 that he thought he could smooth over relations with the president in an hour at the White House. What he did not know, he said, was how badly the general relationship, beyond that of the prime minister and president, had been damaged. He wanted advice on how his government could improve the relationship as a whole.

Some of those in the room suggested that Martin needed to show clearly and in concrete ways that he cared more about the relationship than his predecessor. They suggested that he establish new bureaucratic and political instruments to manage the relationship and to make it a visible priority. Proposals to create a Cabinet Committee on Canada–U.S. relations and to enhance the embassy in Washington were floated. Martin followed this advice when he became prime minister.

The conversation then turned to a broader focus on international relations. Martin wanted to know how his government could make a significant impact internationally. What strategic choice could he make that would set him apart from Chrétien—a choice that would signal to Canadians and to the world that under Paul Martin's leadership Canada would be a major contributor to global affairs? Again, people made recommendations largely about process; a Cabinet Committee on International Affairs should be created. But Martin wanted advice on what he should do, not on what institutions or government machinery he should create to help him make decisions. Inevitably, Martin then heard the predictable recommendations to beef up the foreign service, spend more money on the military, and increase foreign aid.

One of the participants then suggested that Martin might want to consider focusing Canada's limited resources disproportionately on one country for a period of time. Canada's diplomatic—especially foreign aid—resources were notoriously scattered and unfocused, limiting Canada's impact. Why not select a few clear goals that Canada wanted to accomplish in a given country or region, establish benchmarks for success, and really focus diplomatic, aid, and military efforts to achieve these goals? This kind of strategy would be consistent with the Three D approach that allegedly already underpinned Canadian foreign policy. The public would see that Canada could really make a difference internationally and would support greater funding for diplomacy, development assistance, and the military—the three primary instruments of foreign policy.

Afghanistan was the obvious place for such a focused, strategic effort. It was already the single largest recipient of Canadian aid; Canada was on the cusp of deploying two thousand troops to Kabul; and Ottawa was opening a new embassy in Kabul. Afghanistan was also vitally important to the United States, to the international community, and arguably to Canada's security. Canada was already doing a great deal in Afghanistan, but could do much more and in a much more strategic, targeted way. Rebuilding Afghanistan could become Canada's project for the next decade.

Martin listened intently and seemed intrigued by the concept of concentrating a disproportionate amount of resources on one particularly troubled country. But he did not see Afghanistan as the likely candidate. Martin and his staff thought of Canada's ongoing efforts in Afghanistan as Chrétien's initiative, something he had inherited, a "hold-over" from the previous regime.[6] As Tim Murphy, Martin's chief of staff reflected years later: "Paul viewed Afghanistan as something we *had* to do more than something we wanted to do."[7] Therefore, it would not be Martin's project. He would certainly honour Chrétien's year-long military commitment to Afghanistan and the commitments on development assistance for another four years. But Afghanistan would not be a priority for Paul Martin.

The attitude of the new prime minister became obvious early in his mandate. During a Cabinet meeting shortly after becoming prime minister, Martin apparently asked his ministers one of those niggling, basic questions. Why was Canada's military in Afghanistan? To some of his Cabinet, notably Bill Graham, foreign minister at the time, this was an astonishing question. Where had he been for the past two years? How could he be so uninformed about such an important issue? But Martin's question was a window on the man. It reflected the low priority he gave to Afghanistan, and it would remain very low for the next year.

IN EARLY DECEMBER 2003, John McCallum was nearing the end of his eighteen-month tenure as Canada's minister of national defence. On December 12, Paul Martin would succeed Jean Chrétien as prime minister. Martin would immediately make wholesale changes to the Cabinet, putting forward the new face that he so desperately wanted. McCallum would be shuffled out of the portfolio and into the backwater that is the Department of Veterans Affairs, even though Martin thought he had performed well as minister of defence.[8]

But, just prior to that Cabinet shuffle, McCallum had one final international obligation to fulfill. In early December he travelled to a NATO ministerial meeting in Brussels. ISAF was high on the agenda, now that the alliance had formally taken over the mission. This was the meeting where George Robertson "went around to NATO countries with a begging bowl," to use McCallum's phrase, to scare up six helicopters for the Kabul mission. This was also the meeting where McCallum first formally signalled Canada's intent to field a PRT somewhere in Afghanistan, after the Canadian Forces had completed its twelve-month lead-nation assignment in Kabul. It was now looking more and more likely, as Rumsfeld wanted, that NATO would be taking on responsibility for the PRTs. In doing so, the mandate of the alliance would grow to encompass all of Afghanistan.

On the way back to Canada, McCallum, Calder, and the rest of the minister's party stopped off in London. The minister gave a speech at the Royal Institute of International Affairs, Chatham House, a respected think-tank. The speech, written by McCallum himself, argued that NATO's future as a viable military alliance hung in the balance in Afghanistan.[9] If NATO did not succeed in Kabul, it would have very little credibility in future international crises.

But the most interesting and informative part of the minister's visit to London came at an informal lunch in his hotel. The Canadian High Commission in London had recommended that McCallum meet with Arthur Kent, a Canadian expatriate journalist who was living and working in London. Kent had made a name for himself during the 1991 Gulf War, when he worked for NBC television news. He was labelled the "Scud Stud" for his reporting on Iraqi Scud missile attacks on Israel.

But Kent had also been travelling to and reporting from Afghanistan extensively since the early 1980s. He had spent months at a time there during the Soviet occupation, during the civil war between the Northern Alliance and the Taliban, and during the Taliban regime. He had been to Afghanistan recently and had produced an award-winning documentary, *Afghanistan: Captives of the Warlords,* which was broadcast on the American Public Broadcasting System a few months prior to 9-11. He followed that up with another acclaimed documentary after 9-11, *Afghanistan: Legacy of War.*

Kent, a likeable, personable individual, assumed that the minister and his party knew the country where Canada's military was serving. He regaled the lunch guests with his encounters over the years with Afghan politicians and tribal leaders, his travels through the more remote parts of the country, and his deep knowledge of its politics, culture, and history. This man knew Afghanistan and its leaders well. He had travelled this country extensively over many years.

The guests sat silently for about an hour and listened to Kent present a picture of a highly complex, textured, layered society that seemed congenitally prone to conflict and war. And at the end of the lunch, as the guests were walking out of the restaurant, Calder turned to McCallum's chief of staff and said anxiously, "We don't know anything about this country."

December 12, 2003

The new government led by Paul Martin officially took office on December 12, 2003. It was immediately apparent that there would be almost no continuity between his government and that of his predecessor, even though it was the same Liberal Party in office. It was almost as if the electorate had thrown out one administration for another. Prime Minister Martin was signalling a clean break from the decade of Chrétien government.

The Cabinet was almost completely revamped. Bill Graham, a friend of Martin's since they had attended law school together forty years earlier, was one of the few ministers who would remain in Cabinet. He was the only one to keep the portfolio that he had held under Chrétien—Foreign Affairs. Almost every other minister was either demoted or moved to the backbenches. A handful of existing ministers, and notably Anne McLellan, were promoted. A new sheriff was definitely in town.

The structure and priorities of the government, particularly with respect to foreign affairs, Canada–U.S. relations, and national security and defence, also changed significantly. Two cabinet committees—one with the high-minded title of Global Affairs, the other named Canada–U.S. Relations—were established. The prime minister himself was to chair the committee on the relationship with the United States, a clear marker of its importance.

Martin made David Pratt his new minister of defence. This appointment had symbolic importance. It sent a signal to the military establishment—senior serving and retired officers, defence lobby groups, defence contractors, journalists, and academics—that the Canadian Forces and defence issues would enjoy a much higher priority now than they had had under Chrétien. Pratt was the defence community's favourite Liberal. He had been a vocal advocate for all things military and an excellent chairman of the House of Commons Standing Committee on National Defence. Pratt had a deep knowledge of military and defence issues and he was unapologetically pro-American. He had visited the Canadian Forces abroad—in Bosnia—and he was an expert on the conflict in Sierra Leone in West Africa, having visited that country many times in the last dozen years. He was one of the only Liberal MPs to support Canadian participation in the Iraq War, and he was a vocal proponent of Canadian participation in the U.S. Ballistic Missile Defence system (BMD).

The appointment of Pratt as minister of defence indicated that the military was finally going to get the attention it deserved in a Liberal government. Many in the defence establishment expected that Pratt would deliver large increases in the budget for the Canadian Forces— and fast. The Parliamentary Committee he had previously chaired had recommended an immediate five-billion-dollar increase to the defence budget. "Pratt knows there must be an enormous investment in the Canadian Forces and that, without such expenditures, Canada will be without the capability of conducting a foreign policy, let alone a military one," wrote defence expert Barry Cooper.[10] But the conventional wisdom was wrong.

Pratt was certainly well qualified for the job of defence minister and a Martin loyalist. But politics played a role here as well. Martin had promised during his leadership campaign to give much higher priority to the Canadian Forces, again distinguishing himself from Chrétien, who was no fan of the military. "The military suffered more than any department when I brought in measures to fight the deficit [as Minister of Finance]. I accept that. I wanted to repair the military," said Martin.[11] The prime minister had generated expectations that his government would pump significantly more money into the military. But he and his team had no intention of doing so during the first year of his administration; they had other priorities. To pacify the military establishment and buy some time, Martin gave them Pratt—and they loved it. It was a brilliant political manoeuvre. When the Canadian Forces got very little in the Martin government's first budget, there was relatively little hue and cry.[12]

The new prime minister also made an important symbolic gesture early on. He started his first working day as prime minister with a focus on defence. After being sworn in on the Friday before, he paid a high-profile visit to NDHQ on the first Monday morning of his government. No prime minister had ever made this kind of gesture. The defence community duly noted and appreciated the visit. Many were exhilarated, flushed with excitement that, finally, after all these years, the Canadian Forces had a minister who was their champion and a prime minister who would listen.

Not surprisingly, Martin chose a new foreign policy adviser. He brought into his inner circle a senior, well-known, and ambitious mandarin named Jonathan Fried. Fried, a lawyer and expert on trade, was known for his merciless work ethic, as well as his unwillingness to suffer fools gladly. But he was respected, and induced great loyalty among those who worked for him. Fried knew more about Canadian trade law and policy than anyone in the Government of Canada. But he had little experience in international security or defence.

Martin also decided to strengthen the Canadian embassy in Washington, with a new robust congressional liaison function. His office announced that the prime minister would visit President Bush in Washington immediately. And Martin offered the coveted job of ambassador to the United States to his erstwhile leadership rival, former deputy prime minister John Manley.

The U.S. ambassadorship was the most senior and prestigious job in the Foreign Service. Normally it has been given to a career diplomat in recognition of a brilliant career. But Martin wanted a "political" ambassador in Washington, one who was known, who had clout and connections south of the border. The appointment of a high-profile political leader would send a signal to the White House that the new prime minister was taking the relationship much more seriously. Martin had once said, even before he replaced Chrétien, that his ambassador to Washington would have a direct pipeline to the prime minister.

Manley was the perfect candidate for the job. He was widely respected and well connected in Washington. He had an excellent relationship with Colin Powell and Tom Ridge, two of the leading members of the Bush administration and the most moderate. He had connections in the business community on both sides of the border, which he had developed during his eight years as minister of industry and then finance. And highly respected former ambassadors to Washington Allan Gotlieb, Derek Burney, and Raymond Chrétien urged him to take the job.[13] All three thought that Manley was a sound choice.

But Manley refused the appointment. While he felt privileged to be offered the post, he was not persuaded that Martin would take the necessary steps to improve the Canada–U.S. relationship. And after an earlier meeting with the incoming prime minister in November 2003, Manley did not believe that he would have the necessary access to the prime minister to do the job effectively:

> I asked him [Martin], well how do you see it operating, how do you see the relationship between you and the ambassador, what are you going to do on some of the key issues? Martin said, "I haven't had time to think about any of that yet." That was my first clue that this was a bit of a throwaway. I know all the people in the administration [in Washington], I thought I would be a good choice, but I didn't trust the people around Martin to give me access to him. And if you are the ambassador and are not seen to have the ear of the Prime Minister, you are going to cocktail parties—I mean you are not in the loop. So, upon reflection, I decided to turn it down.[14]

Manley felt that Martin never really wanted him to accept the job. The new prime minister never said to Manley, "I need you to do this."

The sentiment was much more akin to, "You can have this if you want it."[15] So Manley took a pass. Michael Kergin, a distinguished career diplomat, kept his job, at least for the moment.

The Illusions of Missile Defence

Paul Martin appeared to differ from his predecessor on the issue of Ballistic Missile Defence (BMD). During the Liberal leadership race, Martin had publicly committed Canada to BMD. While Chrétien had begun discussions with the United States, he had made no commitment to participate in the system. Some of his Cabinet colleagues, and John Manley in particular, were convinced that the prime minister would ultimately have said "Yes" to Canadian participation in ballistic defence.[16] But Martin did commit to take Canada into BMD. In fact, the only time Paul Martin called John McCallum during his eighteen months as defence minister was to tell him unequivocally that he wanted Canada in the BMD system.

The Department of National Defence—both the North and South towers—had been pressing strongly for Canadian participation in BMD for several years. Senior civilian and military officials, especially Ray Henault, Ken Calder, and Vice Chief of the Defence Staff, Lieutenant General George MacDonald—a former fighter pilot and one-time senior NORAD officer—had relentlessly pushed successive ministers of defence to participate in BMD. And they had succeeded. Eggleton, McCallum, and Pratt were all persuaded of the merits of Canadian participation.

However, the Ministry of Foreign Affairs, which had the lead negotiating responsibility, had a more "nuanced" position. Senior officials like Jim Wright, assistant deputy minister for global security policy and Bill Graham's right-hand man, were reserved about Canadian involvement in BMD. They were concerned that the system would stimulate a new arms race, that it might provoke India, Pakistan, and China to produce more nuclear weapons to overcome the limited capability of the system. That kind of dynamic could destabilize the international arms control regime. Foreign Affairs was especially worried that BMD would lead to what it called the "the weaponization of space." Canada's opposition to the weaponization of space was long-standing. Ottawa would need to know a lot more about the nature of the system under development and the implications for Canada before signing on to BMD. Foreign Affairs recommended caution, skepticism, and a go-slow approach.

Foreign Affairs Minister Bill Graham initially shared the skepticism of his department. The House of Commons Foreign Affairs Committee, which Graham had chaired before becoming minister, reported that "the Government should not make a decision about missile defence systems being developed by the United States, as the technology has not been proven and details of deployment are not known. However, the Government should continue to monitor development of this program with the Government of the United States and continue to oppose the weaponization of outer space."[17] Chrétien was also rumoured to be a skeptic. Bill Clinton had once spoken critically about BMD to the prime minister, lamenting the fact that the Americans were spending billions of dollars on a system that he thought would never work. Graham was in no hurry, therefore, to move this issue forward when he became foreign minister.

But the proponents of ballistic defence at NDHQ had one argument that they advanced incessantly, an argument that resonated with Foreign Affairs, with Graham and the prime minister. If Canada didn't sign on to Ballistic Missile Defence, NORAD—the cherished binational Canada–U.S. continental aerospace defence organization—would atrophy. And over time, the United States would likely abandon NORAD completely. Were NORAD to disappear, or be hollowed out, the costs to Canadian sovereignty as well as to its diplomacy would be catastrophic. Ottawa would no longer have the window on the continent's airspace that NORAD provided. Canada could never afford to replicate the capabilities that existed in Colorado Springs. It would cost billions of dollars to do so, well beyond the resources of Canada. The unique and invaluable vantage point that NORAD gave Canada on defence and security thinking, intelligence and operations, would be cut off. Canada could not afford such a catastrophic loss of intelligence, particularly in a post–9-11 world. "One of the strongest arguments in favour of BMD was if we didn't do it, it spelled the death of NORAD. There was this fabulous institution for the defence of Canada and North America and it was up for grabs," reflected Graham.[18]

Officials at DND believed that Washington wanted to assign BMD to NORAD for operational efficiency. NORAD was already responsible for continental aerospace surveillance and defence, and BMD was, after all, a continental aerospace system. These same officials insisted that BMD would come virtually free to Canada. Calder, Bloodworth, and MacDonald had told McCallum in July 2002 that all the United States really wanted from Canada was political support for BMD—not money, not technology, and not territory. As a bonus, Canadian industry might obtain significant industrial benefits from the project.

Those arguments did not exactly compute. BMD had bipartisan support in the Congress and was no longer a wedge political issue. The system was gradually becoming acceptable to governments in Western Europe and Russia.[19] Why would the Americans need Canada's support? NDHQ insisted that they did, if for no other reason than to house the system in Colorado Springs. Putting it there would require Canadian approval. But this argument was also problematic. As early as June 2002, McCallum had met in Ottawa with the U.S. four-star general Ralph E. ("Ed") Eberhart, a decorated veteran of the Vietnam War, now the commander of NORAD. During this meeting, Eberhart, a commanding, charismatic figure, directly contradicted officials at NDHQ. Eberhart didn't think that missile defence would be assigned to NORAD; more likely, it would be housed within NORTHComm, the new U.S. Command created after 9-11, which Eberhart also commanded. Once again, NDHQ had presented a very different picture of U.S. priorities than did U.S. officials themselves.

There was also little evidence that industrial benefits would accrue to Canadian industry. Neither Canadian firms nor the minister of industry had ever raised this prospect with the minister of national defence. Canada's defence industry, one of the most aggressive lobbies in Ottawa, was not pushing Canada to join BMD.

McCallum worked through the arguments in a methodical and pragmatic way. The United States was moving forward with BMD with or without Canada. The system would inevitably have implications for Canadian sovereignty and perhaps for the future of NORAD. Washington didn't want Canadian money or territory, and Canadian industry might benefit. Why wouldn't Canada want to be part of it? What's the downside? The minister couldn't see it. And perhaps, being on the inside, Ottawa could even influence the United States to help ensure that BMD would not lead to the weaponization of space.

So he began to talk about Ballistic Missile Defence with Graham, trying to persuade his colleague and hoping for his support. Here the close relationship between these two men paid dividends and helped to break the deadlock between their respective officials. By the fall of 2002, on the eve of the NATO summit in Prague—where BMD was on the agenda—both Graham and his department were softening. By then the Russians had indicated that they no longer opposed the system. Why would Canada be more Russian than the Russians on this issue? The two ministers agreed that a team of officials from Defence and Foreign Affairs would go to Washington before the Prague summit and meet with their Pentagon counterparts to learn more about the system and what would be expected of Canada should Ottawa agree to participate.

Canadian officials found themselves in a classic chicken-and-egg scenario in Washington. The Americans repeated that they wanted nothing from Canada other than its political support for BMD. Yet the Pentagon refused to give officials details about the system until Canada had signed on. There was no pressure brought to bear on Canadian ministers by their U.S. counterparts. When Rumsfeld and McCallum discussed the issue of BMD at their meeting in Washington, the secretary of defence said only that he was pleased that Canada was showing an interest in the system. Neither Graham nor his predecessor, Manley, heard anything from Powell about BMD. And Chrétien got no pressure from Bush. The tremendous pressure on the politicians in Ottawa came from within Canada, from the military and civilian officials in the Department of Defence. The officials argued that BMD was an urgent matter. They warned again and again that Canada had to sign on very soon or the door might close, with grave consequences for Canada.

Paul Cellucci, the U.S. ambassador to Canada, told McCallum in early 2003 that Washington—particularly the State Department and the White House—wanted Canada in BMD. But what the United States wanted above all was for Ottawa to makes up its mind, and to make it up soon. Cellucci also indicated that NORAD's long-term viability was at risk here and, he added, since Canada had decided not to participate in the invasion of Iraq, "Now would be a good time. A lot of people in Washington," Cellucci elaborated, "were unhappy with Canada, particularly about the comments by the Prime Minister and Dhaliwal."[20] Cellucci thought this was a good time for Canada to do something positive to get things back on track. Without some significant gesture from Ottawa to Washington, Cellucci added, President Bush might cancel his planned trip to Ottawa in May. The White House might well conclude that it was not worth the president's time.

The continuing, relentless lobbying by NDHQ, reinforced by the pressure from the U.S. ambassador, opened up the political space that was needed for a Cabinet presentation on BMD later that year. The foreign minister and his officials were no longer opposed. As Graham recalled, "From a foreign policy relationship with the US it was obvious that we should do this [BMD]."[21] After the Cabinet discussion, Chrétien agreed to give officials a formal mandate to pursue "discussions"—not negotiations—with the Americans on the possibility of Canadian involvement in BMD. In formal discussions, American officials might be more forthcoming with information about the system, about their plans, and about the consequences for Canada.

These discussions had only just begun when Paul Martin became prime minister. Yet one of the first significant acts of his new defence minister, David Pratt, was to send a letter to Rumsfeld that outlined Canada's intention to move forward on the BMD file. The key paragraphs of the letter read as follows:

> Our two nations should move on an expedited basis to amend the NORAD agreement to take into account NORAD's contribution to the missile defence mission.
>
> It is our intent to negotiate in the coming months a Missile Defence Framework Memorandum of Understanding (MOU) with the United States with the objective of including Canada as a participant in the current US missile defence program and expanding and enhancing information exchange. We believe this should provide a mutually beneficial framework to ensure the closest possible involvement and insight for Canada, both government and industry, in the US missile defence program. Such a MOU could also help pave the way for increased government-to-government and industry-to-industry co-operation on missile defence that we should seek to foster between our countries.[22]

The purpose of the letter was clear. It was a strong signal that the new prime minister would no longer dither and that Canada would participate in BMD. Donald Rumsfeld agreed that the Canadian framework provided a suitable basis to move forward.

Foreign Affairs had paved the way for the Pratt letter. The diplomats had moved from skeptics of BMD to full-blown advocates of Canada's participation in the system. Bill Graham explained the change of heart: "Foreign Affairs' view was there is a limit to how much we can constantly say no to the political masters in Washington. All we had was Afghanistan to wave. On every other file we were offside.

Eventually we came onside on Haiti, so we got another arrow in our quiver."[23]

Discussions between officials in Ottawa and Washington went on but went nowhere. U.S. officials gave little information to Canadians. They were not inclined to divulge more until Canada had signed on the dotted line. At about this time, Prime Minister Martin started asking his ministers questions—fundamental questions and questions of detail—about BMD. He was hearing from some of his MPs who were strongly opposed to the program. They equated BMD with the deeply unpopular Bush administration and didn't like the idea of Canada's signing on to the American system at all. A vigorous debate erupted within the Liberal caucus. Over time, controversy over BMD would engulf the Martin government, with serious consequences for the prime minister's reputation. He was labelled "indecisive," a "ditherer." Ultimately, this issue of Canada's participation in BMD would also have a significant influence on Canada's Afghanistan policy.

DAVID PRATT SERVED only eight months as defence minister before Paul Martin's government faced the electorate. During that short time, Canada's Afghanistan mission was on the back burner. "Afghanistan wasn't a priority during my tenure. I was focussing on procurement, defence policy, NORAD and BMD, and the Proliferation Security Initiative," Pratt explained.[24] Canada had just sent two thousand troops to Kabul, and Rick Hillier had taken command of ISAF. The new minister thought that the big decisions had already been made. The mission could run largely on autopilot, at least for a while. Pratt did visit Afghanistan once, but he was not heavily engaged with the mission. And there certainly was no pressure on him from the new prime minister to elevate the stature or profile of an Afghanistan mission that was identified with his predecessor.

A few months after Pratt had sent his letter on Ballistic Missile Defence to Rumsfeld, the 2004 federal election campaign got under-way. Afghanistan and BMD did not figure in the election.

International issues were seldom ballot considerations for Canadians and the election in 2004 was no different. Nevertheless, the Martin government had written into its campaign platform a commitment to increase the size of the Canadian Forces by five thousand regulars and three thousand reservists. The funding to support this expansion—$750 million per year—would be provided in the first budget after the election. Martin was now prepared to honour his earlier statements about rebuilding the military. His ambition for a larger Canadian role in international peace and security was taking tangible shape. And he seemed prepared to allocate a significant amount of money to fulfill his promise.

During the writing of the platform, Pratt had argued that the force expansion should be dedicated to establishing what he called "tier two" special forces—a rapidly deployable army brigade with greater skill and combat capability than the infantry, but somewhat less than Joint Task Force 2. He wanted a robust intervention role for the Canadian Forces in failed and failing states. But the Prime Minister's Office was not at all enthusiastic about his vision.

One Sunday morning, just after the election was called, Pratt presented his idea to a small group assembled in the prime minister's office in the Langevin Bloc on Parliament Hill. These were the people who were charged with writing the campaign document. Pratt drew a schematic on a blackboard illustrating his proposal. Tim Murphy summarily dismissed the idea as "the wrong vision." The Prime Minister's Office and his campaign team wanted to link expansion of the military to the more politically attuned concept of peacekeeping and nation-building, not to intervention in potentially violent foreign conflict. The party platform ultimately called for a "peace and nation-building" force.

After the Martin government was re-elected in the summer of 2004, albeit as a minority, the prime minister began to make his views known about where Canada should contribute meaningfully to peace and nation-building around the world. Afghanistan, again, was not in his sights; Haiti, the Middle East, and Darfur were.[25] Nevertheless, in less than a year's time, Paul Martin would make some historic and far-reaching decisions on Canada's role in Afghanistan. His decisions would unwittingly lead the Canadian Forces back into Kandahar to fight a violent and bloody insurgency. The Canadian Forces had not fought this kind of war since the Boer War, in the early years of the twentieth century. Despite the rhetoric of the election platform, Paul Martin would be taking the Canadian Forces and the country a long way from peacekeeping and a lot closer to David Pratt's concept of intervention in combat in troubled countries.

EIGHT

TOWARD A NEW AGENDA

The election results of 2004 were a bitter disappointment to the new prime minister, Paul Martin. His Liberal Party was reduced to a minority and some of Martin's ministers, including David Pratt, the minister of defence, lost their seats. The prime minister needed to restructure his Cabinet.

Martin had promised during the election campaign to increase the size and budget of the Canadian Forces. He had global ambitions for Canada and wanted an army that he could deploy to trouble spots—Haiti and Darfur—around the world. "Conflict prevention," the prime minister said, "was going to be critical to our foreign policy going forward."[1] The minister of defence was therefore a very important appointment. Martin turned to his old law school chum Bill Graham, who had been foreign minister for the past two and a half years. Graham was a safe pair of hands, an experienced and respected politician. Martin trusted him. Graham was less likely than anyone else to make mistakes in the sensitive and increasingly high-profile defence ministry. "I wanted Bill Graham at DND. McCallum had started the right kind of changes at DND, but more were needed. I thought with Bill's background he could do the job," reflected Martin.[2] And, as Tim Murphy suggested, there would be more action at Defence than at Foreign Affairs. "I called Bill [Graham] after the Cabinet shuffle. The pitch I made to Bill was, 'You will be more effective at Defence. Paul will be his own foreign minister.'"[3]

But there were other factors that influenced the prime minister's decision to move Graham from his dream job at Foreign Affairs. The prime minister understood very well that international issues were more prominent in Quebec than in the rest of the country, so he wanted a francophone to head Foreign Affairs.

And Pierre Pettigrew, the minister of trade, desperately wanted Graham's job and made this abundantly clear to Martin, his advisers, and the media. As one of the few experienced francophone MPs, Pettigrew knew he had some leverage with the prime minister, and he used it to good effect. Other domestic political factors also influenced the shift. As James Travers, the wise columnist and keen observer of the Ottawa scene, wrote at the time: "When Martin needed to move Pierre Pettigrew out of the health ministry to allow the inspired appointment of former B.C. Premier Ujjal Dosanjh, Graham became the designated victim."[4]

The combination of Pettigrew's ambition and the prime minister's inclination to keep a tight rein on foreign policy persuaded Martin to move Graham to Defence. His task was made easier given that Pratt had been defeated in the election and Martin needed to fill the gap at Defence with a competent politician. Moving Graham allowed the prime minister to put one of his most trusted ministers at Defence and to satisfy Pettigrew's insistent demands.

David Herle, one of Martin's most influential advisers, told Graham months after the shuffle that the prime minister had given Pettigrew the job because he and his advisers thought that foreign affairs were more important to the Quebec electorate than to any other in the country. The decision was made for political reasons. Competency was not the issue. When the prime minister grew increasingly frustrated with Pettigrew's lack of attention to important issues like BMD, Afghanistan, and the foreign policy review, Herle conceded to Graham over a drink one night that the move had been a mistake.[5]

WHEN BILL GRAHAM arrived at NDHQ in late July 2004, his initial experience was not unlike that of his friend John McCallum two years earlier. Astonishingly, the transition briefings by officials barely touched on Afghanistan. In both the North and South towers, the priorities were as they had been for years: "Juice up" their new minister to get more money for the military; get him moving on BMD; convince him of the urgency to renew and expand the NORAD agreement; and get him up to speed on work that had been underway for some time toward a new defence policy.

As Canada's one-year commitment as lead nation in Kabul drew to a close in the late summer of 2004, Graham heard virtually nothing from his officials about the way forward in Afghanistan. This was even more surprising given that Canada's contribution to ISAF was highly regarded within NATO circles. Canada's influence in Brussels had risen substantially as a result of the commitment and sacrifice the Canadian Forces had made in Kabul—three CF soldiers were killed in that mission. Canada was also respected because it had been instrumental in bringing NATO into Afghanistan.

When officials did raise the subject of Afghanistan at the end of the summer, they informed Graham that the military was in the process of scaling down its operation in Kabul, in anticipation of the French-German-led Eurocorps' taking over the lead in ISAF from Canada. The plan was for Canada to reduce its two thousand troops in Kabul to about two hundred. The military personnel who remained would constitute a Provincial Reconstruction Team (PRT) somewhere in Afghanistan.

During the NATO defence ministerial meeting in December 2003, John McCallum had committed Canada informally to deploying a PRT after the Canadian Forces finished their one-year term in Kabul. At the NATO summit in Istanbul during the election campaign in 2004, Bill Graham, representing the prime minister in his final days as minister of foreign affairs, formalized this commitment.[6]

Officials in Foreign Affairs and Defence had known since the middle of 2003 that Canada would be fielding a PRT. But they had not yet decided where in Afghanistan the team would go. The Americans had a PRT in Gardez, the Germans were near Feyzabad and Kunduz in the northeast, and the British were in Mazar-e-Sharif in the north. And the Italians were considering Herat in the west. Other countries were lining up as well to get the best real estate, the safer neighbourhoods of Afghanistan.

Officials in Ottawa had not engaged their ministers on the issue of the geographic location for the Canadian PRT. It didn't appear to be especially significant during 2003 to 2004, since the security situation in Afghanistan seemed relatively stable, especially in comparison with Iraq. When Graham arrived at NDHQ in the summer of 2004, officials had not recommended a location, nor had Graham even been briefed that this was an issue. The officials evidently thought this decision didn't really concern the politicians. They could handle it.

True to form, Foreign Affairs and Defence had spent nearly a year squabbling about where the PRT should go and what it should look like. Some suggested it should be in Kabul. Others wanted it in the north, where the security situation appeared most stable. Some officials in NDHQ believed there was a constituency in Foreign Affairs that wanted it located in the west near Herat, so that Canada could get a better window on Iran. The Canadian embassy in Kabul thought differently. "We recommended Kandahar from the start," said the then-ambassador Chris Alexander. "Everyone knew it was going to be a pivotal province. As Kandahar goes, so goes Afghanistan. [A deployment to Kandahar] also fit with the robust capabilities of the Canadian Forces. Canada was among the best-equipped and best-trained militaries in Afghanistan—although the CF leadership doesn't like to say so—so Canada was a natural for Kandahar. Finally, the deployment to Kandahar fit nicely into the evolving mission of ISAF."[7]

At times, Foreign Affairs argued that a diplomat should run the PRT. The idea was anathema to the military. They knew that when push came to shove, the Canadian Forces themselves would comprise the vast majority of the personnel in the PRT. And they were not about to relinquish command and control of their people to a diplomat who would know nothing about managing conflict.

The PRT was a classic case of competing interests and clashing world views between the two departments, between Venus and Mars. And it was a classic case of bureaucratic dithering and bickering over comparatively small issues, so that officials missed the bigger picture until it was too late.[8]

In early October, Graham met with David Reddaway, the new British High Commissioner to Canada. Reddaway informed Graham that the British were keen to engage with Canada in Afghanistan and that they were looking to do more in Kandahar, where the Americans had been holding the fort for the past three years. The High Commissioner hinted that Kandahar was Britain's preferred location for Canada, and he suggested that the defence secretary, Geoff Hoon, was very interested in where Canada intended to send its PRT. Graham still hadn't heard anything from his officials. All he was told was that the Americans were interested in merging ISAF with Operation Enduring Freedom, which meant that the United States wanted NATO forces to move beyond Kabul to southern and eastern Afghanistan. The concept of expanding NATO to the south and east of the country, to take pressure off the Americans, would eventually be labelled "Stage Three" and "Stage Four" NATO expansion. Washington apparently saw a much broader role for NATO in Afghanistan, one that would put the PRTs under the umbrella of the alliance, a point Rumsfeld had made to McCallum a year and a half before.

Italy, too, was interested in co-operating with Canada, perhaps in fielding a joint Canada–Italy PRT in Herat.[9] But Italy was going to deploy in February to March 2005 and Henault claimed that was too soon for Canada. Maddison told Graham that the earliest Canada could deploy was the summer of 2005. For the first time, Henault told the minister that he thought the Canadian PRT should probably go to Kandahar. Even at that time, the Kandahar region was the most unstable and dangerous part of the country, although it was positively tranquil compared to what it would become eighteen months later. "We did a deliberate and careful military assessment of the military capabilities that a PRT would require and the options to deploy our PRT," stated Henault. "Chris Alexander, our Ambassador to Kabul, was involved. The recommendation out of the Embassy in Kabul was to deploy to Kandahar. We looked at both the west and the south. We knew that we had capabilities that were second to none. Through our decision to deploy to Kandahar, we helped the Alliance to make the decision to go to Stage Three expansion. We saw the deployment of the PRT to Kandahar as an element of the overall expansion of the mission."[10]

The concept of a PRT was relatively new to Graham. "It wasn't entirely clear exactly what the PRTs would do or how they would be run at that time. They were an idea that sounded a lot better on paper than in practice. Nobody had had much experience with them," noted Graham.[11]

Later in November Henault advised Graham that the Supreme Allied Commander, Europe (SACEUR), had called him to suggest that Canada send its PRT to work in remote villages in central Afghanistan, around Chaghcharan, halfway between Herat and Kabul, along the route taken during the historic sixteenth-century trek by Babur, the emperor of Mogul India. Although the British army had been in this region since 2002, the Afghan government had no presence there at the time.

Maddison and Henault dismissed the Chaghcharan option out of hand. They argued that this part of the country would give Canada inadequate international visibility. The logistics challenges were, they argued, too difficult, especially since no airport was nearby. This region was one of the poorest and least developed parts of Afghanistan. They told the minister that since Italy would have a high-profile PRT in Herat, a Canadian presence in Chaghcharan would be "under Italian influence." Canada's military leaders were never keen on working with or under their European counterparts. Bill Graham reflected on these discussions:

The objections to the Chaghcharan location were two-fold. One was that it was in the Italian sphere of influence, it was on the periphery of Herat, and I don't think anybody [in the military] liked the idea that they were going to be under Italian command. Second, there was a strong feeling that it was a bit of a cul-de-sac, a trap—you were up in a mountain hole, and if you ever got surrounded you would have to fight your way out. The military who thought about an exit strategy were worried about that particular location. I think Herat itself would not have been as difficult as that particular location.[12]

Henault had a somewhat different recollection of these internal debates: "We were looking at a number of options. Sending the PRT to Kandahar was the best option to enable NATO to expand to the next phase. We were focused clearly on the overall expansion of NATO. This was a decision which was framed within a NATO perspective. Chaghcharan needed a PRT but it was remote and would not be helpful to NATO as it moved from Stage Two to Stage Three. We also looked at Canadian capabilities and where they could best be deployed. We looked at three options—Chaghcharan, Herat, and Kandahar—and did a careful analysis of all three."[13] Rick Hillier, who was then completing his term as the commander of ISAF and, in a few months' time, would replace Henault as chief of the defence staff, was characteristically blunt: "I didn't like the option of a deployment to Chaghcharan at all. There was no upside, no profile because Chaghcharan was so isolated. No one would have noticed that we were there. There was a large downside. It was so isolated that it would have been difficult to protect the PRT if an emergency developed. We had very limited lift capability of our own and the roads were terrible. There was little gain and large risk."[14]

Civilian officials in Calder's organization reinforced the military's preference in the late fall of 2004, when they advised Graham that Kandahar was safer than the Chaghcharan district. But there was a political problem. The Kandahar region was then under Operation

Shouldn't it be more focused on the benefits

Enduring Freedom (OEF)—in other words, under American, not NATO, command. The generals knew that this would be a political problem for the government. The prime minister and Foreign Affairs would certainly want the PRT to be wrapped in a multilateral NATO flag, especially since Canada had been instrumental in bringing NATO into Afghanistan in the first place. But Graham's officials assured him that this was not an issue, as NATO was planning to take over the Kandahar region from American forces in 2006—the so-called Stage Three NATO expansion. And so it did.

In early December Graham received a phone call from the new NATO Secretary-General and former Dutch foreign minister, Jaap de Hoop Scheffer. Graham had known de Hoop Scheffer from their days as foreign ministers. De Hoop Scheffer was calling to urge Graham to send the Canadian PRT to work in the Chaghcharan district in partnership with the Lithuanians. Graham answered that his military advisers had recommended against this deployment because of the operational challenges and the risks in that region. He would consider the Secretary-General's request, but he made it clear that Kandahar was emerging as a preferred option for Canada.

By the late fall of 2004, even though Ottawa still had not decided on the location for the PRT, NATO's preference for Canada was clear. Brussels was pressing Canada to deploy to Chaghcharan; NATO did not seem at all concerned about the need for Canada to be in Kandahar to facilitate Stage Three expansion. It was also clear that Italy was more than prepared to partner with Canada in Herat. "NATO wanted us to be in Chaghcharan and the Italians wanted us to partner with them in Herat," Graham reflected.[15] But what was unclear was what Washington wanted. Henault decided he would call Meyers to ask where the Americans wanted Canada's PRT. And Graham would raise the matter with Rumsfeld when he next had the opportunity. It was looking more and more likely that the Canadian Forces would be going back to Kandahar before too long. Another three months would pass before Canada finally made a decision on where its PRT would be located. In the meantime, Graham and his officials were preoccupied with one or two other major issues.

Making Foreign and Defence Policy for the Millennium

The last big review of Canadian foreign policy was a decade old. Done during the first year of the Chrétien administration, *Canada in the World, Canadian Foreign Policy Review* was published in 1995. The review had been completed before Ottawa understood the new security environment of the post–Cold War era, before the full weight of fragmented and failed states like Yugoslavia, Somalia, and Afghanistan had become clear. The review had also been finished before major changes to the international trading system, before the creation of the World Trade Organization (WTO) that replaced the General Agreement on Trade and Tariffs (the GATT). Nor could the review have anticipated the attacks of September 11 and their consequences for global and national security. Ten years after its publication, it was no surprise that the review was badly outdated.

As the first new prime minister after 9-11, Paul Martin wanted a foreign policy for Canada that reflected the new world order. As finance minister, he had eliminated the federal deficit partly through disproportionate cuts to the international infrastructure of the Government of Canada—notably to the defence and foreign aid budgets. As prime minister, he now wanted to rebuild that lost capacity to help execute an ambitious agenda for Canada in the world.

Unlike some of his predecessors who developed an interest in foreign affairs only after they became prime minister, Martin had been deeply engaged and interested in international issues throughout most of the nine years he served as finance minister. He had been instrumental in creating the G-20 group of finance ministers to address the indebtedness and the periodic financial crises in developing countries. Secretary-General Kofi Annan had appointed Martin, along with celebrated development economist Hernando de Soto, to chair a commission on the role of the private sector in development. "After I was Finance Minister for a few years, [Prime Minister] Chrétien asked me if I wanted to be Foreign Minister. I said no. I did a lot of foreign affairs as Finance Minister. Finance did a tremendous job internationally. Gordon Brown [the British Treasury Secretary] and I played a very active role on a wide range of international issues," recalled Martin.[16]

It was therefore not surprising that immediately upon becoming prime minister, Martin accelerated a review process to modernize Canada's foreign policy. The final product would be the International Policy Statement (IPS). It was to be a defining feature of the Martin government, one of the prime minister's top priorities, an attempt to redefine and transform Canada's role in the world. Martin wanted a new, comprehensive foreign policy that would transcend the boundaries of the traditional "international departments"—Foreign Affairs, International Trade, National Defence, and the Canadian International Development Agency (CIDA). This review, unlike its predecessors, would directly involve every department of the federal government; in an age of economic globalization and transnational terrorism, all domestic policy had a crucial international dimension. Every department of the federal government was in the business of foreign policy now, in one way or another.

One department had to have the "lead," or the "pen." Naturally, this responsibility fell to the Department of Foreign Affairs, which was charged with consulting and integrating the priorities of all departments into Canada's foreign policy for the new millennium. In the first few months of the Martin government, Bill Graham, then still the minister of foreign affairs, and his deputy, Peter Harder, ran this challenging and unprecedented process in cross-departmental collaboration. And Jonathan Fried, Martin's new foreign policy adviser in the Privy Council Office, ran bureaucratic interference with the deputy ministers in Ottawa, to limit the infighting and, if absolutely necessary, impose a solution. It was Fried's job to bring this landmark process to an acceptable outcome in a few short months. There were to be no endless consultations of the public, no round of forums, no hearings. The prime minister wanted this done and done quickly.

In the Prime Minister's Office, two individuals formed a tag team: Peter Nicholson, the director of policy and brilliant former business executive, along with Martin's chief of staff, the politically astute Tim Murphy, one of the sharpest minds around the prime minister whose hand was in virtually every major file of the government. They would both take a keen interest in the development of the policy statement. Eventually, several months after the IPS was launched, the process bogged down; the prose was dreary, the focus totally lost. At that point the wisest and most senior civil servant in Ottawa, Alex Himelfarb, the clerk of the Privy Council, was drawn in to rescue the review.

It did not take long for the review process to revert to type. Very quickly, the agendas of the four key departments—Foreign Affairs, the Department of International Trade, the Department of National Defence, and CIDA—took over, even though Martin wanted a truly inclusive, "horizontal," and integrated approach. The ministers who held these four key portfolios were under constant pressure from Martin to produce a truly bold, transformational policy paper that would chart a new course for Canada. Implicitly, it was clear that the review would have to differentiate the policies of this government from those of its predecessor. This need to differentiate was a constant obsession—almost a pathology—that afflicted the Martin team.

By the time of the election in 2004, each of these four departments was writing its own independent document, in some cases with very little consideration of the views of the other three, not to speak of those of other departments in the federal government. The concept of an integrated, comprehensive international policy statement, even among the four key ministries, was alien to "the system." It was asking too much. Four independent papers would be written, and the Centre—the Prime Minister's Office and the Privy Council Office—would somehow have to integrate these into a holistic document at the end of the exercise.

NDHQ had a bit of a jump on the other three departments. Officials there had already been working on a new paper on defence policy. The bureaucrats in both the North and South towers recognized right after 9-11 that the Defence White Paper, written in 1994, needed "updating" in light of the new global and continental security environment. The department had to give greater priority to the so-called "asymmetric threats" posed by international terrorism. And domestic and continental security needed more attention now that North America itself had been attacked directly. Canada could no longer be the "free rider" on continental defence that it had been for years.

Calder and his staff were charged with revising Canada's defence policy to reflect this new security environment. The joke around NDHQ was that Calder always had a "new" defence policy in his filing cabinet to satisfy the demands of any incoming government—it just needed to be dusted off and "wordsmithed" a bit. Shortly after Graham arrived at NDHQ in the summer of 2004, Calder and the new deputy minister, Ward Elcock—the former head of the Canadian Security Intelligence Service, who had replaced Margaret Bloodworth as deputy minister—presented the latest draft to the minister for his perusal.[17]

Graham was unimpressed. The document seemed warmed over, too bland, excessively bureaucratic in its content and style. It reflected the consensus within NDHQ, rather than a new vision that broke with the past. Even though the Cold War was over, the document failed to chart a new course for the Canadian Forces, an institution that was poised to receive a very large infusion of funds from the new government. "We were finding it was virtually impossible to get a decent document out of the Department," recounted Graham. "Officials were mired in previous thinking rather than willing to think outside the box. I think they [the officials] had decided in their own minds that the military wasn't going to get any extra money and therefore they had to come up with a document that didn't oblige them to do anything dramatic because they weren't going to have any funds to do anything dramatic."[18]

Graham realized, even if his officials didn't, at least not at first, that the document they had given him would not pass muster with this

prime minister and his advisers as an integral component of his transformational IPS. Graham was convinced that Martin was prepared to
provide Defence with a major increase in funding. But this bloated,
notoriously inefficient organization that resisted change would first
have to demonstrate to the skeptical prime minister and his finance
minister that it had a strategic vision for the future that would provide
a framework for the spending of billions of dollars of new money. The
document on offer manifestly failed to do so. To be fair, officials never
saw a visionary policy document that could secure new funding as the
objective.

Throughout the summer and early fall of 2004, Graham and his
staff continually prodded civilian officials and the generals, trying in
vain to stimulate them to think more boldly and inject a strategic
vision into the policy document, one that went beyond the inevitable
inter-service log-rolling that always played out in these exercises. By
late fall, Graham and his chief of staff had become increasingly worried
that neither the civilian nor military leadership at NDHQ was capable
of producing a new defence policy that would satisfy the prime minister and meet the standards he had set. They were also concerned that
NDHQ could not produce a policy paper sufficiently strategic and
focused to help Graham extract the billions from the finance minister
and prime minister that the generals so desperately wanted. And time
was of the essence, as the federal budget was at most six months away.
Graham would have to make his appeal for new funding in three to
four months' time and start "working the town" immediately.

On his way home from a meeting in Europe, Graham read the
recently released British Defence White Paper. It laid out in painstaking detail what the British military would do in the future—and even
more important, what it wouldn't do. The British paper itemized the
equipment and funding the military needed to carry out the role it had
defined for itself over the next generation. Nothing like this was on
offer in the document the Defence Department had produced.
Graham told his officials to use the British paper as a model of a

strategic framework. He thought that such an approach would work with Martin, Finance Minister Ralph Goodale, and the Department of Finance, who were looking for any excuse to limit the increase in funding to Defence that Martin had promised during the election. But the minister's insistence was to no avail. His department simply was incapable of meeting Graham's standards. There was a solution to the minister's dilemma, but it was risky.

IPS and CDS

Ray Henault was scheduled to retire in mid-2005, after serving four full years as CDS, one year longer than the norm. He was now lobbying Graham almost daily to help him become the chairman of the NATO Military Committee, a largely titular yet prestigious job in Brussels that no Canadian had held in twenty years. The position would be open in a year, and while Henault was not specific about the date of his departure from NDHQ, most thought he would retire in April or May 2005, after the release of the new defence policy, and after the budget had passed. He wanted to take some credit for the new money. But Henault and his senior team at the corporate, or "purple," level in NDHQ were not giving Graham much to work with, either in terms of a new defence policy or assistance in the fight for budget resources.[19]

Graham's chief of staff suggested that perhaps Henault's departure should be accelerated by a few months. A new chief of the defence staff could be chosen and appointed quickly, one who could develop a clear strategic vision for the future of the Canadian Forces and Canada's role in international peace and security. The new CDS would take the basics of the policy paper, which were sound, and turn it into a bold strategic vision that charted a new course for the Canadian Forces. Graham agreed, seeing no alternative. "The original game plan was we would do a policy review, get ourselves some money in the Budget, and then get a new CDS. And then we completely reversed the whole order because we couldn't do the review because we didn't have anyone capable of writing it," recalled Bill Graham.[20] Henault would have to be nudged aside and the search for his replacement would have to begin immediately. The prime minister, who appoints the CDS, would have to be persuaded that the change was necessary to achieve his broader, strategic objectives. Graham faced some difficult conversations with his boss and with his most senior officer.

Getting the agreement of the prime minister and his advisers was the easy part. Replacing Canada's top military officer was intuitively appealing. It was another visible demonstration of how the Martin government was making a clean break with its predecessor. If "old guard, old think" generals were standing in the way of the prime minister's transformational defence and foreign policy, they would definitely have to go.

Dealing with Henault was a different matter. When Graham broached the idea of a departure in early 2005, before the release of the budget and before the IPS had been completed, Henault pushed back. He fully intended to stay on until the spring. He argued that he had invested a great deal in the defence policy and wanted to see it through. But Graham, in his quiet, respectful yet firm diplomatic tone, was insistent. Henault, a skilled political operator in his own right, was well aware that the job that he so badly wanted in NATO depended on the support of the minister of defence and the prime minister, who would have to push his candidacy actively in other capitals. Henault realized he couldn't afford a fight with the politicians and reluctantly agreed to step aside and make way for a change of command early in the new year.

The search for his replacement now began in earnest and with haste. Graham decided that he would personally interview every lieutenant general or vice admiral—three star—in the Canadian Forces who expressed an interest in being CDS. There were about six candidates.

Then the Prime Minister's Office threw a wrench into the works. Major General Andrew Leslie, recently back from his tour as deputy commander of ISAF, had come to the attention of the PMO. They had seen Leslie being interviewed on television and were impressed. Tim

Murphy made it clear to Graham's chief of staff that Leslie was their preferred candidate and deserved serious consideration. Leslie would put a brand-new, fresh, attractive, and articulate face on the drab image of the Canadian Forces. Leslie seemed to be the perfect candidate for a government that wanted to show it was making a clean break with the past. Murphy suggested to Graham's office that Leslie enhance his public profile immediately and get some additional media training. He wanted Leslie to appear as the obvious choice.

Promoting a two-star general to CDS would have leapfrogged over the three stars, a radical step. It would have been very controversial among the officer class and the military establishment because it was so clearly a tacit repudiation of the ten or so officers who outranked Leslie. While Graham was impressed with Leslie and liked him personally, he rejected the idea of vaulting him into the CDS job over the other three stars as too risky.[21] After all, Graham had just forced the current CDS out early, against his will, so he was not about to take on the military leadership again by breaking so clearly with military tradition.

Graham began his interviews, excluding Leslie. He would deal with the PMO later. The field quickly narrowed to two candidates. Graham thought that only these two officers had a clear strategic vision and a commitment to change the Canadian Forces to meet the new defence and security challenges of the twenty-first century. The two men were Rick Hillier, just back from his command responsibilities in Kabul and then chief of the land staff, and retired lieutenant general Mike Jeffrey, Hillier's predecessor as head of the army.

Jeffrey had retired before Graham became defence minister, so the two men did not know each other. But both McCallum, whom Graham consulted, and Graham's chief of staff knew and respected Jeffrey. They urged that he at least be considered.

Choosing Jeffrey would have been contentious also, although not unprecedented. Bringing someone out of retirement to lead the Canadian Forces would have been perceived as a lack of confidence in the serving senior officer corps. But Jeffrey was uniquely respected in all the services, and he had paid his dues. No one could or would have argued that Mike Jeffrey wasn't qualified for the job or that he would not make an excellent CDS. He had only two liabilities: He had retired and he was not fluently bilingual.

Graham, his chief of staff, and Jeffrey had dinner one night in a Toronto restaurant to discuss the issue. The minister was immediately impressed with Jeffrey's intellect, self-assurance, and manifest desire to reform the Canadian Forces. But Jeffrey also made it clear that he was not lobbying for the job. He had moved on since retiring, and while he didn't rule out accepting the post if it were offered to him, he would only do so if he had a clear mandate to drive real and potentially controversial change in the Canadian Forces, breaking it out of its Cold War mentality and its calcified bureaucratic habits.

After thinking it through for a few days, Graham ruled out Jeffrey. He concluded that bringing back a retired general could be devastating to morale among the senior officers. Jeffrey himself had suggested that bringing him out of retirement to become chief of the defence staff would certainly bruise egos inside the Canadian Forces and send the message that the government had little confidence in the existing leadership.

Once Graham had ruled out Jeffrey, Hillier became his candidate. But Hillier, the officer with the most operational experience among his peers, was certainly no default choice. Hiller's command of ISAF in Kabul, though relatively uneventful, had strengthened his reputation in Canada, in the United States, and in NATO as a tough-minded, formidable officer.

During his interview with Graham, Hillier put forward a detailed analysis of the international security environment. None of the other candidates did so, despite the fact that a former minister of foreign affairs who had spent his entire professional career in international affairs was the interviewer. Hillier, well prepared, laid out his vision for the Canadian Forces.

Consistent with the emerging themes of the IPS, Hillier claimed that the biggest threat to global peace and security for the foreseeable future would be failed and failing states. Afghanistan was a taste of the future. And, he argued, it would be in these states that the international community would expect Canada to deploy its military, in stabilization, in humanitarian, and even in combat roles. Hillier used the phrase "Three-Block War" to describe the types of missions Canada's military (read "army") had performed in recent years in Bosnia, Somalia, and Afghanistan. The concept of a "Three-Block War" was developed by the U.S. Marine Corps to describe an urban conflict zone, most likely in the developing world, in which one city block needed humanitarian relief, another stabilization, and a third combat troops. This, Hillier argued, was the present and the future. Canada's military needed to be properly equipped and organized to meet the challenges of a Three-Block War. Blue-helmeted peacekeeping operations separating one-time combatants along a ceasefire line were, Hillier insisted, a thing of the past for the Canadian Forces. The general's analysis was a logical and compelling articulation of the international security challenges in the post–Cold War period.

Hillier argued that the current CF "model" did not adequately prepare the military for the effective prosecution of Three-Block War scenarios in failed states. The CF had no comprehensive and integrated vision. Hillier felt the military was afflicted by a silo mentality and its existing model was inefficient and unaffordable. Although the Canadian Forces had been deployed abroad almost constantly for the last several years, they were, in Hillier's view, locked into an outdated Cold War, static structure. Canada's military needed to be more focused and selective in their purposes and in what they were equipped to do. Once and for all, they had to abandon the pretence of full capability across the spectrum and give up the futile attempt to be a small-scale replica of the American or British militaries. The current approach, Hillier argued, was neither appropriate nor affordable for a military of Canada's size. Tough choices needed to be made on mission, equipment, structure, and infrastructure.

Hillier thought it absurd, for example, that the Canadian Forces were still spending tens of millions of dollars each year on anti-submarine warfare from the air and sea in the North Atlantic. He was no fan of the relatively new, but used, fleet of submarines that the Canadian Forces had bought from the British navy during the Chrétien government. He thought that the air force's obsession with fighter aircraft and their demand to acquire the monumentally expensive Boeing C-17 Globemaster were preposterous.[22]

His beloved army was not exempt from criticism. As chief of the land staff, Hillier, a former tank commander, put forward a controversial recommendation to eliminate Canada's aging fleet of Leopard tanks. The general argued that the tanks were useless in a Three-Block War, "a millstone around his neck."[23] John McCallum, then the minister, enthusiastically accepted the advice. McCallum was determined to demonstrate to the prime minister and finance minister a concrete example of the principle of reallocation of resources from lower to higher priorities, a principle at that point new to the federal government and totally alien to the Defence Department.[24]

Hillier's capacity for strategic thought impressed Graham. The general, Graham thought, clearly understood geopolitics, the changing strategic environment, and he had a sharply etched vision for the future Canadian Forces that had clear consequences for operations and procurement. In all of this, he stood apart from the other candidates, not to mention the existing military leadership. Hillier told Graham that if the government appointed him as CDS, he fully intended to implement this vision, with all its attendant consequences. But, he said he could do so only if there was a two-way contract. He would need the political support of the minister and prime minister once the opposition to his reform agenda exploded among the public, the political class, and especially within the military establishment. Hillier was referring in part to the closure of some bases in order to trim the bloated infrastructure of Canada's military, an infrastructure that imposed debilitating costs on the Canadian Forces. He knew that he would need political support when the inevitable howls of outrage began. He also intended to pare down considerably the military hardware the services were requesting, again to create a more strategic, focused post–Cold War military. Here too he would be the subject of withering criticism and attack from current and retired officers who were wedded to the status quo. Hillier would need the government to stand firm in the face of criticism.

Hillier was confident that he could sell his vision internally and externally if he could garner the support of the younger officers, who, like him, had experience in operations during the 1990s and recognized the serious drawbacks of the current model. He claimed that officials in Foreign Affairs and CIDA agreed with his strategic vision and he expected that Canada's allies would as well.

Hillier's arguments were music to Graham's ears. Here was not only a decorated and experienced field commander, but also a visionary leader prepared to put his experience to work to transform the Canadian Forces into a military that was better organized, equipped, financed, and structured to carry out Canada's global responsibilities in the post–Cold War era. Hillier's candidacy offered a tantalizing promise: He would try to create a military that was attuned to the government's foreign policy priorities, rather than one that seemed designed to satisfy the political objectives of the services themselves. If Hillier's vision could inform the defence policy paper, and by extension, the International Policy Statement, Graham was confident that the prime minister would embrace it enthusiastically. And Graham was also more than confident that once Paul Martin had spent an hour or so with the articulate, confident, and charming Rick Hillier, he wouldn't need much convincing about who should be the next chief of the defence staff.

BILL GRAHAM, along with his chief of staff, met Alex Himelfarb and Tim Murphy late one evening in his Parliament Hill office in the

Centre Block to agree on who would replace Ray Henault. Himelfarb and Murphy had excellent relationships with Graham and his staffer. They had worked together on various files over the years and they all knew each other and got along well. After the obligatory pleasantries were exchanged, and the BlackBerrys put away, the serious discussion began.

Murphy immediately pushed the candidacy of Andrew Leslie, and Graham listened patiently. And then he made the counterargument. He pointed out that the appointment would be a very risky and unprecedented decision that could be destabilizing to the leadership of the Canadian Forces. A dozen three-star generals would certainly be unhappy and high-profile resignations might occur. The prime minister's two top advisers then asked Graham whom he favoured. Neither knew Rick Hillier, but Graham presented a compelling picture of the man and his strategic vision. Murphy was still somewhat skeptical and said that, at a minimum, he wanted Leslie promoted to deputy chief of the defence staff. Graham agreed to try to make this happen. The four agreed to the "package."

Graham would immediately send a letter to the prime minister recommending that Lieutenant General Rick Hillier be promoted to general and appointed forthwith as the next chief of the defence staff. Tim Murphy would find some time in Paul Martin's schedule in the near future for Hillier and the prime minister to meet one on one. That meeting happened quickly after Martin received Graham's letter and, as Graham had thought, Martin was immediately sold on the Newfoundlander. "Bill asked me for a new CDS to help him get the defence policy done. Hillier then came to 24 Sussex and he put his perspective to me. I immediately agreed with it," recalled Paul Martin.[25]

The meeting in Graham's Parliament Hill office that day would turn out to be seminal. To celebrate the decision the group had reached, Graham found a bottle of Irish whiskey in his office and the four toasted their work. They instinctively understood that they had just made an important decision. In time it would become clear just how important their choice was.

Hillier's appointment would fundamentally change the philosophy, the strategy, the organization, and the culture of the Canadian Forces. He would become the most important and influential CDS in living memory. As Graham had wanted, Hillier would make defence policy his first priority. Defence policy was historically, and quite appropriately, the domain of civilian officials, and it was unprecedented for a chief of the defence staff to be given this responsibility. But in this case it was necessary. Within a few short weeks, Hillier would transform the existing draft paper, giving the document edge, vision, purpose, and focus and, in the process, would impress both Graham and the prime minister. Within three months the Canadian Forces would receive its largest funding increase in a generation—an additional thirteen billion dollars over a five-year period—and Rick Hillier played no small part in securing the increase.

But most important, within that same three-month time frame, Hillier would persuade Bill Graham and ultimately Paul Martin to send Canada's military deeper and deeper into the conflict in Afghanistan.

Hillier making an influence.

NINE

NAVIGATING BMD

On February 4, 2005, at a hangar at the Ottawa International Airport, Rick Hillier was officially appointed Canada's fifteenth chief of the defence staff. The prime minister, the Governor General, members of the Cabinet, and Danny Williams, the premier of Hillier's native province of Newfoundland and Labrador, as well as hundreds of dignitaries, were there. If there was any doubt that the general was well connected in Washington, it was put to rest that day. Dominating the tarmac just outside the hangar was a United States Air Force plane that was the size of a commercial airliner and looked like Air Force One, the aircraft used to ferry the president around the world. Two American four-star generals and many other U.S. military officers had made the trip to Ottawa that day to honour Rick Hillier.

As Hillier's formal and high-profile inauguration was proceeding, three thousand miles away a young Canadian professor of international relations, Jennifer Welsh, was working late in her "rooms" at Somerville College, Oxford University. Welsh was not writing some obscure academic paper. She was writing Canada's new foreign policy.

Work on the International Policy Statement (IPS) was completely off track by the early winter of 2005. The IPS was bogged down in bureaucratic wrangling and infighting. Officials in Foreign Affairs had produced draft after draft and the prime minister and his senior advisers had personally read each one. To put it mildly, they were not impressed. Foreign Affairs, at one time the home of the cream of the federal civil service, could not produce a decent policy paper, or so Paul Martin and his advisers thought. There was no vision. There was no narrative about Canada's role in the world that anyone could follow. There was no transformational policy, as the prime minister wanted. The IPS had become a Christmas tree, decorated with traditional orna-ments, with no new message about Canada's role in the new global information economy and post–9-11 security environment. Ironically, the document suggested that Canada really had no foreign policy.[1] Martin reflected on this: "Over twenty-five years, due to the combina-tion of Michael Pitfield's centralization initiatives and my budgets, we have totally destroyed the policy-making capacity of the public service, and nowhere is this more manifest than in the Department of Foreign Affairs."[2] A senior public servant was even more scathing: "The Department of Foreign Affairs can't do policy, they have no policy capacity. The Department of Foreign Affairs is a roving travel agency and property management department."[3]

The people around the prime minister had become so frustrated that they took the pen away from Foreign Affairs and brought it into the rarefied world known as the "Centre," the Privy Council Office (PCO) and the Prime Minister's Office (PMO). Typically this happens in Ottawa only when a major file that the prime minister cares about has gone badly off the rails. And so it had. Fried had not been able to extract from the senior bureaucrats in Ottawa a document that would capture the imagination of the prime minister. In fairness, probably no one could have done so. And Pettigrew, the minister of foreign affairs, was mysteriously absent from the file.

It soon became apparent that neither the PCO nor the PMO had the expertise or institutional horsepower to give shape to a document that was the product of endless compromises and had no voice left. Then Tim Murphy had an idea. He had recently read Jennifer Welsh's new book, *At Home in the World: Canada's Global Vision for the Twenty-First Century.* He liked its narrative. Welsh told a story of a bold, confident nation that was well positioned to take on the challenges

and opportunities of globalization. The document from the bureaucrats was neither as clear in its vision nor as optimistic in its tone.

Murphy took a step that was radical by Ottawa standards and
farmed out the writing of the IPS to Welsh, who until then had not
been involved at all in the work that had been going on for months.
Tim Murphy reflected on this decision: "We tried to get them [the key
departments] all swimming in the same direction. Welsh was brought
in to clarify the choices which were getting blurred by the key departments. In fairness, we were incented to be in a lot of places around the
world due to the make-up of our country. But the Department of
Foreign Affairs would always sacrifice a policy outcome for a process.
And Fried, who is a very smart guy, was always giving us advice to
'preserve the process first and foremost.' So we decided to run the IPS
out of the Centre."[4] And Welsh became the Centre's "pen."

Foreign Affairs deeply resented Murphy's decision, since many of its
officials had worked tirelessly on this process for months on end. Many
in the Pearson Building had lost patience with the prime minister and
his staff who, they argued, kept changing the expectations and fiddling
endlessly with text. The Prime Minister's Office fully reciprocated their
frustration. The PMO's frustration became public when *Toronto Star*
reporter Graham Fraser wrote: "Not satisfied with drafts by senior civil
servants, Prime Minister Martin decided that a Rhodes Scholar from
the Prairies should write Canada's first foreign policy update in
10 years."[5]

When Graham's chief of staff visited Welsh in England that
February to check on her progress, he found a typical Oxford office—
charmingly antiquated, damp, cramped, and strewn with books and
papers, with one computer. This was the place where one isolated individual—connected to Ottawa through little more than the internet and
a phone line—was writing Canada's foreign policy for the new millennium. Foreign policy–making had never before been done like this in
Canada. And it had probably never been done like this in any other
advanced industrial state.

Things were very different at NDHQ. Hillier hit the ground running. Even before he was formally appointed CDS, he took full charge of recasting what became known in NDHQ as the Defence Policy Statement, or DPS. By the time Hillier had finished, the prime minister regarded the DPS as the best contribution to the International Policy Statement. "The Defence Review saved the IPS. Hillier's contribution was the outstanding contribution to that effort," reflected Martin.[6] Hillier had outperformed the best minds in the Department of Foreign Affairs and the academic in Oxford.

Hillier made two fundamental changes that gave the Defence Policy Statement life and edge. He put the concept of failed and failing states—states like Afghanistan and Haiti—and the emergence of global terrorism at the heart of the document and then developed the concept of the Three-Block War. To confront these core challenges, Hillier argued in the paper, the Canadian Forces would need to be fundamentally transformed: "In order to address these security challenges, the Government is setting a new course for the Canadian Forces. The recent operational experience of our military and the threats we are likely to face in the future point to the need for a bold vision."[7] This kind of language was, of course, exactly what the prime minister so badly wanted to hear.

Hillier argued that the structure of the Canadian Forces made it very difficult to conduct operations. Canada's military had served around the world despite, not because of, its archaic organization. He called for a new, unified approach to military operations, with transformed command structures, fully integrated units, better coordination with other government departments, enhanced interoperability with allied forces (especially the United States), and better intelligence, surveillance, and reconnaissance capabilities.

This was no easy recipe to follow. Hillier wanted major structural, organizational, and cultural change in the Canadian Forces. He also wanted a substantial increase in the size of the military and in its budget, and new equipment. Hillier was dragging the CF out of the

Cold War mentality that still gripped NDHQ fifteen years after the Berlin Wall had come down; and he was forcing military leaders to focus on the threats and challenges Canada would meet at home and abroad in the twenty-first century.

Hillier's document was exactly what Graham needed and what Martin had asked for. As Martin recalled, "He [Hillier] had a strategic focus that was very clear."[8] The document spoke of transformational change and laid out a blueprint to follow. It would help Graham to wrest billions of dollars from the finance minister and his resistant department. The next federal budget, which would be brought down in March 2005, would deliver the largest increase in defence funding in a generation—nearly thirteen billion dollars. Hillier's plan would convince the skeptics that the CF had changed, that it had a strategy, that it had priorities, and that the new money would be spent to advance those priorities. The new Canadian Forces would be more responsive to the demands of the government and would help the government achieve its objectives internationally.

In mid-February Martin sat down with Hillier, Graham, Elcock, Himelfarb, Fried, Nicholson, and Murphy to pore over Hillier's latest draft. The prime minister went through the sixty-page document page by page, asking question after question. Hillier fired back lucid, confident answers to every prime ministerial query. The general's performance that day impressed the intellectually sophisticated and experienced Peter Nicholson. He said, with obvious admiration, that he had never seen anyone handle the prime minister with such skill.[9] Scott Reid, Martin's director of communications and one of the prime minister's two or three most trusted advisers, described Hillier's effect on Paul Martin: "The Prime Minister liked Hillier. He liked his ambitious confidence. I mean, Hillier says, 'We're gonna do five things, they are very different from what we're doing now, this is how we're going to get them done, and by the way, I'm saying this louder than anyone else in the room.' And the Prime Minister would leave the room after these discussions all fired up, saying, 'Finally, I've got someone who is going to move the ball up the hill.'[10]

That day, after an hour or so of seminar-like discussion, with Martin reading from a personally marked-up, dog-eared copy of the DPS, the prime minister pronounced himself satisfied. That was a significant compliment from a perfectionist like Paul Martin. He wanted a few minor changes made, but he reassured the room that "We have the political will to do this." This was no small commitment, given the enormous financial costs, well beyond what Martin had committed to the military in the 2004 election. Such a significant policy change would certainly provoke opposition inside the Canadian Forces, particularly from the old guard and the retired military establishment who were still fighting the last war—or even the one before that.

In just a few weeks' time, a soldier from Newfoundland had outclassed and outrun the best minds in Canada's august Department of Foreign Affairs. It was his work that gave shape and thrust to the International Policy Statement. He had produced a policy paper that satisfied a demanding prime minister who was now prepared to provide billions of dollars to the military. Ottawa hadn't seen anything like this in many years. With this document in hand, and his forceful, optimistic personality, Hillier jump-started an important psychological shift both within the Canadian Forces and in the government's view of the military.

For more than a decade, NDHQ had actively fostered the impression through the media that not only had Defence suffered badly from budget cuts imposed by Liberal and Conservative governments as far back as Trudeau, but also that the Canadian Forces had been broken, perhaps beyond repair. Canada's once-proud military reputation, so hard-earned with so much loss of life in the great wars of the twentieth century, was lost forever. Or so the military elites claimed.[11] The professionals who made these arguments missed the point.

This story, endlessly repeated, of a depleted and demoralized Canadian Forces made it more difficult for successive ministers of defence to convince their governments to put more money into the military. John Manley, when he was finance minister, expressed his frustration more than once with a military that was always portrayed in the press as broken-down and incompetent. Why would any government want to invest billions of dollars of scarce taxpayer money in an organization that couldn't manage the seemingly innocuous task of procuring boots and uniforms for the first CF mission in Afghanistan without major controversy? Manley publicly reflected a more politically digestible version to the *Vancouver Sun* editorial board: "Instead of asking for more money, the Canadian Armed Forces should first take a hard look at how it is spending the money it has … Certain demands for more military spending are totally unrealistic, and the military needs to be more accountable for its spending. I don't accept the notion that because soldiers went to Afghanistan with improper footwear that, therefore, it's a funding problem."[12]

Politicians like Manley, McCallum, Graham, and Martin didn't think like bureaucrats or military men. They all had spent significant parts of their careers in the private sector and they thought like businessmen. They wanted public institutions that were efficiently run, well organized, creative, results driven, and client centred, and the client of the Canadian Forces was the Government of Canada, not the military establishment or the Pentagon. They were prepared to invest money in an enterprise that had potential, even if it was going through a rough patch. But the Canadian Forces presented an image of itself as an institution beyond repair.

Until Rick Hillier came along. Unlike his immediate predecessors, Hillier was not an NDHQ bureaucrat or an "Ottawa man." He was a soldier, a field commander, and an "operator." Paul Martin approved of Hillier's leadership and straight-talking ways: "I like Hillier. He is a soldier. We didn't ask him to become Deputy Minister of Foreign Affairs. He is a strong leader. He is very articulate."[13] And as Murphy recounted, "We picked Hillier as a change agent. He articulated things we all felt needed to be done. We didn't have any civilian control anxiety."[14]

And he got things done. Give Rick Hillier a task, any task, and he and his team got it done, whether it was cleaning up after the 1998 ice storm that ravaged eastern Ontario and western Quebec, dealing with the consequences of ethnic cleansing in Bosnia, or helping to secure a fragile government in war-torn Kabul. And in each case the task was done very well; Hiller delivered a world-class performance. He was "Mr. Can Do." Hillier didn't see the Canadian Forces as a broken institution. On the contrary, based on his experience working with militaries all over the world, he viewed it as a great institution, both relatively and absolutely, and he infused everyone he met with his confidence. To be sure, Canada's military needed some major structural reforms and more money, but if it got both, along with strategic direction and strong leadership, he believed he could restore Canada's military to its former glory. He set the bar even higher. Hillier thought the Canadian Forces could claim the mantle as the world's best small military.

Almost as soon as he was appointed CDS, a breath of fresh air blew through the stale corridors of NDHQ. Some officials echoed Hillier's optimism and ambition immediately. Tom Ring, the relatively new assistant deputy minister for public affairs—a former naval officer, fellow Newfoundlander, out-of-the-box thinker, and tough-minded, seasoned mandarin—was one senior official who quickly embraced Hillier's goals and his style. After the Defence Policy Statement and the budget, Ring suggested to Graham's staff that the minister should begin referring in his speeches to the CF as "Canada's premier national institution." This was a bit much for Graham to swallow, but it underscored the new mood that Hillier had created in the Department of National Defence (DND). It was this mindset that infused the Defence Policy Statement, animated Hillier's approach, and captivated Bill Graham and Paul Martin.

BMD Rears Its Ugly Head

By the early winter of 2005, after two decades of budget cutting, scandal, and increasing marginalization in Ottawa, the Canadian

Forces and the Department of National Defence were back at the heart of the government's agenda. At the head of the military was a new, dynamic, visionary leader who wasn't afraid to tell the politicians directly what the military needed and tell them bluntly what kind of defence policy the government should have. As one senior Defence official liked to say at that time, "We now own this town."

Then a wrench was thrown into the works. Ballistic Missile Defence (BMD) came back with a vengeance.

Since becoming minister of defence in the summer of 2004, Bill Graham had unwillingly become a one-man promoter of BMD. When he was minister of foreign affairs, he somewhat reluctantly accepted the need for Canada to participate with the United States. In the past, the foreign and defence ministers had always jointly managed the issue. Indeed, it was the minister of foreign affairs who had always had the lead responsibility for BMD. Now, however, the prime minister gave the responsibility to Graham. While officials from the Department of Foreign Affairs remained engaged, Pettigrew almost never intervened. Perhaps because Ballistic Missile Defence was so obviously a political liability in his native Quebec, Pettigrew stayed clear.

One of Graham's first acts as minister of defence was to announce that the government would be signing a new protocol with the United States. This protocol would permit the sharing of missile warning data between NORAD—the binational command that had gathered such data for decades—and the American architects of BMD then housed in Northern Command, the new continental American command set up right after 9-11 that was co-located with NORAD in Cheyenne Mountain, Colorado. This seemed to many to be the first, irreversible step in implementing the intent of the letter that David Pratt had sent to Rumsfeld six months earlier. Canada appeared to be inching its way into BMD through the NORAD door. True to form, this decision touched off a storm of controversy. The NDP hammered the government for going to bed with the Americans on BMD, and Graham now had to manage an ongoing and increasingly acrimonious public debate. BMD was his problem child.

Graham had an almost impossible assignment. The prime minister expected him, single-handedly, to sell BMD to an increasingly recalcitrant Liberal caucus that knew very little about either the substance or the history of missile defence.[15] Many MPs thought that BMD was a proxy for support of the unilateral foreign policy of the deeply unpopular Bush administration. Martin also expected Graham to convince a skeptical media and public that Canada should participate in BMD.

The prime minister had supported Canada's participation in Ballistic Missile Defence when he was campaigning for the Liberal leadership. In April 2003 Martin said on CTV's *Question Period*, "I certainly don't want to see Canada isolated from any moves that the United States might take to protect the continent. I mean if there are going to be missiles that are going off and they are going to be going off over Canadian airspace whether we want it or not, no, I don't think that is acceptable. I think that we want to be at the table." He now vacated this minefield and left it to his defence minister to navigate. What Martin once regarded as "a common-sense proposition," according to Scott Reid, was not as straightforward as he had thought and was getting too hot to handle politically.

The prime minister no longer took a clear public stand on BMD, nor did he express his preference even behind the closed doors of the Liberal caucus room or in Cabinet meetings. As leader of a minority government, he would not spend any of his dwindling political capital on BMD. The file was radioactive politically, especially in Quebec, where the Liberals desperately needed to make electoral gains in the next election. Martin didn't want to be personally associated with BMD, especially in Quebec, but he also didn't want to leave the impression that he had flip-flopped on the issue. So he punted the issue to Graham. Today Martin claims that his most important concern was the impact of BMD on the future of NORAD. Once the NORAD amendment, which permitted the sharing of missile warning data, had been achieved, he had accomplished all he wanted.[16] A more formal Canadian role in BMD therefore became the subject of negotiation and would require further argument to convince the increasingly skeptical prime minister.

Graham had no chance of success under this scenario. Ironically, as he saw it, "The minute we agreed to share missile warning information, the pressure was off to do BMD. Some people probably thought we could have our cake and eat it too."[17] In its first year, the government had let the issue drift instead of acting decisively right after the transition, when Martin's political capital seemed limitless and he headed a majority government. While it appeared that Pratt's letter all but sealed the deal, Martin was hesitant to conclude an agreement with Washington.

As winter turned to spring, and an election loomed, BMD became more controversial. The new NORAD protocol, which the government insisted did not commit Canada to BMD, only served to increase skepticism about the government's intentions. It added fuel to the fire; the government was either duplicitous or indecisive. And the hotter the issue got in public, the quieter Paul Martin became. The silence of the government gave the field to the opponents of Ballistic Missile Defence. The NDP and Bloc Québécois argued again and again that it was the first step to the weaponization of space and evidence of misguided Liberal support for an aggressive and destabilizing American foreign policy. After Graham became minister of defence, Martin would call him regularly, asking for an updated report on where every member of the Liberal caucus stood on missile defence. Graham diligently took on the task.

By early December 2004, BMD was white hot. The prime minister decided to convene a small meeting in the Cabinet anteroom, on the third floor of the Centre Block on Parliament Hill, to discuss the way forward. Graham, Pettigrew, and a handful of the most senior officials from DND, Foreign Affairs, the Privy Council Office, and the Prime

Minister's Office were present for this bear-pit session. No one from the Canadian Forces was invited to attend. The meeting was a policy discussion, and the military had no mandate or direct responsibility for policy. This meeting took place just before Hillier was appointed. Once he took over, defence policy became almost the exclusive domain of the military leadership. But that day, no generals or admirals were invited to participate in the discussion with the prime minister.

Socrates Meets the Mandarins

Martin felt that he had been blindsided by George Bush during his recent and long-overdue visit to Canada, which eventually took place on November 30, 2004. Even though the prime minister's officials had made it clear to the White House before the visit that they hoped the president would not discuss the issue in public, the president went ahead nevertheless. "We were told that Bush was not going to raise BMD in Canada," said Paul Martin.[18] But the president did raise the subject in his private meeting with the prime minister.[19] As former U.S. ambassador to Canada Paul Cellucci reflected, "Quebec was a problem as well as opponents in the Liberal Party who didn't want Canada to get close to the U.S. militarily. But everything was still pointing towards Canada participating in BMD ... in conversations I had with Cabinet Ministers, the Prime Minister, the Prime Minister's Office and bureaucrats it was clear people recognized that BMD was right for Canada. And Martin said 'I want to be at the table.'"[20]

During the press conference following the bilateral meeting between Bush and Martin on November 30, the president expressed his hope that Canada would soon agree to Ballistic Missile Defence. The president was well aware that his Canadian hosts did not want public discussion of this issue, but he very much did. And so he went ahead and raised it at the first opportunity. "We talked about the future of NORAD and how that organization can best meet emerging threats and safeguard our continent against attack from ballistic missiles,"

Bush said, as Martin was silent and thousands of protestors demonstrated outside the building.[21] Years later, Ambassador Cellucci explained why the president had gone ahead and raised the issue in public, with the prime minister sphinx-like beside him. "When the President wanted to discuss something," said Cellucci, "he discussed it whether or not he was told to keep quiet."[22]

This was the first time an American politician had put any pressure on Canada to join BMD. To add insult to injury, the pressure was public, not private—not behind closed doors. The timing of Bush's intervention could not have been worse, given a swirling public controversy, a fragile minority government that depended on the support of the NDP to govern, and Bush's deep unpopularity among Canadians as a result of the war in Iraq. And the intervention clearly antagonized Martin: "After he raised it [BMD] in public, I told Bush we are now a lot further away than we were five minutes ago."[23]

Martin began the meeting with the mandarins by asking what the Americans were up to. What was Bush thinking? Was this issue really so important to the president that he felt compelled to raise it in public, even though he knew he would embarrass his host? Bush's comments had profoundly surprised the prime minister.

Graham made the point that the government needed, once and for all, to make up its mind on BMD. He had been advised that Washington was frustrated and annoyed with the indecision in Ottawa, indecision that had been going on for several years. It was best to bite this bullet, Graham advised, even if Canada was going to say "No" to the United States.

But the prime minister still had questions about the system itself and what Canada's involvement would mean. Did it imply the weaponization of space? What control or influence, if any, would Canada have over the development of the system? Would it be designed to cover Canadian cities if Ottawa signed on? That seemed unlikely. Would the United States ever seek the use of Canadian territory to base radars or interceptors?[24] Would Canada be asked for a financial contribution to the project? Officials were unequivocal that Canada's participation was free, but this too seemed unlikely. And, finally, how would the system work to provide security for Canada? "I wanted to see the configuration to see how it works," recalled Martin.[25]

Scott Reid reflected on these discussions between officials and the prime minister: "There is a Socratic streak in Paul Martin. He asked them [the officials] to tell him the merits [of BMD] from a security and foreign policy perspective. I found that there was a staggering inability to articulate what BMD was, and what we were being asked. We were given answers that resembled newspaper articles … There was no policy-based argument that I could discern other than 'If we don't do this we may piss the Americans off … We've said no to Iraq already and we have to be concerned about how far we can push the envelope.' It was consistently that kind of argument that we got."[26]

Bill Graham made a similar observation. "We got the most inconsistent advice from officials [on BMD]. It was the craziest thing to try and understand. Defence and the Department of Foreign Affairs could never even agree on what they were negotiating. At one time Martin asked a question of one official and got an answer that he just couldn't believe. Forever after Martin felt he had been lied to. So he had no faith. He lost faith. He was furious."[27]

No one in Foreign Affairs, Defence, or the PCO could satisfy the prime minister. No one gave him credible answers to the basic questions that he and other politicians had been asking over and over again for years. Reid was shocked that the officials from Foreign Affairs did not challenge the arguments put forward by National Defence. "Their world view was simply 'We don't want to do anything to alienate the White House.' To get around that you would need an ice pick."[28] Perhaps the timidity at Foreign Affairs was a consequence of the Chrétien government's decision on Iraq. As Reid reflected: "There was a hangover from the Iraq decision that gave a hysterical tone to all the advice that was coming to us. It boiled down to—'You must do this, for God's sake, or you will alienate the White

BMD decision came down to ↗

House.' I was astonished at the paucity of analysis that came to us on most Canada-US files. Most of the advice we got I could have got from a George Will column ... or more to the point, a John Ibbitson *Globe and Mail* column."[29]

Buying More Time

Paul Martin was angry that Bush had taken the issue of BMD to the public. Martin argued that what the president had done, the way he had behaved, put at risk Martin's plan to rebuild the military. Why would the Canadian public have confidence in an expanded and better-funded military if the military could not provide convincing answers to basic questions about BMD but still supported the project? Martin felt that he was being asked to spend an enormous amount of his political capital to sell something in Canada that was deeply unpopular and that, as far as he could see, would give Canada very little.[30] "Paul never understood why we had to do BMD," said Tim Murphy.[31]

Pettigrew agreed. Rebuffing the Americans on BMD would not be a big deal, except in the Pentagon, or so his conversations with Colin Powell led him to believe. Those in both the North and South towers of NDHQ thought this was dangerously naive. They were convinced that Canada would pay a huge price: the withering away of NORAD, and lost access to intelligence and surveillance information.[32] They kept coming back to the same argument; they feared that if Ottawa slapped the Bush administration in the face again on an issue Washington regarded as vital to its national security, and one that would cost Ottawa little or nothing, then the Canada–U.S. relationship would go into the deep-freeze at all levels.

Paul Martin wasn't buying it. He instructed the officials to draft what he called a *de minimus* letter to the Americans indicating that he wanted to explore the notion of negotiating a comprehensive framework on North American defence. BMD would be only one component in the broader agreement. Unpersuaded, the prime minister wanted to buy time.

A Message from the Pentagon

Earlier on the same day that Martin had met with Pettigrew, Graham, and senior officials to discuss BMD, another important meeting took place a few blocks away at NDHQ. Henault, Elcock, and Graham's chief of staff met with Rear Admiral Ian Mack, Canada's military attaché in the embassy in Washington. Prior to Graham's meeting with the prime minister later that day, Mack had flown up to Ottawa to brief officials on what he was hearing in the Pentagon. He delivered a sobering message.

Mack reported that the U.S. officials were not happy that Canada had said "No" so often lately—allegedly seven times. Ottawa had declined to participate in the NATO mission to train the Iraqi army. Canada had not provided a handful of F-18 fighter aircraft to support the U.S. efforts in southern Afghanistan. Although there never was a formal request to Ottawa—Graham received no such request from his American counterpart or from his own officials—some in the Pentagon allegedly wanted the aircraft. Canada had also refused a U.S. request to send a reinforced company of soldiers to Haiti, which seemed on the verge of chaos. And although Canada had promised to send a PRT to Afghanistan, it had not yet decided where the PRT was going nor had Ottawa made any commitment to help NATO expand its mandate beyond Kabul to encompass all of Afghanistan by 2006.

Mack claimed that the tension was particularly obvious among undersecretaries in Washington. Ian Brzezinski in the Pentagon apparently had said that Canada could no longer be perceived as a reliable ally. And on BMD, the Pentagon had gone from frustration to outright annoyance at the dithering in Ottawa. They were especially annoyed because they took Paul Martin's campaign promise as a commitment to participate. Washington knew well that, given the geographic

don't want to put
out for the US, just
sent to put
3 of it

proximity of the two countries, Canada would get the benefits of BMD whether or not Ottawa chose to participate. American officials felt that Canada wanted everything for nothing and BMD was only the latest example of its inclination to seek a free ride.

The bilateral relationship was allegedly in deep trouble and needed attention—and fast. It was suggested that Fried telephone Condoleezza Rice, Bush's national security advisory, to suggest she urge the Pentagon to give more detail on BMD to Canadian officials so that they could satisfy the prime minister. Maybe this would break the log-jam.

Mack suggested that Canada needed to consider seriously doing what he called the "Seven Yeses" to help counteract the negative impact of the "Seven Nos." Some of the "Yeses" were minor—seconding additional senior Canadian Forces officers to the U.S. military. Others were more significant—a robust Defence Policy Statement that demonstrated a commitment to rebuild the Canadian Forces. One of the seven items that Mack suggested was sending Canadian special forces to Kandahar.

Finally ... a Decision

Between December 2004, when Martin convened the meeting to discuss the president's public comments on BMD, and late February 2005, BMD became the dominant political issue for the government. With each passing week, it became more controversial. The NDP and the Bloc Québécois relentlessly attacked the government in the House of Commons, claiming that Martin was about to sign Canada on to a project that would lead to the weaponization of space and destabilize the international arms control regime. Gilles Duceppe, leader of the Bloc Québécois, pressed hard: "Mr. Speaker, before Christmas, the Prime Minister was categorical: without a written commitment from George Bush ruling out any possibility of militarization of space, Canada would not participate in the missile defence shield project ... Will the Prime Minister insist on a written guarantee from George

Bush, or will he sign a blank cheque for the militarization of space?"[33] Not to be outdone, Jack Layton, leader of the NDP, said, "With the evidence now absolutely clear that this is weapons in space, will the Prime Minister simply say no and say no now [to Missile Defence]?"[34]

At the same time, Stephen Harper's Conservatives, who in their 2005 Policy Declaration had supported "Canada's participation in negotiation of a North American Missile Defence System on the clear understanding that any agreement must serve Canada's interest," criticized the prime minister. They accused him of dithering, lacking the courage of his convictions, and failing to follow through on an agreement with Washington on BMD. Martin's minority government was getting picked apart from both the left and the right. The government's vulnerability was the inevitable outcome of having no policy on such a divisive issue for far too long.

As the controversy swirled around him, Bill Graham continued to do what the prime minister had asked him to do months before. He spoke personally to most members of the Liberal caucus to find out where they stood on BMD and tried to persuade them of its merits. His report to Martin was not encouraging. A strong majority of Liberal MPs opposed BMD. Many members of the caucus found it much easier to express their opposition now that Martin had vacated the field. Some even doubted that the prime minister continued to support the program. Only Martin could swing the caucus around, but he was not prepared to do so. As Bill Graham explained: "To have done BMD would have required investing some political capital, to use that overworked phrase. It was never very popular. It required a pretty sophisticated explanation of what it is we would be doing. This was something that would have required the Prime Minister's personal leadership to say 'Well, this is the right thing to do and we're going to do it.'"[35]

In an effort to build support in the Liberal caucus, officials from Foreign Affairs and DND were asked to provide a "technical" briefing to Members of Parliament. Jim Wright, assistant deputy minister for global security policy in the Ministry of Foreign Affairs, and Ken

[handwritten margin note: Harper knew what he wanted/how to act]

Calder briefed the Liberal caucus one cold night in the winter of 2005 in a meeting room in the West Block on Parliament Hill. Briefings from officials to MPs on any subject are rarely well attended, especially if they are held at night after a long day of parliamentary work. But this briefing was an exception. Between forty and fifty Liberal MPs and senators came to hear Wright and Calder. The two officials were unable to persuade any of those who were present. Almost all of the parliamentarians reiterated their opposition to BMD.

The attacks from the Opposition were relentless, and the media focused more and more of their attention on the issue. It was obvious that the government could procrastinate no longer. An election could come at any time and the Liberal Party policy convention was only a few weeks away. Chantal Hébert, a well-respected journalist in Quebec, identified Martin's dilemma: "The Quebec wing of the party will submit a resolution urging Martin to turn down the Bush administration's invitation to participate in the shield. Quebec is a key piece of the puzzle to ensure a Liberal election majority. It is also a hotbed of opposition to missile defence."[36] All this would take place under the full glare of the national media, who would certainly focus their attention on the hostility to BMD among rank-and-file Liberals. The boil had to be lanced. Paul Martin finally made up his mind. Canada would not participate in BMD, but the announcement would not be made just yet. The prime minister wanted to give Washington advance warning before any public announcement. Chrétien's failure to do so on Iraq was still fresh, and Martin wanted this issue to be handled diplomatically, especially since his officials had told him repeatedly how displeased the Americans would be.

When officials at NDHQ heard where the prime minister was heading, they were floored. They could not understand the change in Martin's position, a change that had taken place in just a few months. Elcock, who had served ten years as director of CSIS and was deeply connected to the Washington intelligence community, was incensed. He told Graham's chief of staff that a "No" to the Americans on BMD would deal a "catastrophic blow to the Canada–US relationship."[37] This decision, he insisted, would have even greater impact than Chrétien's decision to stay out of the Iraq War. Elcock was evidently hoping that Graham would talk to the prime minister one last time in an effort to change his mind. But Graham knew that the issue was now closed. BMD was politically a non-starter in a Martin minority government.

The Right and Left Hands

On February 22, 2005, Martin's new ambassador-designate to Washington, former New Brunswick premier Frank McKenna, visited Ottawa to appear before the House of Commons Standing Committee on Foreign Affairs. Martin, in an effort to improve what he had famously labelled Parliament's "democratic deficit," had instituted a new element in the confirmation process: high-profile appointees would answer questions in front of Parliamentary Committees before their appointments were made official. It was an attempt to graft elements of the approval process in the U.S. Congress onto a Westminster parliamentary system. The new process was untested at this point, and that was obvious from McKenna's appearance.

Because McKenna was still not officially the ambassador and did not yet have the requisite security clearances, Foreign Affairs decided not to brief its new ambassador on the latest developments on BMD, even though he likely would be asked questions about this issue during his appearance. Officials at Foreign Affairs naively believed that McKenna could stay clear of policy questions and stick to generalities. McKenna evidently thought the government would participate in BMD, indeed that it had already made that decision. He drew his conclusions, which were reasonable, from the amendment to NORAD, which permitted missile warning data gathered by NORAD to be shared with American officials working on BMD. While McKenna's appearance at the committee did not produce what reporters would call "news," his comments to reporters after his appearance did. During his scrum, when the inevitable question came regarding Canada's position on BMD, the blunt-talking former premier said that the government had already agreed to participate. "We are part of [BMD] now and the question is what more do we need to [do]?... There is no doubt in looking back that the NORAD amendment has given, has created part, in fact a great deal of what the United States needs in terms of being able to get the input for defensive weaponry."[38] McKenna either misspoke or he thought the NORAD amendment made Canada party to BMD, when in fact it did no such thing. McKenna's comment poured gasoline on a brushfire. Finally, the government had stated publicly, through its new ambassador to Washington, its position on BMD. Canada was already in the system. To put it mildly, McKenna's answer surprised officials who knew better.

McKenna had scheduled a lunch meeting with Bill Graham in the Parliamentary Restaurant right after his committee appearance. Graham had been in Cabinet Committee meetings all morning and had not heard about the ambassador's comments. By noon, the Canadian Press had already reported that McKenna had said that Canada supported BMD. The press had assumed that McKenna's appearance before the committee was selected as the appropriate venue to announce official government policy.

Graham's chief of staff brought the CP article to his boss's fourth-floor office minutes before they were scheduled to meet McKenna. He gave the press clipping to Graham, who read it quickly and exclaimed, "What the hell is this?" Given the toing and froing on BMD over the last several months, both men were uncertain whether Martin had changed his mind yet again and failed to inform his minister of defence, or whether McKenna had misspoken before the committee. Did the right hand of this government know what the left hand was doing? Graham headed to the New Zealand Room in the Parliamentary Restaurant to find out.

McKenna, who arrived with two officials from Foreign Affairs, seemed a little shell-shocked from the media attention that had surrounded his committee appearance. Graham and McKenna exchanged pleasantries, sat down, and ordered their food. One of the officials asked Graham's chief of staff to step outside the room. He then informed the minister's aide that the ambassador had misspoken. They re-entered the room. Within minutes the staffer's BlackBerry was alive with emails sent from both Tim Murphy and Scott Reid, who were with the prime minister and Pettigrew at a NATO meeting in Brussels, where Bush and his foreign policy team were also present. The prime minister's staff had heard about McKenna's comments, and they wanted Graham and McKenna to return to the lobby of the House of Commons before question period, where they could meet the press and clear up this "miscommunication."

Correcting the record was urgent, because Pettigrew had planned to inform Condoleezza Rice, now Bush's secretary of state, in Brussels that Canada would in fact not be participating in BMD. "I told Pettigrew to tell Condi it would be no," said Martin.[39] Tim Murphy was preparing to deliver a similar message to Bush's chief of staff, Andrew Card.[40] The plan was to inform the Americans before announcing the government's position in Canada. McKenna, just hours before Pettigrew had planned to deliver his message, had thrown a wrench in the works.

A note was passed to Graham suggesting that he and McKenna meet the press and "clarify" the government's position. He waited for the appropriate moment in the lunch and then diplomatically made the suggestion to McKenna, indicating that it had come from Scott Reid, the prime minister's director of communications. The ambassador straightened in his chair, clearly annoyed, and said he would do no such thing. McKenna retorted that he hadn't heard from Scott Reid in over a month. The Prime Minister's Office had not briefed him on BMD and, McKenna implied, if he had made an error, it was their fault, not his. Reid more or less confirmed this: "I'm reluctant to criticize Frank McKenna. I assumed he had a clear idea of where we were headed on BMD. But I don't know that he had been clearly informed—'Be careful, don't wade too deeply into this lake.' I just assumed that that had occurred already through Fried or Foreign Affairs."[41]

Reid also suggested that McKenna was a strong proponent of BMD, so he might well have been pushing the government a little bit to encourage Martin to get moving. What McKenna did not know was that the government was about to inform the Bush administration of Canada's intentions not to participate in BMD. McKenna didn't stay in Ottawa to correct the record. He left right after the lunch and returned to Toronto. And he made no further public comment for several days as the storm raged on. It was left to Bill Graham to clear things up with the press.

A Lamb in Wolf's Clothing

At 11:15 A.M. on February 25, 2005, Bill Graham, on instructions from the Prime Minister's Office, placed a call from his Parliament Hill office to Donald Rumsfeld to inform the secretary of defence of Canada's decision on Ballistic Missile Defence. There was some concern that perhaps Condoleezza Rice didn't fully appreciate what Pettigrew had told her in Brussels, or perhaps Pettigrew was less than clear with his counterpart. As Martin said, "I expected Bush would want to see me," after Pettigrew had informed Rice.[42] But Bush made no such request. This was a little puzzling given Bush's intervention in Canada on BMD and in light of the prevailing opinion among officials in Ottawa that the Americans really wanted Canada in the system. Why hadn't Bush asked to speak to Martin in Brussels?

Rumsfeld, the man in Washington with responsibility for BMD, needed to be informed directly of Canada's decision to ensure clarity. The call was scheduled in advance. One of Rumsfeld's aides came on the line and asked the minister to hold. Then Graham was advised that the deputy secretary of defence, Paul Wolfowitz, would be taking the call in Rumsfeld's place. Wolfowitz was a legendary figure in Washington. Known to be a brilliant, tough, abrasive, neo-conservative with an uncompromising temperament, he had been a central figure in Republican foreign and defence policy circles for two decades. He was one of the leading so-called "Vulcans" of the Bush administration, the principal architect of waging war against Saddam Hussein immediately after 9-11, and the author of the new U.S. foreign policy doctrine of pre-emptive military strikes against America's enemies. As tough as Rumsfeld could be, many saw Wolfowitz as even tougher. Not only was Graham being snubbed by his counterpart, he was about to be taken to the woodshed by Rumsfeld's ruthless deputy. So one might have assumed.

The two men had never met or spoken to each other before Paul Wolfowitz came on the line. The deputy defence secretary claimed that Rumsfeld could not take the call because he was under the weather with a cold and had not come to the office that day. Graham started with a brief preamble about some of the positive things that Canada had been doing of late in defence—the Defence Policy Statement and the impending increase in defence spending—to help cushion the blow he was about to deliver. And then he informed Wolfowitz that the political climate in Canada was such that it would be a mistake to move forward on BMD. The government might be forced to face a vote in the House of Commons if Canada agreed to participate, a vote that it would surely lose. That was neither in Ottawa's nor in Washington's interest. The Martin minority government simply could not sell BMD to the Canadian public.

Wolfowitz surprised Graham with his response. In a soft-spoken, articulate, and charming tone, George Bush's chief Vulcan told Canada's minister of national defence that he fully appreciated the Canadian position and decision, that he understood the delicacy of the matter in Canada. In a respectful way, Wolfowitz emphasized that the United States was going ahead with the project regardless and didn't need Canada in BMD from an operational perspective. With some generosity, he told Graham that the United States would remain open to continuing discussions on BMD with Canada if "you change your mind. We will keep talking to you about BMD." As Graham reflected, "Wolfowitz basically told me, 'We don't give a damn.'"[43]

Then the deputy secretary of defence shifted gears. He complimented Graham on Canada's efforts around the world. Wolfowitz said that Canada was making a significant contribution internationally, but told Graham that Canada needed to figure out its defence priorities. He knew about Canada's plans to field a PRT in Afghanistan, and he thanked Graham for this important contribution to reconstruction in that troubled country.

Then came a total non sequitur. Wolfowitz had recently seen the acclaimed movie *Hotel Rwanda*, which told the story of the Rwandan genocide and included a character based on Canadian General Romeo Dallaire, who commanded the UN mission in Rwanda. Wolfowitz said it was a terrific movie and he urged Graham to see it. He asked Graham to send him a copy of Dallaire's recently released book, *Shake Hands with the Devil*, chronicling his time in Rwanda. He then asked Graham to help arrange a meeting between Dallaire (a recently appointed Liberal senator) and Wolfowitz the next time the former general visited Washington. The Rwandan genocide and Dallaire's experience as a UN field commander, Wolfowitz said, "illustrated the horrible limitations of peacekeeping and the consequences of limited rules of engagement," a problem that Wolfowitz felt hampered the ISAF mission in Afghanistan.

This cordial, diplomatic conversation with one of the most rigid members of the most ideological administration to govern the United States in decades ended after about fifteen minutes. There had been no harangue. No veiled threats from the Pentagon's chief bureaucrat. No recriminations from Washington. No suggestion that NORAD was at risk as a result of this decision. No hint that the bilateral relationship would in any way be affected as a result of a legitimate decision of the sovereign government of a close friend and neighbour of the United States. Wolfowitz did not even express disappointment that day. In both substance and tone, he was supportive and understanding. Canadian officials had agonized over the repercussions of staying out of BMD and some had predicted catastrophic consequences. It was immediately apparent in Wolfowitz's conversation with Graham that the pessimism of some officials was wholly unwarranted. The Canada–U.S. relationship would weather this difference of opinion, as it had weathered others in the past. The two men had an adult conversation that was appropriate in a mature, sophisticated bilateral relationship that seemed, at least on this day, to transcend ideology, policy, and partisan politics.

Paul Martin had a similar experience when he finally spoke to George Bush about the matter. "I called Bush later. He took a week to get back to me, but my call with Bush was fine. BMD was much bigger here than it ever was there [in Washington]," reflected Martin.[44] And Paul Cellucci, the fiercest advocate in the Bush administration of Canadian participation in BMD, confirmed that Canada's decision on BMD had no effect on the relationship. "It did no damage to Canada–U.S. relations. We just threw our hands up and said these people don't know what they are doing."[45]

GRAHAM'S CHIEF OF STAFF sent a memo to Elcock, Hillier, Murphy, Fried, and Harder summarizing the call with Wolfowitz. The message was simple: It had gone much, much better than anticipated. There didn't seem to be much fallout to worry about. Life went on.

NDHQ was not reassured, not at all. Officials remained convinced that Martin had needlessly inflicted serious damage on the Canada–U.S. relationship. Tim Murphy reflected on the fallout: "The system was panicking, you had all these people who use a decision like BMD to do something to appease the Americans."[46] Despite the evidence that the Canada–U.S. relationship had suffered little or no damage because of Canada's decision not to participate in BMD, the foreign policy and defence establishment in Ottawa felt a renewed sense of urgency to do something significant to offset the negative consequences that they feared. Afghanistan seemed a logical place to start.

TEN

FROM KABUL TO KANDAHAR

O n March 23, 2005, Prime Minister Martin and President Vincente Fox of Mexico were scheduled to meet with President George Bush at Baylor University in Waco, Texas, followed by lunch at the president's ranch in Crawford. Canadian officials were uncertain whether or not Bush would once again raise the controversial issue of Canada's participation in Ballistic Missile Defence. Some officials were apprehensive, but NDHQ had told Bill Graham in no uncertain terms that the Pentagon had warned that Bush would definitely ask Martin about Canada's future plans for Afghanistan. Officials at DND urged Graham to prepare the prime minister to respond to Bush's question, and they implied that Canada's intention to create a Provincial Reconstruction Team in Kandahar would not be enough.

In early March, senior military and civilian officials had briefed Graham on "Global Trends." They began with China, Iran, and North Korea. The nuclear ambitions of Iran and North Korea were once again becoming a grave concern to the international community. Officials also argued that the majority of conflicts in the future would be within states, in what they called the "Arc of Instability," which ran from sub-Saharan Africa through the Middle East to southwest Asia. The nexus between failing states and terrorism, concentrated in this arc, would be the biggest threat to global security.

Officials also discussed the conflicts in Darfur, Sudan, and Haiti. Paul Martin was increasingly concerned about Darfur and wanted some kind of military or diplomatic initiative that would help to stop *janjaweed* militias from perpetrating atrocities on the people of Darfur. These militias, acting as a proxy army for the Sudanese government, were razing villages, raping, looting, and murdering in an effort to force people off the land and over the border as refugees. The conflict in Darfur was not only abhorrent in its consequences for the local population, but it could also destabilize the region because of the large flow of refugees.

Haiti was another trouble spot. Canada's military had been deployed there in the recent past, and political and security conditions were again badly unsettled. Even though a UN force led by Brazil was in the country, Haiti was regressing into anarchy and violence once again. Montreal MP Denis Codèrre, who had recently been appointed the PM's special adviser on Haiti, was pressing the government to do more in that desperately poor country. Montreal's large Haitian community was watching, and Pierre Pettigrew, who had a large Haitian population in his constituency, was also concerned about events in Haiti.

But officials advised against sending the Canadian Forces either to Darfur or to Haiti. In Darfur, the prospects for a successful international intervention were low. Here the North and the South towers at NDHQ were of one mind. The United Nations was not capable of organizing and leading the kind of mission needed to end the carnage in Darfur. With the UN in charge, officials told Graham, Darfur risked becoming another Rwanda. To stop the slaughter in Darfur, a large, well-armed NATO-led combat force would need to be in place for years, as in Bosnia. Brussels had no appetite for such a mission, especially one that would be "out of area"—i.e., outside Europe. And opposition by the Sudanese government to any Western troops in their territory led NDHQ to dismiss the prospect of a military operation as fanciful. Only if Sudan were invaded could NATO forces be inserted into Darfur, and an invasion of Sudan was unthinkable, at least to Canada's Department of National Defence. A deployment to Darfur would make Afghanistan and Iraq look like a picnic, or so officials claimed. Notwithstanding the moral imperative to stop the slaughter, Graham was told that there was simply no feasible military option.

This moral imperative to stop the crimes against humanity that were being committed in Darfur weighed heavily on the prime minister's mind. The UN General Assembly had just passed a resolution giving legal weight to the "Responsibility to Protect" (R2P). The resolution emphasized that governments had obligations toward their citizens and when they abused these obligations, when they abused their own citizens, the international community had a moral responsibility to intervene within states to protect innocent civilians who were the victims of systematic violence or genocide. Sovereignty no longer trumped criminal behaviour. Canada had been a strong supporter of R2P for several years, prominent Canadians had been involved in its development at every stage, and the Canadian ambassador to the United Nations, Alan Rock, had been instrumental in steering the resolution through to passage by the General Assembly. Canadian fingerprints were all over this, along with a strong sense of pride and Canadian ownership.

The attitude within the Department of National Defence was very different. R2P was regarded as dangerous and recklessly naive, divorced from geopolitical and military realities. Deployment of several thousand troops would make little difference in many of these fragile or war-torn states, and Western governments, officials argued, were unwilling to suffer the casualties that would inevitably flow from these kinds of actions.

The Department of National Defence had a simple approach to Haiti. The country had always been and would always be a mess. The Brazilian troops were not committed to the UN mission and it showed on the ground. Brazil was allegedly looking for an exit strategy. (By early 2006 the Brazilian commander on the ground would commit suicide.) The UN bureaucracy had not provided adequate support to the mission in Haiti and no contribution from Canada would make any difference whatsoever. It would be a waste of scarce Canadian military resources, officials argued, to send the CF back to Haiti in any significant numbers. This pessimistic analysis resonated with Graham, who had visited Haiti when he was foreign minister. He often recalled a conversation he had had with Colin Powell, whom Graham held in great esteem. Powell thought that the only way to help Haiti was to make it a protectorate and send in tens of thousands of U.S. marines to secure the country indefinitely. Powell admitted there was no appetite for that kind of strategy either in the international community or in Washington.[1]

This briefing on global trends set the stage for Graham's first substantive discussion on Afghanistan with his newly appointed CDS, Rick Hillier.

Go Big or Stay Home

Hillier had been CDS for only one month, but already he had managed to develop a considered and integrated Canadian plan for Afghanistan. His plan went far beyond deploying a single PRT as an exit strategy from Kabul—the strategy that Henault and Maddison had supported. Instead, Hillier wanted a deployment that would get Canada deeper and deeper into the most troubled part of Afghanistan. It was heavy lifting. And it was an initiative that would impress the Pentagon and even George Bush.

Any barriers to Hillier's proposal to increase Canada's presence in Afghanistan that might have existed at Foreign Affairs melted away after Canada declared it would not join the BMD program. A new consensus, led by DND, was rapidly emerging in Ottawa: Canada, and in particular the Canadian Forces, needed to do something significant for Washington—something that the Pentagon really valued—to compensate for the refusal to participate in Ballistic Missile Defence. Michael Kergin, former Canadian ambassador to Washington, put it this way: "There was this sense that we had let the side down ... and then there was the sense that we could be more helpful, militarily, by taking on a role in Afghanistan ... We could make a contribution in a place like Kandahar."[2] Tim Murphy went further: "We would have done this anyway, but there was pressure to be seen to be doing something as a result of BMD."[3] Paul Martin clearly felt the pressure: "There was a view coming out of the military and the Department of Foreign Affairs that we had to do something in order to repair the relationship in terms of both Iraq and BMD. I didn't agree," said Martin.[4]

AT THIS TIME, NATO was beginning to broaden its mandate well beyond Kabul to encompass all of Afghanistan. It was to be done in four stages—each stage a further expansion of NATO's responsibilities. The third stage would extend NATO operations to the southern part of Afghanistan, including Kandahar province, then under U.S.–led Operation Enduring Freedom (OEF). Graham was told that the British, the Dutch, and the Norwegians were interested in participating in the third stage. The Dutch were allegedly keen to work in a joint Provincial Reconstruction Team led by Canada. It was expected that Stage Three would take effect in early 2006, so military planning and government approvals were required right away if Canada were to be involved. The Canadian Forces needed to begin preparations to move out of Kabul—where by this time they had scaled back from a 2,000-person deployment to a 750-person reconnaissance unit at Camp Julien—and head south.

A Canadian PRT in Kandahar was now a given. There was no place left in Afghanistan for Canada to deploy, or so went the conventional wisdom. Other countries had taken the relatively safe real estate. And the CF leadership had ruled out a partnership arrangement with the Italians in Herat and had rejected Brussels' repeated requests to go to the Chaghcharan region. But Hillier wanted to do much more than send a two-hundred-person PRT to Kandahar.

The new CDS put on the table an Afghanistan package consisting of five elements. The first would be the PRT in Kandahar, beginning in the late summer of 2005. It would stay in place for at least two to three years, given the challenges of reconstruction in that part of Afghanistan.

In addition, he argued that Canada should deploy JTF2 special forces in the same region. This was the highest value-added military contribution that Canada could make to the ongoing combat in Afghanistan, a contribution that Washington would greatly appreciate. JTF2 were considered to be the only special forces in NATO (or in the world for that matter) that were as capable as their British and American counterparts. Elements of JTF2 had been in Afghanistan in the past. And they had impressed the Americans.

Hillier also recommended that Canada respond positively to a British request to lead and command for nine months, beginning in the fall of 2005, the Kandahar region multinational headquarters. This headquarters, which commanded the forces of eight countries, including the United States, was then under OEF, but NATO planned to take over in early 2006. Canada could pave the way for that transition by taking on the lead of the headquarters. It would require about 350 members of the Canadian Forces and a one-star general to do the job. Hillier argued the CF had the capability to run the headquarters and that doing so would give Canada an important and unique window on the situation on the ground in southern Afghanistan.

To add to the Kandahar package, the CDS proposed that Canada deploy for one year (beginning in February 2006) a combat infantry task force of about eight hundred to one thousand troops. This unit would work with the Americans under OEF, and eventually under the NATO flag, to conduct stabilization and combat operations throughout Kandahar province. The task force would not be deployed to protect the PRT; it would have a robust capability to defend itself and would not be geographically co-located with the task force. To be sure, it would be advantageous to have a combat unit that could be rapidly deployed to assist the PRT if it found itself in a particularly threatening situation. But that was not the primary reason for the task force.

Hillier argued that Washington would greatly value a Canadian combat force, given the overstretch of its forces in Iraq and Afghanistan. Of equal importance, the combat task force would give

Canada another important window on security in Kandahar as it engaged in operations and gathered intelligence throughout the region. The Canadian Forces had not been in Kandahar since 2002. As they were relearning the terrain of the province, the task force would be invaluable. Hillier had raised with Graham earlier the possibility of deploying a task force and the two men had agreed that the military planners would explore its feasibility. Graham had also told Wolfowitz during his telephone conversation with him about missile defence that Canada might field an infantry task force in Kandahar in 2006.

5   The fifth and final element was a fifteen-person team, including a CIDA member—labelled a Strategic Advisory Team—that would go to Kabul to work in important ministries of the Afghan government, such as Defence and Finance. These officers would advise the Afghan government on public administration. They would also provide the CF with good information and some influence on decisions that the Karzai government might make that could affect Canada's ongoing efforts in Afghanistan.

The plan was big and bold. It was quintessential Rick Hillier. He argued with great confidence and clarity that the Canadian Forces could meet the challenge, that Ottawa should focus on the opportunity rather than the risk. Not only the United States, but also the United Kingdom, NATO, the UN, and the Afghan government would respect Canada's contribution. Canada would no longer be on the margins.

This mission would open doors for Canada in Washington, at a minimum those in the Pentagon, which had allegedly closed due to Canada's refusal to participate in military operations in Iraq. It would also prevent doors from closing in pique because of Ottawa's refusal to participate in BMD. Donald Rumsfeld was desperate to backfill U.S. forces in Afghanistan, so that the U.S. Army could concentrate on the rapidly deteriorating situation in Iraq. It was now becoming clear that Iraq was engulfed in a civil war, a war that the Bush administration and the Pentagon had not anticipated and were unprepared to manage.

Ever since the autumn of 2002, the Bush administration had shifted its attention from Afghanistan to Iraq, even though Afghanistan was far

US pull out

from secure. Some former members of the administration claim that the Bush foreign policy team had shifted its focus away from Afghanistan to Iraq even before the Taliban were ousted.[5] One comparison makes the point. In 2005, the United States had about 20,000 troops in Afghanistan and about 150,000 in Iraq, even though both countries were of comparable geographic size and population. McCallum got an early indication of this shift in priorities in his meeting at the Pentagon in 2003, when Rumsfeld was aggressively looking for countries to commit troops to Afghanistan to free up U.S. forces for the coming invasion of Iraq.

But winning the respect of the United States and other allies was not the only argument Hillier made for his proposals. Canadians would be justifiably proud of their government and their military for undertaking a difficult and important assignment. The Canadian Forces could make a real difference on the ground, both in reconstruction and in the stabilization of the security situation. And the prime minister would have transformed Canadian foreign and defence policy in a bold action, one that would make a mark for Canada in the world.

There was comparatively little discussion about the operational challenges of southern Afghanistan in general or of Kandahar specifically. Officials described the region as by far the most unstable and dangerous part of the country. Unlike the last time the Canadian Forces had been in Kandahar, the Taliban had regrouped and reorganized inside Pakistan and now regularly crossed the notoriously porous border, a frontier that the Pashtun communities living on either side—and the Afghan government—had never recognized. The Canadian Forces, and in particular the infantry task force and JTF2, would be engaged in direct combat. There would be casualties. It would be a dangerous assignment, people would get killed, and the government would need to prepare the Canadian public for certain losses.

No official, civilian or military, used the word *war* to describe what was going on in southern Afghanistan. At that time, no civilian or military leader understood that Taliban attacks signalled the beginning of a new war. The military rarely, if at all, used the word *insurgency* with the politicians to describe what was happening in southern Afghanistan. Moreover, the term *counterinsurgency warfare*, which is so widely used today to describe NATO's role in southern Afghanistan, was never used in Graham's presence to describe what the Canadian Forces would be doing in Kandahar. Even as late as January 2006, months after the Canadian Forces first started arriving back in Kandahar, Defence Department officials were still referring to the Kandahar deployment in their briefing notes as "a more robust peace support role, which will likely entail even greater risks."[6]

"The mission was described to me as twofold," recalled Bill Graham. He continued:

> The PRT would be doing the Three *D* work [the integration of defence, diplomacy, and development assistance], but we needed combat troops because there was trouble, we had to pacify the region. But nobody foresaw the summer offensive of 2006. The Light Armoured Vehicle (LAV) III was considered the perfect vehicle for the terrain, the perfect tactical response. We needed lightly equipped, agile soldiers who would go into the villages, "make love to the people" and "kill the bad guys." We sold ourselves that we could do this and that it was possible. That was what I would call prior to the "Iraqization" of Afghanistan. Nobody who planned the mission anticipated this. Nobody used the word *war* to describe the mission. We were convinced that the Loya Jirga went well. Presidential elections went well. I think everybody was convinced that Afghanistan was a lot further down the road to recovery than it really was. And those were pretty superficial benchmarks. We were probably drinking too much of our own bathwater.[7]

It was not only the minister of defence and the military who thought that way. Chris Alexander, formerly Canada's ambassador to

[handwritten margin note, top left: "never wanted to call it a war"]

[handwritten margin note, left: "3D important for describing the mission"]

Afghanistan and now the United Nations Secretary-General's deputy special representative to Afghanistan, admits that he too did not expect the Taliban to come back with the force that they have and fight the way that they have. "We were taken by surprise," he said. "Why? Because we live in hope. Commanders feel relentless pressure to be optimistic."[8]

Graham and his civilian and military advisers devoted a lot of attention to the political repercussions of the mission. Hillier was proposing to redeploy Canadian troops out of NATO's ISAF mission and into Operation Enduring Freedom led by the United States. And while the plan was for NATO to take command during Canada's deployment in Kandahar, the CF would be without the cover of a NATO flag for several months at least. Also, there was still some uncertainty as to whether NATO, which had missed more than one target date already for Stage Three, would move into the south at all.[9] Given the unpopularity of the Bush administration in Canada since the invasion of Iraq, having large numbers of Canadian Forces in an American-led mission would be politically awkward for the government. It could make it more difficult to persuade the prime minister.

Graham certainly recognized the political sensitivity of the mission, but he did not think that these political constraints would be insurmountable. And Foreign Affairs was comfortable with this proposal and would not stand in its way this time.

The Department of Finance would likely be the problem. This mission would be expensive and it was not budgeted for in the "fiscal framework" of the government. The estimate was at least $1.2 billion, or $600 million for each of two six-month rotations. These numbers dwarfed Canada's commitment to development assistance in Afghanistan, which then totalled $600 million over seven years. The ratio of military to development spending was more than 10 to 1, almost exactly the obverse of what successful counterinsurgency demands. At the time, however, no one framed this problem as counterinsurgency.

Hillier's extraordinary powers of persuasion made Graham comfortable with the package, and he agreed to recommend it to the prime minister. If Martin approved, the mission would constitute the largest and most significant deployment of the Canadian Forces since the end of the Cold War.

March 21, 2005

Graham wrote to the prime minister within days of his briefing by Hillier. By mid-March, NDHQ had heard nothing and was becoming anxious. Graham's office checked with the Prime Minister's Office and was told that the prime minister had not focused on the letter yet. The meeting with Bush was quickly approaching and the South Tower was getting nervous that Paul Martin had not yet decided where he stood on the mission to Kandahar.

On March 20, three days before Martin was scheduled to meet Bush, word came that the prime minister would convene a meeting the next day to prepare for Waco. Graham, Pettigrew, and a few of their top officials were invited to attend. But, they were told, the subject for discussion would not be Afghanistan; it would be NORAD.

Now that the dust had settled, Paul Martin apparently wanted to understand more deeply the implications for NORAD of his decision not to participate in BMD, and he wanted to discuss NORAD renewal. It appeared that the prime minister wanted to be well prepared to emphasize to Bush that his "No" to BMD did not signal a weakening of Canada's commitment to NORAD or North American security.

As usual, the meeting was held in the Cabinet anteroom on the third floor of the Centre Block around a large circular table. Graham, Hillier, and Elcock from DND; Wright from Foreign Affairs; Fried, Himelfarb, and Murphy from the Prime Minister's Office; and, of course, the prime minister were present. Very quickly, it became apparent that Martin didn't really want to talk about NORAD; he was preoccupied with Darfur. No one was prepared to discuss Darfur. Nevertheless, Darfur became the subject of the meeting.

The prime minister said clearly that he wanted Canada to play, and to be seen to be playing, an important role in helping to resolve the crisis in Darfur. He felt that to mobilize public support for a major increase in military funding, Canadians would want to see their foreign policy anchored in an identifiable "Canadian role." "On forgiveness of African debt," Paul Martin said, "I led and said we will forgive it. This kind of action helps our sense of well-being as a country. Our military policy should support that."[10] Public support for rebuilding the Canadian Forces, in Martin's view, was directly linked to a role that Canadians could endorse. He believed that while approval for the military was high, it could erode quickly if Canada were perceived to be doing America's bidding around the world. From this perspective, Canada's role in Afghanistan had not been satisfying to Canadians. But a concerted effort in Darfur, to help stop genocide, would be something Canadians would immediately support.

And it was also the Liberal thing to do. Many members of Martin's caucus wanted to see Canada more engaged on Darfur. Recently appointed senator and internationally renowned army commander retired Lieutenant General Romeo Dallaire (the man Paul Wolfowitz was so interested in meeting) had become the public champion of intervention in Darfur to stop the killing. Dallaire likened the international community's failure to act in Darfur to the world's inaction a decade earlier in Rwanda, when over eight hundred thousand Tutsis had been killed in a genocidal frenzy. The world had stood by and watched the slaughter. Dallaire had been in command of a weak and ineffective UN peacekeeping force that could do little else but witness the Rwandan genocide. Now, Dallaire was making a passionate and compelling case for Darfur and he was making it loudly and clearly.

"Darfur is the most visible symbol of the failure of multilateralism today," the prime minister said with conviction.[11] And Canadian public opinion, as well as his government's commitment to Africa, suggested that Darfur was the place where Canada should concentrate its military and diplomatic efforts. Martin told the assembled group that he wanted to inform the UN and the African Union (who were at that time in charge of an ineffective peacekeeping mission in Darfur) that Canada was prepared to put in sufficient troops as part of an international coalition to do whatever was necessary in Darfur. The Darfur crisis, in Martin's view, needed what he called "catalytic leadership" from some country, and he wanted Canada to be that country. Darfur would be Canada's new project on the world stage. No crisis was more pressing and no symbol greater than Darfur. Afghanistan would have to take a back seat.[12]

The prime minister also pointed out the obvious about Haiti. International efforts were a recognized failure, and he asked whether Canada should not be playing a bigger role. Pettigrew definitely thought that Canada should, and he suggested that Ottawa develop a Haiti strategy.

Martin then turned to the Middle East and said that it was one of his priorities.[13] The region was so volatile that the Canadian Forces might be able to play a role in the region, although he was not clear on what that might be. Years later Martin clarified what he had in mind: "James Wolfensohn [former head of the World Bank] called me and said he would put a plan forward at the G-8 summit in Gleneagles for $3-billion for economic reconstruction for the Palestinian Authority. It was felt this could lead to a peace agreement. I spoke to some G-8 leaders and it was approved. I thought there was a chance for peace and that the Israelis wouldn't want a United Nations force but might accept some foreign troops, including Canada's. I wanted to ensure I had the capacity to commit troops to that if it came about."[14] Martin's optimism was not borne out by developments in the region. The demand for a peacekeeping force grew out of badly deteriorating security rather than progress. By the summer of 2006, full-scale war had erupted between Israel and Hezbollah fighters in southern Lebanon and a much-strengthened UN peacekeeping force was deployed between the two parties inside Lebanon.[15]

Martin had made his foreign policy priorities clear: Darfur, Haiti, and the Middle East, in that order. Afghanistan was a distant fourth at best. "Afghanistan was not a priority for me the way Darfur, Haiti and the Middle East were. Afghanistan had become our biggest aid commitment, and it shouldn't have been," reflected Martin.[16]

Then Hillier started a conversation on Afghanistan. He laid out three options, with costing—the full-blown five-element package, which had already been recommended to the prime minister, and two smaller options. Hillier made a concise and persuasive presentation on why Afghanistan should be Canada's principal focus for the next two years, and why all the elements in the package supported one another and would bring significant political and military benefits. No one in the room challenged him on the politics, the policy, or the military dimensions of the proposal.[17] Except Paul Martin. The prime minister responded that he was concerned Afghanistan would consume resources, both military and financial, even though it was not central to the kind of foreign policy Canadians wanted their government to pursue. He also rejected Hillier's implication that a large Canadian role in Afghanistan would build public support for the military. Martin thought the opposite more likely. "I made four demands of Hillier before I agreed to the mission," recalled Martin. "I want in, but I want out. We do peacemaking and reconstruction and win hearts and minds. I am going to make a big demand on Darfur soon and you have to tell me I can have all the troops I need. And you must have the capacity for Haiti if that blows up again. I told him none of this could be constrained by Afghanistan or I wouldn't agree to the mission."[18]

The prime minister's attention was on Darfur. Officials from Foreign Affairs, DND, and PCO all told him that there was almost no possibility that the UN could get a resolution through the Security Council that would authorize a peacekeeping force for Darfur that included Western troops. China had significant oil interests in Sudan and would certainly veto this kind of proposal. But Martin wasn't persuaded. He thought that the UN might reach a consensus on

[handwritten left margin: Parallel to who was already suspicious of liberal convention]

[handwritten right margin: Hillier didn't follow any of this!]

Darfur within a year, and he insisted on the flexibility to be able to contribute significantly to any international force if it were created. Martin's optimism may well have been justified. In the spring of 2007, the government of Sudan tacitly agreed to the presence of a twenty-six-thousand-strong mixed UN–African Union peacekeeping force in Darfur that would be deployed within a year.

Officials misread Martin when they thought that the prime minister and his staff would see Hillier's package as a way to distinguish his government from that of his predecessor. It was now painfully evident that Martin would link anything to do with Afghanistan—no matter how big, or bold, or different from anything that Canada had done in the past—to Chrétien's government and would, therefore, find the proposal unappealing. Martin viewed Afghanistan, Scott Reid explained, as an inheritance from the previous government. The prime minister felt that Canada, as a member of NATO, had an obligation to stand with the alliance in Afghanistan, but his interest in Afghanistan ended there.[19]

only a NATO obligation.

Hillier gave the prime minister unequivocal assurances that the complete package that he recommended in Afghanistan would not inhibit the Canadian Forces from contributing significantly to an international force for Darfur (or Haiti or the Middle East), beginning in early 2007.[20] As *Toronto Star* reporter Bill Schiller reported, "Martin made it plain … that he didn't want to be patronized … He didn't want any 'Yes, Minister' business. He looked Hillier squarely in the eye and demanded his commitment. He got it."[21]

Hillier thought that by early 2007 the Canadian Forces, and particularly the army, would be sufficiently regenerated to mount a second mission elsewhere. And since the official plan was to withdraw the combat infantry task force and the headquarters elements from Kandahar by early 2007, scarce resources would be available for other missions.

The prime minister ended the meeting with two decisions. First, he instructed the ministers of foreign affairs and defence and their departments to work together to develop a strategy for Darfur, where Canada would lead an international effort to help resolve the crisis.

2 results from PM meeting.

Second, on Afghanistan, he agreed that Canada would do more than send a PRT to Kandahar. He would think about the options that had been presented to him and he would speak to the finance minister about the fiscal flexibility that would be needed. He would get back to Graham in due course. Paul Martin did not think it was urgent to sort all this out before he met George Bush the following day.

After the Ranch

After a meeting between two heads of government, officials in Ottawa normally get "debriefed" on the essential points and on any follow-up that might be required. Within hours of Martin's meeting with Bush on March 23, official Ottawa got its debrief. Afghanistan was one among many issues that were discussed. The president made clear how much the United States had valued Canada's contribution in Afghanistan over the last several years. But he did not press Canada to do more, and Martin made no firm or specific commitments to Bush.[22]

Officials at NDHQ did notice, however, that the prime minister suggested in public in Texas that Canada would do more in Afghanistan, although he offered no specifics. They speculated that Martin was getting more comfortable with the package of options as he learned more and thought more about Afghanistan. The intervention by Hillier and Graham had at least put Afghanistan on Paul Martin's radar screen. Nevertheless, the Privy Council Office told NDHQ that the prime minister was still concerned, notwithstanding Hillier's assurances, that if he approved the full package he might not have sufficient troops available when he needed them to make a commitment to Darfur, Haiti, or the Middle East. Martin wanted further assurances.

The prime minister had also raised Darfur with Bush and had suggested that Canada might consider taking a leadership role to help resolve the crisis. Bush liked the idea. In a public speech, Colin Powell had deliberately used the word *genocide* to describe what was happening in Darfur. The use of that word by an American secretary of state carried precise international legal obligations. The Convention on Genocide mandates states to take all necessary actions, including the use of force, to stop genocide. Powell was well aware of the consequences of labelling the conflict in Darfur *genocide*, not only the legal consequences but also the political and moral obligations. How could the lone remaining superpower and self-professed leader of the free world permit genocide to continue unchecked?

President Bush was under increasing pressure, in particular from the Christian right in the United States, which sympathized with the Christian tribes that were the target of the *janjaweed*, to take forceful action to stop the killing. But the Bush administration was not about to engage in Darfur, or anywhere else in Africa for that matter. It had its hands full in Iraq. More to the point, as Paul Wolfowitz told Bill Graham when they spoke, Africa was not central to U.S. national interests and Washington would not commit forces there. Presumably this is why Bush liked Martin's proposal to break the deadlock on Darfur at the UN. Secretary of State Condoleezza Rice, who attended the Bush-Martin meeting, agreed that some country had to take the lead on Darfur. Her comment was music to Paul Martin's ears. "Bush believed in the idea that he was bringing democracy to the world," reflected Tim Murphy, one of the participants in the Crawford meetings. "Martin told Bush, 'We can do things you can't in places like Darfur where we can be the face, we can be the lead, and we can make a difference,'" recalled Murphy.[23] "Bush agreed with me on Darfur," said Paul Martin.[24]

Waiting ... and Waiting

NDHQ was still waiting for a response from the prime minister to the Afghanistan proposal. Important meetings of senior military officials would take place very soon in Washington and Brussels, and officials needed to know whether or not Canada should attend these sessions. Would Canada be going big in Kandahar? Would Martin go with the full package or would he shave some of it off?

didn't want to pay for it

At the end of March, word came from officials in the Privy Council Office that the Finance Department was unhappy about the cost of the Hillier package. It wasn't until April 20, almost three weeks later, that NDHQ got further word. They were told the issue would go to Cabinet in early May and that the prime minister was not comfortable with the cost of the full package.

In that Cabinet meeting in May, Paul Martin decided that he would exclude from the package a lead role for Canada in the multinational headquarters. Adding that element to the mix drove the cost too high for the prime minister and for the finance minister as well. As Tim Murphy reflected, "It was recommended that we approve the 'Goldilocks' option, which was the priciest one. I talked to Ralph Goodale [the Finance Minister]. We picked the middle one which we were told would not add to the risk of the mission."[25] But Hillier refused to take no for an answer. The prime minister's only objection was cost, so Hillier decided that the Canadian Forces would find a way to fit the headquarters assignment within the funding envelope that the Finance Ministry was offering. Some of Hillier's staff suggested that it was impossible to find the funding within the envelope, but the general wasn't having it. The Canadian Forces would find a way. This initiative was far too important to be watered down over money. "You cannot underestimate the desire of soldiers to prove themselves in combat," said Paul Heinbecker, a former senior foreign policy adviser to the Mulroney and Chrétien governments, "nor of commanders to finally show their skill in managing real battlefields."[26]

The full package was approved at Cabinet. Canada would be going big … very big, into Kandahar beginning in late 2005, eventually ramping up to over two thousand troops for a one-year assignment.

Eighteen months after the decision, it was apparent that this mission was the most dangerous Canadian military operation in decades. Forty-five Canadian soldiers died in the first few months of the deployment. Canadian deaths in Afghanistan are proportionally higher than those of other NATO countries.[27] The mission in Afghanistan changed the public image of the Canadian Forces from a military largely engaged in peacekeeping and humanitarian work—a public perception that ignored Canada's long military history—to one of an army engaged in full-scale combat and counterinsurgency warfare. Canada's military was at war, and it was at war in ways the whole country could see and feel. There is little doubt that some of the senior leadership in the Canadian Forces relished the explosion of the myth that the Canadian Forces were primarily peacekeepers. The mission was a chance to rebuild parts of the military from the ground up, to transform it into an efficient fighting machine. Hillier made that point publicly to reporters in July 2005 at an informal, on-the-record media luncheon. Being a soldier meant "you go out and bayonet somebody. We are not the Public Service of Canada," he declared. "We are not just another department. We are the Canadian Forces and our job is to be able to kill people."[28]

The mission to Kandahar prompted the first national debate about Canada's role in Afghanistan fully five years and three missions after the Canadian Forces had first set foot in Afghanistan. It would sharply divide Parliament and the Liberal Party. It would also mark the beginning of a vigorous public debate about the appropriate role for Canada and its military in global peace and security operations.

No one in government or in the military predicted where the decision to go big to Kandahar would lead. No one expected that within a few months the Canadian Forces would be engaged in counterinsurgency warfare. No one predicted the widespread consequences from a package of military options. But Hillier's proposal was like a stone thrown into a stream. The stone is small, but the ripples are wide.

wasn't a good image change

ELEVEN

SCUMBAGS AND DUTCHMEN

O nce the prime minister decided that the Canadian Forces were going to Kandahar and directed the military to prepare to go to Darfur if conditions permitted, Foreign Affairs and NDHQ went to work. The prime minister appointed two special envoys, Romeo Dallaire and Robert Fowler, then Canada's ambassador to Italy and Martin's point man on Africa.[1] Fowler would try to fashion a diplomatic initiative on Darfur and Dallaire would work on the military dimension.

Rick Hillier again rose to the occasion. He immediately dispatched a few dozen military officers to Khartoum and Addis Ababa, Ethiopia, to report back on the situation on the ground. The new Chief of the Defence Staff came up with an innovative way for Canada to help. He recommended that Canada donate 110 Grizzly armoured personnel carriers, which were aging and of little use to the Canadian Forces, to the seven thousand–strong African Union (AU) peacekeeping forces operating in Darfur. The force was badly armed and badly equipped. An armoured mobility capability on the ground would be, according to the experts—including Dallaire—a significant "enabler" to help the AU achieve its objectives. Even the old Grizzlies could make a difference to the capacity of the African force to operate on the ground and protect civilians in Darfur.

It was not obvious that the Canadian Forces, a military that had allegedly been stripped to the bone in the 1990s due to budget cuts, would have surplus armoured vehicles to contribute to an African peacekeeping mission halfway around the world. Here Hillier was at his best, ready to break with patterns that were deeply embedded and resistant to change in the Canadian Forces. Before Hillier became CDS, almost no piece of "kit," no matter how obsolete, was eliminated, just in case it might be needed some day, somewhere, for something. But Hillier wanted the Canadian Forces to get rid of equipment that it didn't need and that was expensive to keep. The Grizzlies were taken out of storage, put in good working order, then put on a train to Montreal, loaded onto a ship bound for Senegal in West Africa, and transported across the African continent to Darfur, where they were needed and could be used.[2]

This tangible military contribution and the search for a diplomatic solution satisfied the prime minister, at least for the moment. The military turned its attention to Kandahar.

Preparing the Ground

As the summer of 2005 approached, it became apparent that Ottawa had not "shaped the public environment," to use Tom Ring's phrase, for the upcoming mission to Kandahar. Ring advised strongly that Bill Graham and Rick Hillier needed to hold a joint press conference formally announcing the mission, followed by a speaking tour of the country during the summer to explain the purposes of the mission and to prepare Canadians for the inevitable casualties. Once again, the minister and the CDS agreed. Speaking engagements and interviews were scheduled throughout the country.

Graham delivered a sophisticated message to the public about what this mission meant for Canada, why it was the right mission, what Canada would be doing for the people of Afghanistan, and how and why it would be dangerous for the Canadian Forces. Afghanistan was a fragile state that needed expertise, development assistance, and military help to stabilize the region of Kandahar, and the Afghan government had asked Canada to undertake this mission. The defence minister acknowledged that Kandahar, the former home of the Taliban, was the most dangerous and unstable region of Afghanistan and casualties were inevitable. The Canadian Forces would help to stabilize this region and provide security, an essential precondition for humanitarian relief and reconstruction.

Graham did not describe this mission as part of the "War on Terror." Nor did he link the mission to the death of Canadian citizens in the World Trade Center on September 11, the language the Harper government would use a year later. Graham never used the word *war* at all to describe the Kandahar operation. No one in Ottawa expected the Canadian Forces to be fighting a war.[3] As Tim Murphy recalled: "We knew it was a sharper end of the stick. It was to be a reconstruction mission which was dangerous. We would do the Three *D* model there [defence, development, and diplomacy]."[4] Graham's emphasis was on reconstructing a war-torn region of Afghanistan, where some fighting would be necessary to create space for reconstruction: "Our role in Afghanistan is quintessentially Canadian: we are helping rebuild a troubled country and we are giving hope for the future to a long suffering people. This is a clear expression of our Canadian values at work."[5] He emphasized that the mission would engage all three of Canada's departments working together—the Three *D* model—and quoted Brigadier General Tim Grant (he would subsequently become Canada's commander in Kandahar) who "spoke of how we will reach out and win over the local population while also bringing stability to the region, with what he calls, and I proudly agree, our 'warrior diplomats.'"[6]

It was a complex message describing a complex mission. It was not black and white, but very little was black and white in the security environment of the early twenty-first century. Graham gave the speech in four major Canadian cities during the summer of 2005. The media billed it as the "pre-body bag speaking tour;" Graham was preparing Canadians for casualties.

wasn't actually a direct threat to Canada though.

Hillier's public statements on the mission through that summer were blunt and direct. In stark contrast to Graham's, the general's language was black and white, even if the mission was not. Hillier made clear, in graphic language, how he understood the mission. It was about getting at the "ball of snakes" and the "detestable murderers and scumbags" that inhabited Kandahar province and threatened Western societies. That kind of language got headlines. It also buried the more sophisticated, nuanced message that Graham was trying to communicate, a message that more accurately described the purposes the government had approved.[7] The politicians were not pleased with Hillier's comments. They didn't see his description as an accurate reflection of the mission they had approved and now had to sell to Canadians. "His comments about scumbags put the nature of the mission in a totally different light and we lost our ability to persuade people it was what I call 'peacekeeping heavy,'" recalled Bill Graham.[8]

With his straight talk and colourful language, Hillier dominated the news throughout the summer. He became a household name and a national figure. In the two years following his appointment, he was quoted in the press more than six hundred times. No CDS in recent memory had achieved this kind of recognition. Nor had any senior officer courted controversy so openly.

Hillier intended his message to prepare the public for casualties. The reaction was mixed. Some Canadians regarded the general's comments as refreshingly honest and courageous. But many others recoiled at his aggressive language, which they thought insensitive, vulgar, simplistic, and "American" in style. Some in Ottawa worried that the general's language reflected an underlying recklessness. Hillier was using up his political capital so quickly that Paul Martin began to worry that his new CDS might undermine his credibility with the public before this mission got underway. Martin raised the issue with Graham and offered to speak to Hillier, as an experienced public figure to a relative novice, to urge the general to be cautious in his public speeches. That didn't happen, but Graham did have a discussion with his CDS, and,

as a result, Hillier was more careful in public. But Canadians had heard
the basic point. The Kandahar mission was now defined as an operation to root out terrorists who might someday, somehow, again do
violence to North America.

New Developments

June 2005 was not a good month in Afghanistan. It was the second
most violent month since the Taliban had been ousted in 2001. Suicide
bombings, which were relatively unknown in Afghanistan up to that
point, were now becoming commonplace. These kinds of attacks were
not part of Afghanistan's recent history. "When I visited Kabul in 2005
Karzai told me that the Afghans don't do suicide bombings, that the
recent suicide bombings were isolated incidents," recalled Graham.[9]

Taliban insurgents were crossing the Pakistan–Afghan border with
impunity and in increasing numbers. The South Tower now began to
think that the solution to Afghanistan was in Pakistan. President Pervez
Musharraf of Pakistan tolerated the presence of Taliban fighters in his
country and the ISI, Pakistan's Security Services, which Musharraf did
not fully control, were aiding and abetting the Taliban, their one-time
ally. The Taliban were easily able to recruit from the *madrassas,* or religious schools, inside Pakistan. These fighters could enter Afghanistan
across a porous border that the Pashtun communities living on both
sides had never recognized.

Military commanders began to realize that if this insurgent flow into
Afghanistan was not stopped, NATO would not succeed in the south.
The smell of a new insurgency in southern Afghanistan was in the air.
To make matters worse, the opium yield had increased from the
previous year and the CF would be operating in the second-highest
opium-producing province in the country. It was not an auspicious
time to send the Canadian Forces back to Kandahar, the most dangerous part of a country that appeared to be getting more dangerous with
each passing week.

There was also an emerging political problem in Brussels. As the alliance assumed responsibility for security across Afghanistan, NATO was now demanding that member states remove their so-called "national caveats." These caveats, or restrictions, ran the gamut from Germany's refusal to ferry soldiers from other NATO countries in its helicopters, to prohibitions on the use of tear gas, to the refusal to permit soldiers to operate at night.[10] The caveats were symptomatic of the deeper philosophical divide within the alliance over how to manage the conflict in Afghanistan, one that has still not been resolved. Some countries—the United States, the United Kingdom, Canada, and the new members of NATO from the former East Bloc—had no caveats, and allowed their troops to go wherever they were needed in Afghanistan and to engage in any type of combat or counterinsurgency operation. Other NATO members, including Germany, France, Italy, and Spain, put precise restrictions on their forces (some legislated by their national Parliaments) that, in some cases, effectively prohibited them from engaging or assisting the troops of other countries in counterinsurgency warfare.

The caveats had been an issue for Donald Rumsfeld for some time. He had publicly excoriated those NATO countries—which he famously labelled "Old Europe"—that had caveats, and he browbeat his colleagues to remove the restrictions. Up until now, the caveats had not been a serious issue in Ottawa. But as the CF prepared to move into the dangerous south, removing these caveats became increasingly important. Canada would find it much easier to find a NATO member to take over once its tour was finished if there were no restrictions on what countries could do and where they would go. It would be easier, in other words, to develop an exit strategy. It would also be easier for the Canadian Forces to get help from others if the situation in Kandahar deteriorated badly. The caveats got in the way, every way.

And they continued to get in the way. "Old Europe," particularly France and Germany, remained unyielding on the issue of national caveats. They consistently refused to go anywhere near the south and east of Afghanistan. Michèle Alliot-Marie, the French defence minister, told Graham at a NATO meeting in Berlin in the late summer of 2005 that the American-led Operation Enduring Freedom and the NATO-led ISAF missions were very different and not necessarily compatible; the former concentrated on combat, the latter on reconstruction. ISAF's expansion throughout Afghanistan would not change NATO's mission of reconstruction. She was not opposed in principle to Stage Three expansion to the south, but she was concerned about its timing. Since NATO had taken responsibility for ISAF in 2003, it had extended its scope to the north (Stage One) in 2004, to the west (Stage Two) in 2005, and was scheduled, in the third stage, to expand the mission to the south. The French were worried that the Americans, in their haste to shore up their sagging fortunes in Iraq, might pull out of southern Afghanistan quickly after ISAF took over, taking their heavy-lift aircraft and other assets with them, and leaving ISAF vulnerable in this more hostile environment. Alliot-Marie wanted to slow down Stage Three to give NATO more time to ensure that conditions in Kandahar were suitable for the ISAF mission and its mandate of reconstruction and stabilization. In 2005, the French clearly did not think of the ISAF role in the south as an aggressive combat mission in a war zone.

Don't Brag

The NATO meetings in Berlin also gave Graham the opportunity to meet his American, Dutch, and British counterparts. And it would be the first time Graham would be meeting Donald Rumsfeld since Canada had decided not to participate in the Ballistic Missile Defence program seven months earlier.

On September 14, 2005, Graham and Rumsfeld and a handful of advisers sat down in a Berlin hotel meeting room to discuss a range of issues.

Rumsfeld cut through the pleasantries. The Canadian delegation expected a stinging rebuke from him on BMD. But it wasn't until halfway through the meeting that Rumsfeld brought up the issue in the context of NORAD renewal. The secretary of defence echoed what Paul Wolfowitz had told Graham months earlier. Contrary to what Canadian leaders heard repeatedly from their advisers in Ottawa, Rumsfeld had no problem with the Canadian decision on BMD. However, he did say that he didn't like Canadian politicians "bragging" in public about their rejection of American requests to join the project. Rumsfeld told his counterparts that Canadian participation was not necessary to the success of BMD and that the Bush administration had never asked Ottawa to join. That assertion was more than a little disingenuous and self-serving on Rumsfeld's part. While it was technically true that neither the president nor any American Cabinet secretary had ever directly asked a Canadian counterpart to join BMD, Bush, when he was visiting Ottawa, had publicly urged Canada to participate. It was those public comments that had so troubled Paul Martin. Rumsfeld concluded the NORAD/BMD part of the discussion with talk of NORAD renewal and, in particular, his interest in expanding the agreement to cover maritime surveillance. Canada had asked that maritime surveillance be included, but the secretary said that he didn't want to get burned again. The United States was receptive to further co-operation, but would not be "pushy" about it.

Then the conversation turned to Afghanistan. Rumsfeld emphasized how important Canada's role in the south was, particularly in the training of the Afghan National Army. Predictably, he returned to the enduring problem of the national caveats. The United States was fighting in the south and national caveats were consequently a serious problem. The Bush administration wanted to concentrate its military resources in Iraq and Rumsfeld clearly wanted NATO allies to relieve American troops in the south. Rumsfeld asked for Graham's help to persuade other NATO states to remove their caveats because, he argued, Canada had credibility in the alliance. The secretary implied that his credibility was wearing thin. And it clearly was.

The Dutch Start to Waver

Later that same day Graham met with Henk Kamp, his Dutch counterpart. As an important part of Stage Three, the Dutch were planning to deploy a PRT and combat troops in the south central Afghan province of Oruzgan, the birthplace of Mullah Omar, the former Taliban ruler of Afghanistan. At this time Oruzgan was considered one of the two or three most dangerous, isolated, and unstable provinces in Afghanistan. No international aid agencies or NGOs had a permanent presence there; it was simply too insecure. The Dutch assignment was at least as dangerous as Canada's. Hillier thought that Canada and NATO could not succeed in their mission in the south if the Dutch did not secure Oruzgan.

While the Canadian delegation in Berlin knew there was controversy in the Netherlands over the planned deployment to Oruzgan, they were nevertheless surprised when Kamp suggested that the Dutch government might renege on its commitment. Kamp claimed that the Dutch needed a partner nation that would contribute two to three hundred troops to their PRT in Oruzgan, and that while they were in the midst of negotiations with Australia, there were no guarantees that Australia, not a member of NATO, would participate. Kamp was clear: Without a partner nation, the Dutch would not go to Oruzgan. This was a sobering message coming as it did when Canada had already set up its PRT in Kandahar. "The Dutch were very nervous about going there [to Oruzgan]," recalled Bill Graham. "And what we were told was the Dutch have been nervous about everything since Srebrenica."[11]

Hillier often referred to what he called the "Srebrenica syndrome," which allegedly afflicted the Dutch military. Dutch soldiers, part of a UN peacekeeping force, had been unable to prevent the massacre of eight thousand Bosnian men and boys by the army of the Republic of Srpska in the city of Srebrenica in 1995 during the war in Bosnia. The Dutch were shell-shocked by their experience, Hillier explained, and that was why they were so nervous about Oruzgan.

In late October, the Dutch requested a NATO assessment of conditions in Oruzgan before they committed troops. Two weeks later they were making demands on Canada and the United Kingdom. The Dutch wanted additional troops to help them secure the region. If they didn't get the support, the Dutch hinted that they might walk away from their commitment. The CF had neither the excess capacity to meet this request nor the willingness to reinforce the Dutch when Canada was preparing to take on a very dangerous and demanding mission in Kandahar. NDHQ, with Graham's support, rejected the Dutch request.[12]

The Hague also hinted that it wanted U.S. troops to remain in Zabol province, which borders Oruzgan to the southeast. The Americans were ready to draw down their forces in Zabol and Rumsfeld flatly rejected the Dutch request. NATO, the United Kingdom, and the United States were now impatient with the Dutch, who, they felt, were putting the Stage Three NATO mission at risk with unreasonable demands.

As the uncertainty continued, Rumsfeld called Kamp. The conversation was a disaster. Jaap de Hoop Scheffer, the NATO Secretary-General, phoned Graham and told him that Rumsfeld had bullied Kamp and had made matters worse with his less than subtle intervention.[13] The Netherlands apparently finally understood that Canada was also unhappy. Given the long-standing and close relationship between the two countries, anchored in the major role Canada had played in the liberation of Holland during the Second World War, the Dutch moved quickly to reassure Ottawa. The Dutch ambassador to Canada, Karel de Beer, met Graham in his office on Parliament Hill in late November. The ambassador promised that the Dutch Cabinet would make a final decision that week. He emphasized that both the foreign minister and the prime minister supported the mission, but Kamp, the defence minister, was still hesitating. The ambassador pointed out that the Dutch had different intelligence assessments of the situation on the ground than did Canada and saw the mission as

wouldn't Canada's be the same as the US?

Chief of Defence Staff
Ray Henault taking questions
on May 22, 2001. He subse-
quently became chair of the
Military Committee at
NATO.
(CP PHOTO/Tom Hanson)

Foreign Affairs Minister
John Manley answers
questions in the House
of Commons in Ottawa
on November 7, 2001.
Manley worked closely
with U.S. Secretary of State
Colin Powell and Secretary
of Homeland Security
Tom Ridge on enhancing
security after September 11.
(CP PHOTO/Jonathan Hayward)

Defence Minister Art Eggleton at Remembrance Day services in Toronto on November 11, 2001. He was the longest-serving defence minister in fifty years. *(CP PHOTO/Aaron Harris)*

Prime Minister Jean Chrétien and President George W. Bush share a laugh at a meeting in Detroit, Michigan, on September 9, 2002. The two leaders discuss tightening security against an attack by terrorists while keeping the border open to trade. *(CP PHOTO/Jason Kryk)*

U.S. Secretary of Defense Donald Rumsfeld at the Pentagon, March 28, 2003. Rumsfeld told Defence Minister John McCallum early in 2003 that he wanted Canada to lead the ISAF mission in Kabul. *(Reuters/CORBIS)*

U.S. Deputy Defense Secretary Paul Wolfowitz answering questions on June 3, 2003. He subsequently told Minister of Defence Bill Graham that he understood Canada's decision not to participate in the Ballistic Missile Defence program. *(TORU YAMANAKA/AFP/Getty Images)*

Defence Minister John McCallum taking questions in Ottawa on June 19, 2003, on the decision to deploy the Canadian Forces as the lead of the International Security Assistance Force (ISAF) in Kabul. (*CP PHOTO/Jonathan Hayward*)

The repatriated remains of Corporal Robbie Beerenfenger, Canadian Forces Base, Trenton, October 5, 2003. Beerenfenger was one of three fatalities in the Canadian Forces during Canada's one-year leadership of the ISAF mission in Kabul. (*REUTERS/Jim Young*)

Prime Minister Paul Martin and President George W. Bush arrive for their joint news conference in Ottawa on November 30, 2004, as part of Bush's first visit to Canada. The president embarrassed and angered Martin when he said publicly that he wanted Canada to participate in the Ballistic Missile Defence program.
(CP PHOTO/Paul Chiasson)

U.S. Ambassador to Canada Paul Cellucci, who had pressed Canada hard to join the Ballistic Missile Defence program, in Ottawa on February 24, 2005. Cellucci told the press that despite Canada's refusal to participate, the United States would not allow a missile to hit North America.
(CP PHOTO/Fred Chartrand)

Defence Minister Bill Graham at the Canadian Forces Base, Edmonton, seeing off soldiers heading to Afghanistan in the summer of 2005. *(CP PHOTO/Larry MacDougal)*

Corporal Jean Rene d'Amours wipes away his tears at CFB Valcartier, Quebec, as he prepares to depart for a nine-month mission in Kandahar on December 4, 2006. *(CP PHOTO/Jacques Boissinot)*

Chief of the Defence Staff Rick Hillier arriving at the Canadian Forces' Provincial Reconstruction Team near Kandahar City, May 2, 2007. Hillier was the architect of Canada's mission to Kandahar. *(CP PHOTO/Ryan Remiorz)*

Afghan president Hamid Karzai at his presidential palace in Kabul on May 17, 2007. ISAF leaders and diplomats speak of Karzai as the "mayor of Kabul" because of his limited authority in Afghanistan. *(AP Photo/Musadeq Sadeq)*

A Canadian Forces Leopard tank crew dismounts at Ma'Sum Ghar, a forward operating base in Kandahar. The thirty-year-old Leopards, which General Rick Hillier had ordered scrapped, were deployed to Kandahar to help the Canadian Forces fight an unexpected and intensifying insurgency. *(CP PHOTO/ Ryan Remiorz)*

Prime Minister Stephen Harper tours the Canadian forward operating base in Ma'Sum Ghar, Kandahar, May 23, 2007. Harper extended Canada's mission to Kandahar by two years until February 2009. *(CP PHOTO/Tom Hanson)*

more dangerous than did the Canadian Forces. The Dutch felt that winning hearts and minds was central to their mission in Oruzgan, but worried that they would fail given the deteriorating security situation in the south. They wanted assurances from the Americans that their troops would cover the Dutch flank if things went badly wrong. Kamp had made similar representations directly to Graham on more than one occasion. "The Dutch were much more cautious, their intelligence was much gloomier than ours," recalled Graham. "Henk [Kamp] used to say to me, 'Our intelligence is not as rosy as what you're telling me.'"[14]

These conversations should have been alarming, given the difference in the intelligence estimates of Canada and the Netherlands. But NDHQ insisted this was just a manifestation of the "Srebrenica syndrome." By early December, moreover, NDHQ was reporting that the Dutch "were about to make the right decision." As Christmas approached, however, there was still no definitive word from the Netherlands.

Their indecision rippled outward. Tony Blair's government in London, which was committed to a large deployment in Helmand province in the south, was not prepared to make its final decision until the Dutch government had made up its mind. Political observers in The Hague began to suggest that the Dutch government would not have the support of Parliament. NATO Secretary-General Jaap de Hoop Scheffer allegedly then lobbied his former political colleagues to deploy troops in Afghanistan.

The NATO Stage Three mission was hanging in the balance, even though Canada had already set up its PRT in Kandahar, had sent special forces to the region, and was in the final stages of planning the deployment of an infantry task force and brigade headquarters. The Americans, who saw their long-sought merger of OEF and NATO unravelling before their eyes, now made contingency plans. The Pentagon told the Canadian Forces not to worry. If the Dutch did not follow through, the United States would plug the gap in Oruzgan. And

(handwritten margin note: it doesn't make sense that the western world would just reject such assumptions)

the British were even considering swapping Helmand province for Oruzgan, if that would break the log-jam.[15]

After months of acrimonious parliamentary debate, in February 2006, the Dutch government did make "the right decision" to honour its commitment to NATO. The Dutch Parliament agreed that the Netherlands would send troops to Oruzgan in partnership with the Australians.

With the benefit of hindsight, the Dutch appear to have been prescient in the fall of 2005. They saw a much more unstable and violent southern Afghanistan on the horizon than did Canada, Britain, the United States, and NATO. The Dutch were right. And so, as it turned out, were the Russians. The former Soviet Union had had a painful decade-long experience in Afghanistan in the 1980s and knew the country well. Bill Graham reflected on a conversation he had with Russian defence minister Sergei Ivanov during an official visit to Moscow in the summer of 2005. "Conversations I had with Sergei Ivanov, the Russian Defence Minister, reflected the Dutch view. They [the Russians] watch this area closely and see it as a subset of the Chechnya problem," recalled Graham. "Ivanov said to me there are camps all over the place in Afghanistan, training all sorts of people all the time, it's a hornets' nest down there. He wished us well."[16]

BY THE END of 2005, Paul Martin's minority government had been defeated on a confidence motion in the House of Commons and a general election was underway. After repeated requests from Hillier, Martin agreed to visit Afghanistan in January 2006. A Canadian prime minister had not visited Afghanistan since October 2003, when Jean Chrétien paid a brief visit to Camp Julien and met with President Karzai. Martin's trip was being planned as the government fell.

The trip was not to be. Paul Martin would never visit Afghanistan. His term as prime minister would end a few weeks later. Surprisingly, the mission to Kandahar was not an issue in the election. The Conservatives under Stephen Harper supported the deployment.

Although the NDP and the Bloc Québécois saw the mission as little more than an extension of Bush's foreign policy, neither made an issue of the Canadian Forces in Afghanistan in the election campaign. That would change radically within a few months' time.

`war stayed out of the election, how important is cpp to Populace?

TWELVE

THE CHALLENGE OF INSURGENCY

N o political or military leader thought that the Canadian Forces would be fighting an insurgency when the Canadian government committed military forces to Kandahar in 2005. They knew that the mission was dangerous, that stabilization and reconstruction risked casualties, but no one thought about "war." "I had no sense that it was war. I surely didn't think that it was war," said Paul Martin, the prime minister at the time. "I had no understanding that we would be as aggressive as we have been. Of course, our soldiers have to have the capacity to defend themselves, but I didn't think it was going to be combat all the time. It was not presented to me as a counterinsurgency operation. Our purpose was reconstruction."[1]

'Shouldn't they have the intellegence to know this? dumbasses!

Insurgency: The War of the Future

Yet for the first time since the Boer War, when the Canadian Forces deployed to Kandahar, they would be fighting an insurgency. It should not have come as a surprise, given the history of Afghanistan and the changing nature of warfare. Insurgency is the war of the future, argued Canada's chief of the defence staff, Rick Hillier, and large-scale state-to-state warfare is largely a relic of the past.[2] This is not to say that "classic" war—the confrontation between command-and-control, technologically sophisticated militaries within a confined battle space—is not possible. It certainly is. But it is increasingly unlikely. Over the last thirty years, that kind of war between states has become less and less common.

The first few decades of the twenty-first century will likely see military escalation at the top and at the bottom. Nuclear arms races in different parts of the world—escalation at the top—will become increasingly common. And insurgencies will dominate the battlefield at the bottom.

Today, and for the foreseeable future, military power and advantage is concentrated overwhelmingly in one state, the United States, with no military challenger in the offing. Those states that are hostile to the United States, or fear its intentions, will seek nuclear weapons as the ultimate deterrent against invasion and guarantor of their survival. Once one state acquires nuclear weapons, others in their neighbourhood will follow. New states, and even private groups, will join the nuclear club.

Insurgents will also challenge weak governments, or authoritarian governments, or governments dominated by a rival tribe or ethnic group. They will do so through "low-intensity" and "asymmetrical" warfare in an effort to compensate for their military inferiority, turning weakness into strength. They will, in other words, escalate at the bottom. Insurgents will wage low-intensity warfare against governments and their armies over long periods of time, with patience, determination, and endurance, over and over in the coming decades.

That is the scenario that the Canadian Forces are most likely to confront for the next few decades. The argument was hard to make at 101 Colonel By Drive before Rick Hillier became chief of the defence staff. It flew in the face of the culture of the Canadian Forces—how its members thought, trained, and armed themselves, at least until 2005. Fighting an insurgency is still new and unfamiliar territory for the Canadian Forces.

Insurgency is deeply political warfare, where military and political strategies reinforce each other. Insurgents depend on a mass base of support, which they win or lose through politics. They use military strategies to build political strength and alienate people from their governments, to create the political preconditions for success. In insurgencies, there is no neatly defined "front," and once the front is gone, the "safe space" behind the lines disappears for civilians as well as soldiers. In insurgency, Rupert Smith argues, the fundamental aim of war has changed. Both the insurgents and those who resist "are fighting each other amongst the people, over the will of the people…. to influence the intentions of the people."[3]

The trappings of conventional war are all too familiar. Armies invest in precision-guided munitions, tanks, warships and submarines, and long-range bombers. Insurgents, on the other hand, buy their small arms—a Kalashnikov or AK47 rifle, an RPG-7, a portable surface-to-surface missile, a Stinger or a Russian portable surface-to-air missile (SAM)—on the black market and make their own bombs, or improvised explosive devices (IEDs). In Afghanistan, these kinds of attacks would prove lethal to Canadian soldiers.

The latest version of homemade bombs is suicide bombers, either on foot or in vehicles. What makes them so effective is that they are part of everyday life—routine, familiar, almost indistinguishable until it is too late. "When action occurs," a senior officer in the Canadian Forces explained, "it is most often a fleeting attack—an IED, suicide bomber, or quick ambush. The attack occurs, creates havoc and leaves death, destruction, and casualties in its wake—often without anyone seeing the enemy or firing a single shot in anger. The initiative often seems to lie almost entirely with the antagonists. They decide where, when, how, and who to attack." General Hillier agreed. "A series of bombs can terrorize a city," he said, "even when these bombers do not threaten fundamental security. Perception of threat can be as important as the threat itself."[4]

Conventional armies trying to counter human explosives have little choice but to disrupt the general population, in the process alienating the very people they are trying to protect. As military personnel terrify local populations—kicking down doors to conduct house-to-house searches, stopping and searching vehicles, shooting at people who approach too quickly or too closely, and bombing from the air—insurgents find it easy to recruit among people who become deeply distrustful of their own government. Yet governments cannot simply stand by and watch as bombs explode in the cities and on the roads, as insurgents take control of villages at night. If they do not respond, governments lose legitimacy as protectors of their citizenry and providers of public security. They are, as one analyst observed with a tinge of despair, "damned if they do and damned if they don't."[5]

Many of the same dilemmas confound outside military forces that come to the assistance of governments challenged by insurgents. In some ways, the dilemmas facing outsiders are far more pointed simply because they are outsiders. They are strangers with strange customs, who, no matter how hard they try, often understand little of local culture. They cannot speak the language, are much less able to read local traditions, to make intuitive sense of what is happening on the ground, and to decode the important nuances. Heavily dependent on local leaders for intelligence, for interpretation, and for advice, they themselves cannot distinguish who is friend and who is foe. Outsiders are at the mercy of "insiders," their agendas and their grudges, their desire for vengeance as well as their knowledge and skills.

In the midst of an insurgency, soldiers are separated from the people whom they have come to help. To protect against suicide bombers and explosive devices, the Canadian Forces in Afghanistan, no different from other militaries, work out of a heavily fortified American base—the Kandahar Air Field—with secure fencing around the perimeter, and Camp Nathan Smith just outside Kandahar where Canada's Provincial Reconstruction Team (PRT) is located. Anyone unknown who approaches the base is treated with suspicion and interrogated. The military leaves the base only to patrol in an armed convoy. Soldiers do not mingle easily with the population and even when they do spend the night in a village, they generally leave after a short time to move on to the next one. They are cut off, separated, foreign. They become intruders, even occupiers—a foreign body that is unwelcome to the

local population—although they are fighting wars "among the people."
The commandant at the Royal Military College asked Colonel Bernd
Horn to go on a study tour to Kandahar to bring back "lessons learned"
for the soldiers who are now being trained. "It has long been recognized
that culture is to insurgency what terrain is to conventional mechanized warfare," Horn concluded. "However … in the current environment, it is sometimes difficult to breach the cultural barrier."

Horn also spoke of the anger soldiers often feel. "It is not unusual
for soldiers who are attacked to feel angry and betrayed. They deeply
believe that they are serving in Afghanistan to create a better society for
its people, yet they are continually attacked by seemingly invisible
antagonists who appear to operate effortlessly in the very Afghan
society that the soldiers are trying to improve and protect."[6]

Three incidents in February 2007 tell the story. When an Afghan
man approached a Canadian convoy travelling down a road and
refused to stop, even though the soldiers tried, through hand signals, to
warn him, the soldiers shot him. The soldiers were afraid—legitimately
afraid—that he was a suicide bomber, a human explosive device. If
they shot him, they risked killing an innocent person and further
enraging and alienating the local population. If they allowed him to
approach or approached him, they could be blown up. Ten days later,
Canadian soldiers fired at a sedan that didn't stop at a roadblock,
killing the driver instantly. "The Afghan civilian approached in a
civilian vehicle and failed to heed repeated warnings from both the
Afghan National Police and the Canadian Forces to stay away," said
Major Dale MacEachern. The soldiers were so worried that the driver
might be a suicide bomber that they asked the Afghan soldiers to pull
the dead driver from his car and search for explosives. Nothing was
found. The same day, a suicide bomber walked right up to the main
gate of Bagram Air Base, north of Kabul, and killed twenty-three
people and injured scores of others.[7]

Colonel Horn described the vicious cycle that insurgency creates.
"The nature of the conflict fuels a spiral of antagonism," he said. As

Constantly worried about
suicide bombers.

coalition forces continue to be targeted by IEDs and suicide bombers, he argued, they have no choice but to take the necessary actions to protect themselves. But their defensive action comes at a cost. "As convoys drive aggressively down the centre of the road," explained Horn, "they force local Afghan traffic to scurry for the shoulder. As they physically bump traffic out of the way, or threaten vehicles that follow too close by pointing weapons ... they risk alienating Afghan nationals ... Coalition forces, particularly as a result of the defensive actions they have been forced to adopt, often appear as a force of occupation."[8] Canada's soldiers and their Afghan counterparts face only difficult choices. That is the genius of insurgency. Insurgents, when they succeed, make certain that there are no good choices.

NATO air strikes have badly damaged the relationship between soldiers and the local population. In the last six months of 2006, NATO launched more air strikes, largely in the south, than it had in the past three years: more than 2,600 air missions, an average of 15 a day. They inflicted a significant number of civilian casualties, created more than eighty thousand internally displaced people who fled the bombing, and antagonized the local population who see no difference between the Taliban and ISAF bombs. One seems as bad as the other. It is these internally displaced people who live in camps who are most seriously at risk of hunger and illness. "Neither the Taliban nor the Americans leave us alone," said an Afghan woman who now lives in the Marghar refugee camp in the province of Kandahar. "We left our houses and came to this camp to escape from the aerial bombings. My house was destroyed and all our possessions were buried. Two of my cows were buried beneath the debris, and now I have nothing to eat, nothing to feed my children with."[9]

The loss of civilian life so enraged Afghans that the upper house of the Afghan Parliament passed a resolution in May 2007 urging that all air strikes stop, that NATO soldiers not go out on patrol, and that negotiations be started immediately with any Taliban who were willing to join the government. The horror at the inability to protect their villages, to keep them out of the fighting, goes to the heart of the Pashtun tradition of limiting the fighting and negotiating with an adversary.

NATO air strikes and artillery fire killed more than one hundred civilians in one week in June 2007. A visibly anguished and infuriated President Karzai criticized the "careless operations" and pleaded again for caution. "Afghan life is not cheap," he said, "and should not be treated as such." The president was scathing in his criticism. "The extreme use of force ... and the lack of coordination with the Afghan government is causing these casualties. You don't fight a terrorist," he insisted angrily, "by firing a field gun from thirty-seven kilometers away into a target.... You don't hit a few terrorists with field guns."[10] The president's inability to stop the air strikes and artillery fire only further weakens his government in the eyes of the local population. General Dan McNeill, the commander of ISAF in 2007, understood how damaging the air strikes were and emphasized, over and over, how carefully his commanders reviewed targets before they authorized a strike.[11] Nevertheless, the political costs of the death of innocent civilians—particularly women and children—are incalculable, both to NATO forces and to the Afghan government.

The Face of the Insurgency

Insurgencies thrive in the darkness, at night. National armies come to a village or a town during the day, to show the villagers that they are there, that they can provide protection from the night terrors; but as darkness falls, they often retreat to the safety of their base camps or, at the most, stay a night or two, or a week. Then they move on. As they vacate the space, the insurgents take control. David Kilcullen, a young Australian who had studied *Jemaah Islamiya*, a militant Islamist movement in Indonesia, and the rebels in East Timor and is now a U.S. official, visited the southern provinces and emailed back a description of the "night letters" that farmers receive from the Taliban. "They [the

Taliban] have been pushing local farmers in several provinces [Helmand, Oruzgan, Kandahar] to grow poppy instead of regular crops, and using night-time threats and intimidation to punish those who don't and [to] convince others to convert to poppy." The Taliban did not need more opium, argued Kilcullen, but were working to detach the local people from the legal economy and weaken the governments of the provinces and districts. "They also use object lessons," he continued, "making an example of people who don't cooperate—for example, dozens of provincial-level officials have been assassinated this year, again as an 'armed propaganda' tool—not because they want one official less but because they want to send the message 'We can reach out and touch you if you cross us.'"[12]

These tactics of night time intimidation are typical of insurgents who seek, above all, to separate the local population from their government. In at least three of the southern provinces, the Taliban target not only the desperate and the frightened, but also the moderate mullahs, the local Afghan leaders who are most difficult to corrupt, and the "foreigners" who are best connected to local leaders.

Who are these faceless "insurgents"? The answer to this question is hotly contested, both inside and outside Afghanistan. The Taliban are certainly the most powerful and important element in the insurgency, but they are part of a larger, loosely connected group of disaffected warlords, drug traffickers, and commanders who have joined the insurgency for politics or for profit. Gulbuddin Hekmatyar, a notorious warlord, and his *Hizbi-i-Islami* party that fought actively during the Afghan civil war, have allied with the Taliban in a transparent marriage of convenience. Afghan tribes who feel excluded by the ruling Popalzai tribe and some frustrated fighters from the Northern Alliance also move in and out of the insurgency. Finally, there are the "soft" Taliban, those who join the insurgency because they are desperately poor and the Taliban pay so much better.

Today's Taliban is not the Taliban that swept to power in 1996. Mullah Dadullah, the head of military operations in Helmand and

Kandahar provinces who was killed by NATO forces in May 2007, reportedly made operational decisions with little consultation with the top Taliban leaders who remain in Quetta, in Pakistan. He was only one among several local leaders with considerable autonomy. Mullah Akhtar Mohammad Osmani, who operated in both Pakistan and Afghanistan as an important "financial officer" and was killed in a targeted American air strike in December 2006, was another.[13]

A sophisticated political strategy to contain the insurgency must make room for these differences and for the simultaneous negotiation and fighting that is so familiar to Pashtun tribal leaders and so deeply embedded in the culture. Negotiating with tribal elders or local Taliban sympathizers before villagers are convinced that NATO will stay the course, and protect them from the night terrors, Chris Alexander argued, is premature and will not work. Some Pashtun tribal leaders, he added, remember that the United States once supported the mujahideen and worry that they could support the Taliban in the future. Here Alexander touched on a deep worry among some Afghans. Several voiced their fear that the United States and its allies could again switch sides as they have in the past.[14] Yet a refusal to negotiate, Alexander continued, an unwillingness to open space to bring in the Pashtun tribes that feel excluded from the present government, will only build support for the Taliban.[15] "We ... have to be very careful ... about tarring everyone with the same brush. Taliban are religious students. There will always be Taliban in Afghanistan and we should welcome that. The ones who are the problem for NATO and indeed for Afghanistan," Alexander concluded, "are the militant ones, the extremist ones, the ones who are fighting ... But there are thousands, probably tens of thousands, who are willing to join this government to help rebuild their country if they are invited, welcomed, in the right way. And we all need to think about how that hand of cooperation can be extended and how the process of reconciliation in Afghanistan can be deepened."[16] In Pashtun culture, timing is everything.

"Going Outside the Wire"

In August and September 2006, the Taliban did something insurgents usually do not do early on. They massed their forces and prepared for a conventional battle, hoping to inflict high casualties on ISAF forces and push through to the city of Kandahar. The stakes were very high. If Kandahar had fallen to the Taliban, the morale of the Karzai government might well have broken. ISAF responded with Operation Medusa.

Brigadier General David Fraser, at the time the commander of ISAF forces in the south, recalled the battle. His forces were spread very thin, but, said Fraser, with considerable pride in his soldiers and his officers, "We did it the smart way. They [the Taliban] chose the ground that was most advantageous to a strategy of attrition which would inflict casualties. We became guerrillas. For the three weeks before we launched Operation Medusa, we talked to and gave money to every village leader in the area. In exchange, we asked them to get rid of the Taliban. We had limited success." Fraser and his officers could see the Taliban massing for an attack. "Just before the battle, we told villagers to get out of the way of the fighting that was coming. We defeated the Taliban with only four casualties," he said. "Then the Taliban fighters tried to bug out one night. Not many made it out. We saved the city and, in so doing, saved the country," he concluded with confidence.[17] Canada, he said, had saved Afghanistan from the Taliban. If the Taliban had taken Kandahar, he mused, Karzai's government would have fallen.

NATO leaders claimed that Operation Medusa was a stunning success, that more than one thousand Taliban fighters were killed, and that the back of the Taliban in the area had been broken. Freed of the Taliban, villagers were now welcoming back government officials. The truth, unfortunately, was less straightforward.

The Canadian Forces did not have enough troops to seal the battlefield and consolidate their victory. Many of the Taliban escaped, regrouped, and quickly infiltrated again and inflicted casualties on the

Canadian Forces with roadside bombs. "We destroyed infrastructure, tore up villages, to trap the Taliban," said a Canadian officer. "We antagonized the local population, but we didn't rout the Taliban. They were back at us the next day. We lost face with the locals."[18] The Canadian Forces suffered more casualties from a suicide bomber a few days later than they had in battle. Very quickly after the battle, the Canadian Forces were struggling again with the familiar challenge of protecting villages—and themselves—against insurgent attacks.

Operation Medusa was certainly an important tactical victory. It stopped the Taliban from an all-out assault on Kandahar. But it was not, as some Canadian officers claimed, a decisive strategic victory. Canada's ministers of foreign affairs, national defence, and international co-operation put it better in a joint document they submitted to Parliament: It was a "tactical defeat" for the Taliban fighters, who reverted immediately to insurgency.[19] They might have lost a battle but they had not lost the war. And Canada's top soldier, Rick Hillier, took from Medusa the lesson that insurgency could at times blend with more conventional warfare to create new kinds of challenges in the long wars ahead.[20]

The operation that the Canadian Forces conducted in the Panjwai district two months later, in December 2006, speaks directly to those dilemmas. Canadian soldiers moved forward in heavily armed convoys during the day. Colonel Horn vividly described the atmosphere as Canadians left the security of the base at Kandahar Airfield: "The three-vehicle convoy pulled away from the Task Force Afghanistan (TFA) headquarters building seemingly invisible to the normal hustle and bustle of people and vehicles scurrying about the inner confines of the Kandahar Airfield. However, those in the vehicles were keyed up— they were going outside the wire.... There was no mistaking the charged atmosphere or the seriousness of what was about to transpire—to these troops it was clear that they were at war."[21]

Horn recalled how the convoy travelled down a crowded highway, with cars and trucks of all sizes and in all states of repair moving in both directions. "In such a saturated state of constant motion, it was virtually impossible to differentiate friend from foe. In total, the threat environment was extreme, yet non-existent. What was a threat and what was the simple reality of existence in a destitute third world nation?" he wondered.

When the Canadian soldiers arrived at the village, they arranged to talk with the village elders in a *shura,* or council meeting, and listen to the needs and requests the village elders made. Before they left, they distributed blankets, cooking oil, and other supplies that the villagers had requested and then handed over responsibility to Afghan soldiers when they withdrew. Villagers had to trust the Afghan National Army to provide security that night. The record is, not surprisingly, mixed. Some of what Canadian soldiers gained during the day was given up at night.

Poor Governance in Afghanistan

After Operation Medusa was over, farmers told UN officials that Afghan policemen, behaving like gangs, swept in behind Canadian forces to ransack homes, burn shops, and extort valuables. The head of the United Nations Mission in southern Afghanistan, Talatbek Masadykov, who oversees development assistance and UN programming, could barely contain his disgust. "This is a case of bad governance," he said. "Maybe half of these so-called anti-government elements acting here in this area of the south, they had to join this Taliban movement because of the misbehaviour of these bad guys."[22] Villagers complained that the police stole their cash, cellphones, and watches, and their motorbikes.

The Afghan government is weak, remote, and often corrupt in its dealings. The first governor of Kandahar, Gul Agha Shirzai, a notorious warlord appointed by President Karzai, enriched himself through corrupt practices and infuriated the local population.[23] Corruption is so endemic that Kandahar's director of customs has threatened to resign. "I feel shame," said Azizullah Sakzai, "because our administration is very weak and cannot control corruption. I can't continue like this."[24]

The reliability, integrity, and the credibility of Afghan institutions, a senior Canadian officer explained, is so questionable that soldiers are often unsure whether or not to trust the officials they meet. "Rampant corruption and criminal activities," he concluded, "pose serious challenges."[25]

Canadian officers worry about the quality of the Afghan National Army (ANA). It is the strongest institution among the security forces— some of the others have recruited criminals and drug traffickers as members—but its numbers are small, it often lacks equipment, and it is able to fight only when it is supported by international forces. Afghan soldiers are not yet capable of standing on their own feet and need more training before they go out into the field. The chief of the Canadian defence staff, Rick Hillier, is nevertheless relentlessly upbeat about the progress the ANA is making. "The progress we have seen is incredible," he said. "We have the best ANA battalion with us in Kandahar, attrition is down, and training is far better." In two to four years, he insists, the ANA will be able to operate without international assistance.[26]

The Afghan National Police (ANP) is an entirely different matter. Five years after the Taliban were forced from office, a joint report by the Pentagon and the State Department found that the police force in Afghanistan was largely incapable of carrying out routine law enforcement.[27] For the first two and a half years of the new government, there was no systematic police-training program outside Kabul, and only in 2004 were thirty police advisers sent across Afghanistan. It is little surprise that the police force in the south is shockingly inadequate.

To plug the gap, in the summer of 2006, the government created a new eleven thousand–strong Auxiliary Police from existing tribal militias. These new recruits received only two weeks of training rather than the standard eight weeks. This band-aid solution, officials say, made the problem worse. Afghan police are paid about seventy dollars a month while the Taliban are reportedly offering twelve dollars a day; badly trained and poorly paid police are especially susceptible to infiltrators and criminals. To make matters worse, Afghan commanders in the northern and western parts of Afghanistan are alarmed by what they see as the rearmament of southern Pashtun militias.[28] The Afghan police are the face of the government to the public, often the only point of contact with villagers, so it is not surprising that public confidence in the government is dropping.

Colonel Horn was graphic in his description of the Afghan police in the autumn of 2006: "Young, untrained, and answerable to the governor of their respective province, they resemble and behave more like common thugs than police. Some wear no uniforms, and are notoriously corrupt, unreliable, and untrustworthy. Complete detachments watching checkpoints or outposts are regularly found fast asleep and usually 'wasted' on hashish or marijuana." Horn's chagrin was obvious. The vast majority of the Afghan police, he explained, can neither read nor write. Large elements are suspected of being sympathetic to, if not in league with, the Taliban and with narcotics traffickers. "The population fears the ANP," Horn said, "which is corrupt and feeds on them through brutality and extortion.[29]

Brigadier General Greg Young, a Canadian with the Combined Security Transition Command, began an emergency program to transform the police in 2006. The RCMP increased its trainers from two to ten in Kandahar province, and more are on their way; in 2007, twelve Canadian civilian police and trainers were working in Afghanistan and an additional twenty-four military police helped with training.[30] There is some progress. Two classes of police cadets with better training have graduated, explained General Young, and are being fed into the ranks of the Afghan police.[31] More telling is the behaviour of a senior police officer in Kandahar. The newly appointed police chief did something in January 2007 that would have been unthinkable even six months earlier. He arrested one of his own officers and launched an investigation into an alleged rampage by police, which ended with the death of a civilian. "The message for police," said General Asmatullah Alizai, the chief of police, "is that they should be honest, work for our nation and respect people."[32] General Young was encouraged, but acknowledged that the road ahead is long, very long. Rooting out the corruption and the brutality is a project of many years.

The costs of weak institutions in Afghanistan are incalculable. A recent assessment of the Afghan government by American intelligence was devastating. President Karzai's government and security forces, the report concluded, are struggling to exert their authority outside Kabul. Increasing numbers of Afghans viewed the Karzai government as corrupt, unable to deliver the reconstruction that it has promised, and too weak to protect the population in the south from the Taliban.[33] The government is losing its legitimacy.

The Canadian Forces understand these dilemmas all too well. "Putting an Afghan face on everything we do," said Colonel Horn, "is key. But if the Afghan face is an ANP that extorts money at checkpoints, steals and bullies the people; and if the Afghan face is an appointed governor who was a previous warlord who continues to use the drug trade to enrich himself, or is tied to the drug trade; and if the Afghan face is locally appointed officials based on tribal connections who are corrupt, then the Coalition's actions and presence is seen as supporting a corrupt government incapable of providing security or governance."[34] Damned if you do, damned if you don't …

Where the Poppy Grows

Every problem in the south is made worse by poppy production. General Dan McNeill, the commander of ISAF, thinks that weakening the narcotics economy is NATO's biggest challenge. "If we don't," he insisted, "we will fail."[35] In Afghanistan today, Taliban fighters and drug traffickers are using the same criminal networks, said a senior

American official. "What we think is happening is that there are links at the local level. There is certainly the use of networks—networks of informants, networks of smuggling routes, communications, finances."[36] Some Taliban fighters are courting farmers by promising to protect their fields from any attempt to eradicate the poppy crop. A corrupt police force has become even more corrupt because it is on the payroll of poppy growers and exporters.

The crop in 2006 broke all records—an estimated 6,100 metric tonnes compared with 4,100 in 2005—and early indications are that in the south of Afghanistan, the crop will be even bigger in 2007. Students harvesting the crop can earn the equivalent of twelve dollars a day in comparison with four dollars for harvesting wheat. Poppy cultivation and opium smuggling account for about a third of Afghanistan's economy. Sixty percent of the activity is concentrated in the southern provinces, and Kandahar's position at the junction of the trucking routes puts the city squarely at the heart of the illegal trade.[37] Afghanistan is now the world's largest exporter of opium, accounting for ninety-two percent of the world supply. A report issued by the United Nations Office of Drug Control and the World Bank concluded that a handful of politically connected traffickers dominated the drug trade: "The drug industry in Afghanistan is becoming increasingly consolidated. At the top level, around 25–30 key traffickers, the majority of them in southern Afghanistan, control major transactions and transfers, working closely with sponsors in top government and political positions."[38] Smuggling is intimately connected with all layers of government, which get paid off. A mid-level smuggler, interviewed by a journalist, explained what he did when he ran into a problem in Afghanistan: "I simply make a phone call. And my voice is known to ministers, of course. They are in my network. Every network has a big man supporting them in the government."[39]

The pernicious impact of the poppy crop makes its eradication an obvious strategy, but it is far easier said than done. The Karzai government, working with NATO support, has tried and failed dismally. The campaign of poppy eradication has misfired in both directions: It has failed to reduce poppy cultivation and it has enabled the alliance between drug traffickers, farmers and villagers, and the Taliban. "In the villages, they had their crops destroyed," said one worker in Kandahar. "There is no water, no jobs, nothing to do—isn't it fair that they go and join the Taliban? Wouldn't you do the same thing?"[40] Poppy eradication has made it much easier for the Taliban to infiltrate villages and farms.

The poppy crop creates a Hobson's choice. Ignoring it or attempting to eradicate it fuels the insurgency. Both strengthen financial and social ties with the Taliban. One obvious strategy is to provide farmers with alternative livelihoods. Farmers would be paid high prices—the value of opium crops foregone—to grow other crops. The international donor community would heavily subsidize agriculture in Afghanistan—for years—until security had improved and the ties between the drug traffickers and the Taliban were broken. Although NATO governments have repeatedly promised farmers assistance to plant alternative crops, they have failed to deliver anything like the money that is needed. Some argue that NATO or an equivalent "Poppy Board" must buy the crop legally to break the back of the narco-economy. But this strategy brings its own risks. Buying the crop may encourage farmers who presently do not grow poppies to convert their fields. Nor is it clear why the drug lords who run the narco-economy would stand quietly by as farmers lined up to sell their poppy crop. And what would the "Poppy Board" do with the crop they bought? Burn it? Process it as commercial morphine? Export it? All this in a country with a very limited legal system.

General McNeill recognizes that poppy cultivation is a serious challenge to the security of Afghanistan. "ISAF can interdict convoys of poppy as they travel around the roads and cross the borders," he argued with a glint in his eye and steely determination in his voice. "We don't want to hurt the farmers, we want to hurt the traffickers and the profiteers."[41] Interdiction is difficult, however, and draws forces away from what they normally do.

None of the obvious alternatives are without cost. Yet another instance of damned if you do, damned if you don't ...

A Local Insurgency

All the classic elements of insurgency are present in Afghanistan. A weak government, a corrupt police force, an army that cannot yet fight on its own, dire poverty, and a black market economy that thrives on drugs. But much in Afghanistan pushes in the other direction—a growing economy, an education system that is pulling kids into schools, a health care system that is beginning to deliver benefits, and a revitalized network of elected local councils. The future of the insurgency in Afghanistan rests with the fine details—better services, the tangible improvements in the lives of women, the village councils. These are hard to see from a distance.

In Ottawa, far away from Kandahar, some Canadian officials see the insurgency as part of a more general global network of militant Islamists who are trying to overthrow existing governments and restore the caliphate and the unity of Islam. The Taliban can be contained only by defeating militant Islamists wherever they are. This argument is made in Washington—and in Ottawa—by officials who see a global threat of Muslim militants, all connected to one another. Their answer is a global "War on Terror."

That argument is flawed in several important ways and is dangerous as a prescription. A close look at many of the insurgencies in Muslim societies tells us that they are almost all local, inflamed by local grievances, with a local political agenda. Whether it is Hamas in Palestine or Hezbollah in Lebanon or the Union of Islamic Courts in Somalia or *Jemaah Islamiya* in Indonesia, Islamic organizations are all locally based, with local ties and local purposes. Militants in each certainly know militants in others, funds flow back and forth, and small numbers of fighters will go when they are called. Osama bin Laden was the first—and so far the only—to knit together successfully the threads of local movements into a global network, with a global agenda.

The Taliban are local, sons of the soil of the Pashtun. What makes the insurgency in Afghanistan so salient to the outside world is the relationship that once existed between the Taliban and al-Qaeda. How strong that relationship is today is impossible to know. Mullah Omar in a recent interview claimed that he had seen bin Laden only once or twice since 2001, but he strongly defended his refusal to hand over bin Laden in 2001 as consistent with *Pashtunwali*, the Pashtun tribal code that treats guests with honour. Very likely, connections exist between the Taliban and a resurgent al-Qaeda that appears to be organizing again on the frontier of Pakistan, where the Taliban is centred. The two certainly are in close proximity to each other, but they are not one and the same. The Taliban are local, Pashtun, rooted in southern and eastern Afghanistan and in the frontier and tribal areas of Pakistan. Their ambitions are local, while al-Qaeda's are global.

American foreign policy traditionally operates at the global and national level, ruefully remarked Henry Crumpton, who was responsible for the CIA's covert strategy against the Taliban in 2001, but today the battlefields are also regional and local. "It's really important," said Crumpton, "that we define the enemy in narrow terms. The thing we should not do is let our fears grow and then inflate the threat."[42]

David Kilcullen agrees. It is important, he argues, to find ways to address local grievances in Pakistan's tribal areas, in Aceh province in Indonesia, in southern Lebanon, and in the southern and eastern provinces of Afghanistan, so that they are not all joined together in a single map of global jihad. When the Bush administration speaks of the Sunni insurgency in Iraq, of Hezbollah, and of al-Qaeda in one breath, drawing no differences among them, it strengthens the insurgents and inflates their importance. "You don't play to the enemy's global information strategy of making it all one fight," he argues. "You say, 'Actually, there are sixty different groups in sixty different countries who all have different objectives. Let's not talk about bin Laden's objectives—let's talk about *your* objectives. How do we solve that problem?' You've got to define the enemy," Kilcullen concluded, "as narrowly as you can get away with."[43]

The insurgency in southern Afghanistan is local and deeply rooted. It is overwhelmingly likely that some sort of Taliban insurgency is a given in Afghanistan, at least for the foreseeable future. The life cycles of insurgencies are not a year or two or three, but a decade or a generation, and the Canadian Forces are now on the front lines of that insurgency.

THIRTEEN

HARPER'S WAR

Stephen Harper's Conservatives made defence and national security a central pillar of their campaign in the 2005 to 2006 election. On the campaign trail they pledged to commit five billion dollars to the budget of the Canadian Forces over five years. During the campaign, the Conservatives released a paper on the Canadian Forces, "Canada First," which accompanied their election platform. Written by Gordon O'Connor, the Tory defence critic and a retired brigadier general, it put the emphasis squarely on domestic and continental defence. It called for major investments to assert Canadian sovereignty in the Arctic, as well as new "territorial defence units" in every major Canadian city.[1] This last proposal led the increasingly desperate Liberals to produce a tasteless television advertisement alleging that the Tories wanted "soldiers in the streets." While the ad never aired on television, it did appear briefly on the Liberal Party website and television newscasts then showed the short clip. The Liberals consequently found themselves in the midst of a heated controversy in the middle of the campaign.

The Conservatives had said very little about the Afghanistan mission during the election. The "Canada First" plan centred on protecting Canada at home and in North America, and had only a thin overseas dimension. The Conservative election platform could not have been more different from the Defence Policy Statement that emphasized intervention in failed and failing states, which Rick Hillier had written for the Martin government. The Tories wanted to improve the Canada–U.S. relationship and to deal explicitly with the accusation that Canada was a free rider in North American defence and security. The emphasis was on the home front, what the Americans called "homeland defence," not on overseas "adventures."

Prior to the election the Conservatives had shown no serious interest in Afghanistan, although they did support the Kandahar mission. O'Connor and his colleague MP Cheryl Gallant, whose riding includes CFB Petawawa, the military base of many of the soldiers sent to Kandahar, had requested briefings on the mission shortly after it was announced. But O'Connor expressed no interest in going to Afghanistan to assess the situation on the ground. Graham had asked O'Connor more than once during the summer and early fall of 2005 to accompany him on the trip to Afghanistan that he planned for that October. Graham intended to visit both Kabul and Kandahar and to see the PRT in action, which had begun its work that summer. Each time Graham approached him, O'Connor declined and claimed that he had important business to attend to in his constituency that precluded his going to Afghanistan.

It was not only O'Connor who was uninterested. The House of Commons Standing Committee on National Defence paid little attention to Afghanistan. Graham's office had urged the Liberal chair of the committee to hold hearings on the Kandahar mission to help educate parliamentarians and the public. But the committee had other more pressing priorities to investigate; it was focused on the process of defence procurement. When the government was defeated, the committee still had not scheduled hearings on the mission to Kandahar.

We Don't Cut and Run

On January 23, 2006, Stephen Harper was elected Canada's twenty-second prime minister at the head of a minority government. Gordon O'Connor, the retired army general, lobbyist, and author of "Canada

First," was appointed minister of national defence. Peter MacKay, Harper's erstwhile leadership rival, became foreign minister.

Even though Canadians paid very little attention to foreign and defence policy during the election, Canada's new mission in Afghanistan would soon became the dominant national issue. After thirty-seven soldiers were killed, *Maclean's* magazine named the "Canadian Forces Soldier" the newsmaker of the year for 2006. By the end of that year, Canada's military suffered more casualties in a single twelve-month period than it had since the Korean War of the early 1950s. By some measures, the war in southern Afghanistan was more dangerous to Western troops than the bloody civil war raging simultaneously in Iraq.[2]

Once Canadians woke up to the reality that their soldiers were fighting and dying, their indifference to Canada's role in Afghanistan dissipated quickly. The mission in Kandahar would become synonymous with Stephen Harper's prime ministership, a defining feature of his government. The public and the media quickly forgot that the Liberals under Paul Martin had made the decision to send Canada's military into the most dangerous region in Afghanistan. This was now Stephen Harper's war.

LESS THAN ONE MONTH after the Harper government was elected, the combat infantry task force began operations in Kandahar province. It became apparent that conditions in Kandahar were far more dangerous than the Canadian Forces had expected. "There is a school of thought," said General Rick Hillier, Canada's chief of the defence staff, "that argues that the victory of the insurgents over U.S. forces in Iraq encouraged the Taliban to take on ISAF. They [the Taliban] learned that insurgency could defeat well-equipped forces. It came as a strategic surprise in 2004–2005. What was surprising was not their numbers, or the ferocity of their attack, but their tactics."[3]

The Dutch proved to be prescient in the pessimism that they had expressed before they committed their forces to Oruzgan several months earlier. Casualties began to mount through the spring as the Canadian

Forces engaged Taliban insurgents in villages outside Kandahar City. The national news was dominated by stories of CF combat operations in Kandahar province, and by pictures of the coffins coming home to cities and towns across Canada. By early May, Canada's army, still operating under Operation Enduring Freedom and waiting for NATO to take command, had sustained eight fatalities and twenty-eight wounded in the four months since Harper was sworn in as prime minister.

To put this in context, before February 2006, Canada's military had suffered eight fatalities over the previous four years. In four months, the Canadian army lost as many soldiers as they had lost in four years. It was now starting to look like Canada's troops were at the epicentre of an unanticipated, well-organized, and lethal insurgency, fed from sanctuaries inside Pakistan. As Bill Graham reflected, "The hornets' nest we poked had a hell of a lot more hornets than anybody thought."[4]

The mission became more and more controversial and unpopular with each passing week. Other NATO countries, particularly the Dutch, were questioning NATO's strategy in southern Afghanistan. They thought that it was overly aggressive and confrontational, likely to provoke and destabilize when NATO's purpose was to contain the insurgency and to stabilize the south. Canadians, uncomfortable watching their soldiers in combat on the nightly news and unaccustomed to watching military funerals for fallen soldiers, were seeing both with increasing frequency throughout the spring of 2006. The Canadian public and the soldiers' families would have to watch these pictures for another year until Canada was scheduled, in the NATO tradition of burden sharing, to hand off its responsibilities to another member of the alliance.

Then something odd happened in Ottawa.

The Friendly Professors Revisited

On a warm evening in early May 2006, John McCallum, now the Liberal finance critic, and his former chief of staff were eating dinner at a bistro in downtown Ottawa. They were catching up after the sobering election defeat of the previous winter. As they were finishing their meal, a mutual friend came into the restaurant, saw them, and headed to their table. It was Bill Graham, who had become leader of the Opposition after Paul Martin had resigned as Liberal Party leader following the election.

Graham told McCallum that several hours earlier, the Prime Minister's Office had called to ask him to meet with Harper later that day on an urgent matter. Graham of course agreed. He met with Harper alone, one on one. The prime minister told a stunned leader of the Opposition that he planned to extend Canada's commitment to the mission in Kandahar to 2009, two years beyond the original date. Harper asked for Graham's support and that of the Liberal caucus.

Earlier that day Harper had convened a meeting with his chief of staff, Ian Brodie, Hillier, and Elcock, when they effectively made the decision to extend the mission. Neither the minister of national defence nor the foreign minister was present. Gordon O'Connor confirmed that officials made the recommendation directly to the prime minister.[5] "There was a meeting of senior officials from Foreign Affairs, CIDA and Defence that made a recommendation to the Prime Minister to extend for two years," recalled O'Connor. "The two years was an estimate of the time we needed to make progress. It was brought to Cabinet before the Prime Minister announced the decision to extend ... The Prime Minister spoke to me and Peter MacKay before we made the announcement, but it was primarily the Prime Minister's decision."[6]

O'Connor's absence from the discussions seems somewhat unusual—and troubling—but it might have reflected his well-known views on the mission to Kandahar. O'Connor, like Hillier, had spent years in West Germany during the Cold War.[7] Unlike Hillier, he had not served with the Canadian Forces in failed states like Bosnia in the post–Cold War period. He was known as one of the "sausage generals" who had served in the safety of Germany. During the transition from the Martin to the Chrétien government in February 2006, O'Connor had been briefed by his officials on the proposed extension of the mission to 2009.[8] Senior officials at NDHQ soon learned that Gordon O'Connor was no fan of the Kandahar deployment. He thought it far too dangerous. However, it was a legacy from the previous government and he was forced to defend it in public, at least for another year. But Prime Minister Harper saw things differently from his defence minister, and acted on the advice of officials to extend the mission.

Gordon O'Connor reflected on the rationale for the extension. "In one year we could not make progress. We took over the government on February 4 [2006], just at the moment our troops were going into combat. We inherited this mission. We realized that we couldn't complete the job in one year. We needed to do both security and development. I personally checked to see what was going on in development even though this wasn't my responsibility."[9]

Bill Graham was taken aback by Prime Minister Harper's intention to extend the mission in Afghanistan. Already the mission had proved far more dangerous than Graham had imagined when he recommended it to Martin. The infantry task force had been operational for only two months, yet it was sustaining significant casualties. Harper had been prime minister for only three months. What was the compelling reason to extend the mission now? Why the urgency? Harper was not clear. He simply asked Graham whether he could count on the support of the party that had sent the Canadian Forces to Kandahar and the party leader who had recommended the mission when he was minister of national defence.

Graham made no commitment to Harper that day. He told Harper that he would consult his caucus and get back to the prime minister in due course. Harper asked him to do so quickly, as he planned to make an announcement soon.

Shortly thereafter Graham requested a meeting with Hillier to get a detailed briefing on the reasoning behind the proposed extension. "The raison d'être Hillier offered for going to 2009 was two-fold," Graham recalled:

Within Afghanistan, 2009 was a threshold year when one could ascertain whether one was being effective or not, because that is the year Karzai's mandate ends, and we could say democracy was or wasn't taking hold by then. So it was a logical thing to commit to 2009. Secondly, our going there was inextricably linked up with our partners, the British and the Dutch. The Dutch and British had agreed to stay until 2009. [In fact the Dutch hadn't committed to 2009, but only until 2008.] Therefore, since we were committed to them as part of the team, Hillier argued we needed to commit to 2009. Who started the 2009 business I don't know. Maybe it was the British that started it and dragged us and the Dutch along. I'm sure it wasn't the Dutch because they were always very cautious about this stuff.[10]

A year after the extension was approved, Hillier made a similar argument: "The one year timeline was much too short a window for NATO. The mission would have been a failure if we had extended for only one year. We needed the time badly and we are seeing the results on the ground."[11]

The ongoing challenges of Kandahar were not central to the discussion about the extension, even though eight Canadian soldiers had been killed in less than four months' time. The conversation revolved around NATO and Canada's obligations to its allies.

Within two weeks of his meeting with Graham, Harper announced that he intended to extend the Kandahar mission for an additional two years, until 2009, and that he would put this issue to a vote in the House of Commons. It is not unprecedented in Canada's Parliament to hold a vote on overseas military deployments, although in a Westminster parliamentary system like Canada's, military deployments are the exclusive purview of the executive—the Cabinet and the prime minister. But the Conservatives had taken a page from Paul Martin's book. They had committed in their election platform to address the "democratic deficit" and expand the role of Parliament. They would put all foreign

(margin note:) didn't take into account Canada itself

military deployments to a vote in the House of Commons. Even though the Harper government was in a minority and might lose this vote, the prime minister evidently felt it necessary politically to hold a vote.

really?

There was a significant inconsistency in the Conservative approach to expanding the role of the House of Commons. The government would allow only six hours of parliamentary debate on the extension of the mission to Afghanistan. This was a woefully inadequate amount of time for considered debate in a Parliament that was largely ignorant of Afghanistan and had spent almost no time in debate or discussion of the mission until very recently, when the casualties began to mount. Gordon O'Connor claimed that the debate was limited because "everyone knew what everyone's position was; further debate would not have clarified anything."[12] Not surprisingly, the Opposition parties were outraged at having the debate cut so short. They felt that Parliament was being used as a rubber stamp to give the Harper government political cover for the extension of an increasingly dangerous, controversial, and unpopular mission. To add fuel to the fire, the government gave no substantive reason for extending the mission, nor did it explain the urgency. *dumb dumb* When it looked as though the government might lose the vote in the House, the prime minister made matters worse when he announced that he would extend the mission for one year regardless of the will of Parliament. For many commentators and critics, Harper was displaying his lack of respect for Parliament even as he was manipulating the vote for political purposes.

Editorialists across the country were mystified. What was going on here? Why was a new prime minister, who led a minority government, taking a political risk to extend a mission put in place by his predecessor? With public support for the mission waning, perhaps it was nothing more than a shrewd political strategy to take a potentially divisive issue off the table well in advance of the next election, which would likely not come for a year or so. Or perhaps Harper was extending the mission to appeal to his political base early in his prime ministership.

The Conservatives were now visibly demonstrating that they were much stronger than the Liberals on defence, much more committed than their predecessors. The prime minister was not simply talking the talk—he was walking the walk.

Perhaps, as Bill Graham speculated, Canada's allies had pressured Ottawa to extend its deployment. The escalating violence in Kandahar was making it increasingly difficult to find a replacement nation for Canada. NATO and Canada might need more time to persuade one of their allies to fill the gap. Gordon O'Connor rejected this argument out of hand: "The allies put no pressure on us [to extend]. This was our decision and our decision alone."[13]

Senior officials, both military and civilian, had their own agenda and in this case their agenda seems to have been decisive. There was no doubt that Hillier and Elcock wanted the Canadian Forces to stay in Kandahar for a longer period of time. The ink was barely dry on Martin's signature approving the Kandahar deployment when Hillier and Elcock began to suggest that the government should seriously consider extending the mission beyond 2007.

But their advice ignored the political priorities of the Martin government. Paul Martin was preoccupied with Darfur and Haiti. It was crystal clear to Graham that the prime minister's priority was to have the capacity by 2007 to deploy troops to one or both. An extension of the Kandahar mission could well eat up that capacity and put the prime minister's priorities at risk. Moreover, it was not certain that the government had the political will to finance the existing mission in Afghanistan for an additional year. Pressing for another billion dollars per year for an extension beyond 2007 would not sit well with the finance minister and the prime minister, especially after they had just agreed to pump thirteen billion dollars into the Defence Department.[14]

Prime Minister Harper, on the other hand, had different priorities from his predecessor. Yet he has still said relatively little in public about why he took the risk of extending the mission just three months into his minority government. In Parliament, the government limited debate and reduced its argument to "Canada will not cut and run from Afghanistan," suggesting that a refusal to extend the mission in Kandahar until 2009, an arbitrary date, was tantamount to abandoning the Afghans. Months later, O'Connor argued in public that the Canadian Forces were in Afghanistan for "retribution" for the 9-11 attacks. The implication was that Canada would continue to fight in Afghanistan as long as the Americans, the principal victims of 9-11, were fighting or as long as they asked for Canada's help. A failure to extend the mission would not only abandon the Afghans but also the United States.

Nothing could be further from the truth. After 2006, Canada had other military options in Afghanistan. It could contribute in many different ways. Canada could, for example, send additional PRTs to other parts of the country or take a major role in training the Afghan National Army, a suggestion that Rumsfeld had originally made.[15] But the Conservatives would not discuss these options, which they labelled "cutting and running."

Rolling the Dice

True to his word, on May 17, 2006, Stephen Harper put the extension of the Kandahar mission to a hastily arranged vote in the House of Commons. The prime minister was putting his government at risk. Both the NDP and the Bloc had made their intentions known; each party would vote against the extension. They did not support the mission now that it was clear the CF were fighting a war under the umbrella of the United States. They were also enraged by the truncated debate, which they thought offensive and contemptuous of Parliament. Harper therefore needed the support of two dozen Liberals to carry the vote.

The government would not have fallen if it had lost this vote, as the resolution was not a matter of confidence. The weight of Parliament's views on the mission, moreover, did not seem to be the prime minister's main concern. Harper said that if Parliament did defeat his motion he would extend the mission for one more year; and, further to that, if he had trouble securing parliamentary agreement to extend the mission again, he would seek a mandate from the people of Canada. Nevertheless a defeat on the motion would certainly have been a serious if not a debilitating political setback early in the Harper government. Had he lost the vote, Harper's judgment would certainly have been questioned. Harper badly needed the support of Bill Graham and as many members of Parliament as he could bring with him.

After agonizing over the issue, Bill Graham decided that members of the Liberal caucus would be free to vote according to their conscience. The Interim Liberal leader would not impose his view on his colleagues. The Liberal Party was in the early stages of a leadership race and the front-runner, Michael Ignatieff, announced that he would support the Conservative motion to extend the Kandahar mission. Ignatieff had far more caucus support than any of his competitors at this point—about a quarter of the Liberal members of Parliament—and these MPs were expected to follow Ignatieff's lead. But the majority of Liberal MPs and leadership candidates, some of whom, like Bob Rae and Gerrard Kennedy, were not in Parliament, opposed the extension. Some rejected the mission on substantive grounds, while others objected to the parliamentary process that Harper had adopted to get the extension "approved." They would not support the extension.

Even John McCallum, the former minister of defence and now a strong and vocal supporter of Ignatieff's leadership, voted against the motion to extend. McCallum found the parliamentary tactics of the government appalling. As he said in public, the government had two options. The prime minister could make an executive decision and live with the political consequences, with no vote in Parliament. Foreign military deployments are usually handled this way in Canada. But if the government wanted the imprimatur of Parliament, McCallum felt that the government was obliged to ensure that MPs had sufficient time—weeks, if not months, as was the case in the Netherlands—to examine the issue carefully and make an informed judgment. The

didn't allow for
parliament to

prime minister was following neither course of action. Nevertheless, McCallum's friend Bill Graham would vote in favour of the extension. Hillier's arguments had convinced him that extending this mission was the right thing to do.

The party that decided to send Canada's military to Kandahar was deeply divided over extending this deployment. The motion to extend would pass, with about twenty-five percent of the Liberal caucus voting in favour. Harper had gambled and won. The divided Liberal Party immediately lost credibility on the mission in Afghanistan and struggled with the issue throughout the rest of the leadership campaign and into the next year.

Sins of Omission

By spring 2006 it was glaringly apparent that the security situation in southern Afghanistan had deteriorated badly. Kandahar and adjacent provinces were in the grip of a new, intense insurgency—the most serious challenge to the government since it was created after the United States and the Northern Alliance drove the Taliban out in late 2001. Southern Afghanistan was now engulfed in an unexpected war, one that neither the Canadian Forces nor NATO nor the United States had predicted. Everyone was caught off guard.

Lieutenant General David Richards, the British officer in command of ISAF, took the unusual step in the summer of 2006 of publicly pressuring NATO states to commit an additional two thousand troops to reinforce the counterinsurgency campaign in southern Afghanistan. He suggested that the mission could fail unless the troops on the ground were strengthened. His request fell largely on deaf ears. Old Europe—France, Germany, Italy, and Spain—had no intention of deploying their forces to fight an escalating insurgency. Months went by before the Americans and the British, whose armies were stretched thin in Iraq and Afghanistan, finally agreed to provide more troops for southern Afghanistan. There was no other option. No one else was prepared to fight and die in the south. Canada had been pressed to do more, but Ottawa had declined. The Canadian army was at its limit and could stretch no farther.

Canada's military leaders were also surprised by how quickly and how thoroughly the war consumed the Canadian Forces. Hillier had promised Paul Martin that, beginning in February 2007, the Canadian Forces would have the capacity to mount a second international mission elsewhere. Hillier made this unequivocal commitment even though, from the outset, he clearly wanted to extend the Kandahar mission beyond 2007. He believed that while the mission in Kandahar would be challenging, the Canadian Forces would still be capable of managing a second, simultaneous operation somewhere else. Running two missions simultaneously was in fact consistent with the Defence Policy Statement that Hillier had penned. However, by spring 2006, as the conflict in Kandahar escalated, the new government began to signal that this optimism was no longer warranted. In testimony before a Senate committee after the vote on the extension, Gordon O'Connor said, "We can maintain Afghanistan, as is, into the future basically forever, but we would be greatly challenged for a substantial commitment elsewhere in the world."[16] Hillier reinforced the message later that year when he made it clear that the war in Kandahar precluded the Canadian army from mounting a second operation for the foreseeable future. The mission in Kandahar was consuming resources and manpower at a rate unforeseen either by military leaders or by the government. "I underestimated the demands of the Afghan deployment, what it would consume," said Hillier. "It includes a conventional force component—which I did not foresee—which demands so many enablers [support elements]. Our C-130s [Hercules transport aircraft] are dying by the month and we have no replacement in sight. The intensity of the fighting required all our enablers."[17]

The casualty rates in the Canadian Forces in summer 2006 were higher than those of any other NATO country operating in the south. The situation on the ground deteriorated so badly that the commander requested and received a squadron of the aged Leopard tanks to reinforce the Canadian troops. During Graham's tenure as minister of defence, no one had raised even as a possibility the deployment of the tanks that Hillier once labelled "a millstone around his neck." On the contrary, Hillier had recommended that the Leopards be scrapped and permanently eliminated from the army. The tanks were to be replaced by a lighter so-called "Mobile Gun System," then under development in the United States. This platform was agile and mobile enough to be useful in a Three-Block War environment while the tanks were not. Suddenly, as casualties mounted, the old Leopards were drafted into service to help manage the deadly situation in Kandahar. By early 2007 the Harper government would announce the purchase of one hundred used Leopard 2 tanks from the Dutch army. The millstone around Hillier's neck has now evidently become an essential capability to fight the war in southern Afghanistan.

At one point during discussions with Graham, Hillier had suggested that sending Canadian CF-18 aircraft to bomb targets in Afghanistan might be necessary. But Graham rejected this option and got no push back from the CDS. "I was opposed to putting in CF-18s," recalled Bill Graham. "I didn't see how they fit with this mission. I remember Hillier telling me 'It's sort of like the cavalry ... the modern cavalry is your air force, they go over the top, you call them in for precision strikes.' All of which is great in theory, but the problem is the strikes are never very precise, they kill the people you are trying to win over to your side."[18] Although Canada didn't send in fighter bombers, other NATO states did. During 2006 NATO flew some 2,600 bombing sorties in Afghanistan, killing scores of civilians. The "collateral damage" from these air strikes has been a serious strain on the relationship between the Karzai government and NATO. It also threatens to undermine continued support among the Afghan population for the ISAF troops in their country.

Staying in Kandahar

The Canadian Forces are now locked in this unexpected war until February 2011. The Harper government extended the mission a second time through a vote in Parliament in autumn 2007. Recent experience shows that the longer a country commits to multilateral missions, the harder it is to withdraw. The Canadian Forces were in Bosnia, for example, for nearly fifteen years. As challenging a conflict as Bosnia was, it pales in comparison with the complexities of Afghanistan. It will also be much harder to find a replacement nation for Canada in Afghanistan than it was in Bosnia, where the European Union clamoured to take over that NATO mission.

It is almost always far easier to get in than it is to get out. Henault and Maddison understood the difficulties of withdrawing troops and consequently were adamant in 2003 that Canada commit for no more than one year to the leadership of the ISAF mission in Kabul. They insisted as well that Ottawa begin to develop an exit strategy and find a replacement nation for Canada before the mission had even started. Paul Martin understood this as well: "I went in for one year. But I knew at the end of the first year we probably wouldn't be able to get out. It would likely take a second year to get out. And that after a period of time we might rotate back in. By committing to two years, Harper has taken the pressure off others to replace us."[19]

The decision to extend the mission of the Canadian Forces in Kandahar creates formidable challenges for Canada's military and for its government. Canada is now at war. Canada slipped into war in Afghanistan, step by step, incrementally, without fully understanding that it was going to war, until it woke up to mounting casualties and grim battles. Paul Martin looked back at the decision-making process and saw the gaps: "We didn't have detailed discussions about the challenges of Afghanistan."[20] The government first committed only to a short-term combat mission in 2002, then to a short-term stabilization mission in 2003 to 2004, then to provincial reconstruction, and then, almost imperceptibly, to battle—all for short periods

of time. In 2006, thirty-four soldiers would die in combat in
Kandahar, the largest number since the Korean War. Canada was
most certainly at war.

Canadian soldiers are now locked in a battle for the "hearts and
minds" of Afghans, a battle that will shape the future of Afghanistan.
It will also shape the future of Canada's armed forces and it will colour
government thinking about the use of its army as an instrument of
foreign policy for years to come. It will shape Canada's development
assistance program, who is sent abroad, and under what circumstances.
It will shape Canadians' thinking about Canada as a global power for a
generation.

FOURTEEN

THOSE VEXATIOUS DETAINEES

Although Bill Graham had supported the Kandahar mission, he was deeply concerned about one issue. What would the Canadian Forces do with the prisoners they would take—the "detainees," to use that wonderfully sanitized term that the Pentagon manufactured so it could claim that those who were captured did not have the usual rights of prisoners under the Geneva Conventions. Prisoners captured in Afghanistan by the Canadian Forces had been transferred to the American authorities and, in some cases, to the Afghans. The Canadian Forces did not hold on to prisoners; Canada did not have nor did it intend to establish detention facilities in Afghanistan. The military leadership had consistently told the government since 2002 that the CF had no capability or expertise to run prisons, and the cost of building them was prohibitive. The practice of transferring detainees to a third country would have to continue. And with several hundred CF troops and JTF2 operatives actively engaging insurgents in Kandahar over the coming year, the CF would likely take many prisoners.

This issue of transferring Afghan prisoners to the Americans had been controversial ever since the Canadian Forces first set foot in Afghanistan in early 2002. Once in U.S. hands, many of the detainees were sent to the prison at the American naval base at Guantanamo Bay, Cuba. Amnesty International and other human rights groups alleged that once in Guantanamo, detainees were subject to cruel and inhuman interrogation techniques. No one really knew what happened at Guantanamo. The Americans provided little information about the prison and only very limited access, which further fuelled speculation about inappropriate treatment of prisoners behind its walls.

Graham, an international lawyer with a strong interest in international humanitarian law, had serious concerns about the Canadian Forces continuing to transfer detainees, perhaps in large numbers, to an unknown fate in Cuba. His discussions with officials on the fate of detainees began in mid-2005—when American abuse of prisoners at the now-notorious Abu Ghraib facility in Iraq was still fresh in people's minds. Graham's concerns, however, were not widely shared among civilian and military officials and lawyers in the Department of National Defence, where officials thought of the detainee issue as a nuisance, an obsession of the political class rather than a serious issue. The Department of Foreign Affairs, which should have sounded the alarm, was oddly silent.

Nevertheless, for Bill Graham this issue was vital, and he would push his officials hard to get a resolution that satisfied his standards. Here, as on other issues, Graham and Hillier saw eye to eye as the general broke ranks with conventional thinking inside NDHQ and sided with his minister.

Ottawa could not explain convincingly why the Canadian Forces did not set up their own detention facilities in Afghanistan. And, more to the point, Ottawa could not explain why the CF did not transfer all detainees to the Karzai government, now a democratically elected regime that Canada supported so strongly. It was logical to hand the prisoners over to the Government of Afghanistan, even though there were legitimate concerns about the human rights practices of the Karzai government and of the Afghan National Security Forces. Why would Ottawa want to court further controversy by continuing to transfer detainees to the Americans? Moreover, the American detention facilities were filling up. The United States allegedly wanted only high-level targets, which the Afghans would undoubtedly hand over to the Americans after receiving them from the Canadian Forces.

Graham and Hillier agreed that it was time to start negotiating a detainee transfer arrangement with Kabul. The agreement would have to stipulate that any prisoners handed over by Canada would be given Third Geneva Conventions rights, and that prisoners were accessible to both the International Committee of the Red Cross (ICRC) and the newly created Afghan Independent Human Rights Commission. Finally, the agreement had to stipulate that Canada and Afghanistan would both keep "accurate written records accounting for all detainees."[1]

But the agreement would not make provisions for the monitoring of transferred detainees by the Government of Canada or the Canadian Forces. The CF leadership and military lawyers adamantly opposed this kind of arrangement. They argued that the military had neither the capacity nor the skills to monitor detainees and ascertain whether they had been maltreated or tortured in Afghan jails. This seemed a compelling argument at the time. Two highly controversial cases—those of Canadians Mahar Arar detained in a Syrian jail and William Sampson imprisoned in Saudi Arabia—exposed the failure of Canada's diplomats to assess accurately whether or not the two men had been tortured. Despite having visited both Arar and Sampson in jail, Canada's diplomats concluded that the men had not been tortured. Subsequent inquiries determined otherwise. How could the Canadian Forces be expected to do a better job of determining whether Afghans—whose languages they did not speak—had been tortured while in custody, when Canada's diplomats could not determine whether Canadians had been maltreated in Syrian and Saudi jails?

ON MAY 31, 2005, the Afghan foreign minister, Dr. Abdullah Abdullah, visited Ottawa. Graham told him that Canada and Afghanistan needed to conclude an agreement on the transfer of detainees quickly, as the Canadian Forces were due to start arriving in Kandahar in three months. Abdullah agreed. Negotiations continued between NDHQ and Kabul through the summer and into the fall, but it seemed that the

Afghans were dragging their feet. In October, Graham visited Kabul and met with the foreign minister again, who told him the agreement was now little more than a formality; the Afghans had accepted Canada's terms and were about to sign the agreement.

Graham then met with his counterpart, the new Afghan defence minister, Abdul Rahim Wardak, who had replaced Fahim. Wardak was a mujahideem fighter during the Soviet–Afghan war and a former university lecturer. He seemed much more sophisticated, worldly, and cultured than his predecessor, whom he had served as deputy.[2] Wardak, speaking fluent English, bemoaned the small number of detention facilities in Afghanistan and asked for Western funds to build more prisons. Directly contradicting the foreign minister, the new defence minister claimed that the lack of facilities might preclude a transfer agreement with Canada. There appeared to be confusion within the Karzai government about whether a detainee arrangement would be concluded before the CF had arrived in full force in Kandahar. When Graham returned to Canada, he asked his officials to sort out this confusion and to try to bring this issue to a quick conclusion.[3]

The federal election that ended the tenure of the Martin government began within weeks of Graham's return from Kabul. The detainee agreement had not been signed when the election got underway. It appeared that the new government would have to handle the issue after the election.

However, during the election campaign, Hillier visited Kabul and, along with Canada's new ambassador to Afghanistan, David Sproule, met with Defence Minister Wardak. During the meeting, Hillier managed to obtain the Afghan government's approval of the elusive agreement on detainees, with all the terms and conditions that Canada wanted. The general signed the agreement for Canada, even though Graham had not delegated this responsibility to him. Hillier insisted that the Department of Foreign Affairs had seen and approved the agreement at every stage and explained why he took this unusual step of signing the agreement: "Wardak was a friend of mine. We got to know each other when I was Commander of ISAF and he was CDS in Kabul. Wardak asked if I could sign the agreement since he had such great respect for me. Sproule agreed. Without question, Foreign Affairs saw the agreement and approved it. If my flight had been delayed twenty-four hours, Sproule would have signed the agreement. He wouldn't have signed anything that Foreign Affairs hadn't seen."[4] Foreign Affairs did see the agreement, explained a senior official in the department, but when it raised objections, was told in no uncertain terms by Defence to "mind our own business. We didn't press any further."[5]

Hillier's decision to sign the agreement—typical of his can-do atti-tude—would come back to haunt him in eighteen months, when the detainee issue blew up and engulfed the Harper government in its first real crisis.

BRITAIN AND DENMARK had also negotiated detainee transfer agreements with Afghanistan, with one significant difference. The British and Danish agreements provided for the continuing right to follow-up visits to the prisoners they handed over to the Afghans. But the politicians in Ottawa did not know about those agreements until November, just before Hillier signed the Canadian agreement in Kabul, but months after negotiations had begun between Ottawa and Kabul. The NDP spoke about the Danish agreement during a parliamentary debate on the Afghanistan mission—a debate that Bill Graham had insisted on having in order to help educate parliamentarians and the public about this deployment. During the debate, the NDP, who had somehow obtained a copy of the Danish agreement, referred to one of its clauses that prohibited the application of the death penalty against transferred detainees and asked whether Canada would insist on a similar provision in its agreement. Until the parliamentary debate, Graham had not been apprised of the Danish agreement. As soon as he heard about it, Graham asked for a copy. He insisted that a similar provision prohibiting the death penalty be inserted in the Canadian agreement.

Graham and his staff also noticed a clause providing for follow-up visits by the Danish military. The minister re-engaged the military on this subject to try to include similar provisions in the Canadian agreement. But the leadership of the Canadian Forces and their lawyers remained steadfast in their opposition to such a clause. They would agree only to an article prohibiting the death penalty. In addition to their claim that the Canadian Forces had no experience or expertise in monitoring or evaluating the treatment of prisoners, the military leadership argued that insisting on follow-up visits would smack of paternalism and would be offensive to the democratically elected Karzai government. In a perverse kind of logic, they argued that perhaps the Danes could get away with this kind of clause, but Canada, which was a major player in Afghanistan, could not afford to offend the Karzai government. But the Dutch, who were also major troop contributors in Afghanistan, were evidently not worried about offending sensibilities in Kabul. They would eventually sign an agreement with Kabul that included provisions similar to those of the Danes.[6] It was this opposition by Canada's military leadership to monitoring that set the stage for a government crisis.

The protections built into the agreement that Hillier had signed proved inadequate. Since the Canadian Forces arrived in Kandahar in 2005 to 2006, the Afghan Independent Human Rights Commission, Amnesty International, and the UN Commissioner for Human Rights, Louise Arbour (a former justice of the Supreme Court of Canada), had concluded that abuse, torture, and extrajudicial killing were routinely inflicted on people in Afghan custody. The U.S. State Department, in its annual human rights assessment in 2006, confirmed that local authorities in Afghan prisons "routinely torture and abuse detainees." Canada's embassy in Kabul made a similar assessment in a report it sent to Ottawa, a report that came to light only in 2007.[7] Yet oddly, as then Foreign Minister Peter MacKay has since confirmed, "The human rights reports are not normally copied to the Minister of Foreign Affairs, nor is the Minister briefed on their content."[8] Former Defence Minister Gordon

O'Connor also claimed that neither he nor his predecessors had been made aware of the reports on the abuse of prisoners.[9]

These assertions of prisoner abuse are no small matter. Under international law, Canadian soldiers cannot knowingly hand prisoners over to authorities that engage in torture. If they do, they are liable under international criminal law.

The issue exploded in spring 2007 when the Military Police Complaints Commission, a civilian body created after the Somalia Inquiry to investigate complaints about the conduct of the military police, received a request for an investigation into the treatment of three detainees transferred to the Afghan authorities by Canadian soldiers. The three men handed over to the Afghan National Police on April 8, 2006, had allegedly been abused, not by the Afghan police but by Canadian soldiers, before they were transferred.[10] The ghosts of Somalia wafted through the corridors of Ottawa and, very quickly, General Hillier ordered a board of inquiry and, in short order, three other investigations were set up. One, the investigation by the independent Military Police Complaints Commission, will determine whether the Canadian Forces violated international law and the Canadian Charter of Rights and Freedoms when they transferred detainees to the Afghan National Police, a police force that allegedly routinely engages in torture.

The story got worse. The three detainees who were allegedly abused by Canadian soldiers could not be found in Afghan prisons.[11] The prisoners could have bought their way out of prison, as many do; the record keeping of the Afghan National Police could be very poor; or, at the very worst, the detainees could have been tortured or killed. Canada, unlike some of its NATO allies, had no explicit right to visit detainees in Afghan prisons, although both Canada and Afghanistan did commit to keep "accurate written records accounting for all detainees." Ottawa depended in part on the very new and under-resourced Afghan Independent Human Rights Commission to follow the fate of the detainees, but far more so on the International

Committee of the Red Cross (ICRC), the oldest and very best independent international agency that works to protect prisoners of war.[12]

Even though the ICRC was central to the monitoring of the Canada–Afghanistan agreement, the Government of Canada did not consult the ICRC when it was drafting and negotiating the detainee agreement with the Afghan authorities. It was known at the time that the Red Cross did not want the responsibility of monitoring. Nor did the ICRC appreciate being used as a "talking point" by governments that wanted to defend their human rights record.

To make matters worse still, Gordon O'Connor evidently misunderstood the role of the ICRC. He told the House of Commons, "The Red Cross or the Red Crescent is responsible to supervise their treatment once the prisoners are in the hands of the Afghan authorities. If there is something wrong with their treatment, the Red Cross or the Red Crescent would inform us and we would take action."[13] Some of his officials also suggested this was the case during testimony before a Parliamentary Committee. Not at all, said the ICRC. "We were informed of the agreement, but we are not a party to it and we are not monitoring the implementation of it," said Simon Schorno of the ICRC. "Silence does not mean," he continued, "that all is well." The ICRC only informs the Government of Afghanistan of any concerns. It does not report to Canada. "This was clearly explained [to then Minister of Defence Gordon O'Connor and former Minister of Foreign Affairs Peter MacKay]," said Schorno, "during our president's visit [to Ottawa in September 2006]." Finally, on March 8, 2007, O'Connor acknowledged that he had been wrong: The Red Cross would provide information only to the detaining nation.[14] He issued an apology to the House of Commons. Again, the Defence Ministry did not fully understand the political consequences of its treatment of political prisoners. And again, Foreign Affairs was silent.

Foreign Affairs is normally central to the negotiation and signing of all state-to-state agreements. Notwithstanding Hillier's claim that Foreign Affairs "had the lead" on these negotiations, it is now clear that

Canada's diplomats took a back seat to the leadership of the Canadian Forces.[15] The low profile the diplomats kept in the negotiations on the transfer of detainees is surprising—and worrying—given the department's expertise in human rights and international humanitarian law. Bill Graham rightly regarded this agreement as critical to the success of Canada's mission in Afghanistan, yet the negotiations went ahead without serious advice from the strongest experts Canada has. The very limited role of Foreign Affairs, their failure to push back at the Department of Defence, is one more troubling example of the weak civilian oversight of Canada's military.

Had experts from Foreign Affairs been deeply involved, they might have known the terms that the British, the Dutch, and the Danish had successfully negotiated with Afghanistan. They might have warned the Canadian Forces about the human rights record of the Afghan government and explicitly cautioned the CF about their obligations under international law. They might well have argued that the agreement the Canadian Forces had drafted was not adequate in its protections of the rights of detainees and that members of the CF might find themselves compromised under international law.

The diplomats and their lawyers would surely have pointed out that a state-to-state agreement signed by General Hillier, rather than a minister of the Crown or an ambassador, might well not have legal standing. Normally, military officers do not sign international agreements on behalf of the Government of Canada. More to the point, it is highly unusual that any official or minister would sign any agreement of this significance during a federal election.

By early 2007 it was glaringly apparent that the agreement Hillier had signed in late 2005 was inadequate to fulfill Canada's obligations under international law. *The Globe and Mail* decided to make the detainee issue its *cause célèbre*. Through the winter and spring of 2007 *The Globe* relentlessly exposed the flaws and contradictions in Canada's policy on detainees. A political crisis engulfed Canada's new government. All three Opposition parties called for Gordon O'Connor's

[margin handwritten note: to should have recognized the apparent problems]

resignation. They claimed that he had misled the House of Commons on the nature of the detainee agreement for over a year when he insisted that the Red Cross was monitoring detainees transferred by the Canadian Forces and reporting back to the Government of Canada. The defence minister either had lied or was incompetent, claimed the Opposition parties and the press, and he understood neither Canada's policy on detainees nor its international obligations. He had to go.

Then a bomb went off in Ottawa. Graeme Smith, an intrepid twenty-seven-year-old reporter for *The Globe* based in Afghanistan, tracked down and interviewed thirty former detainees who claimed to have been transferred by Canadian officials to Afghan authorities and then tortured while in custody. Ottawa had maintained up to that point that there was no evidence of detainees being tortured in Afghan custody. Yet the government also claimed that Canada had no knowledge of where transferred detainees were located.

Even though the revelations reported in *The Globe* were unsubstantiated, the detainee issue was quickly reaching a tipping point. The government went into damage control, silenced the hapless defence minister, and shifted the responsibility for public communications on this issue to the prime minister and other members of the Cabinet. At one point Stockwell Day, the minister of public safety, suggested that Correctional Services of Canada officials were in Afghanistan to monitor detainees and determine whether they had been tortured. But the Afghan ambassador to Canada, Omar Samad, contradicted Day. It soon became clear that Samad was right and Day was wrong.

By early May 2007 the controversy over the detainees had become the dominant issue in the House of Commons and in much of the national media. The government was accused of incompetence, duplicity, and lack of transparency. Amnesty International and the British Columbia Civil Liberties Association had sought an injunction in Federal Court to stop further transfer of detainees to Afghan authorities, on the grounds that these transfers "expose detainees to a substantial risk of torture."[16]

The government initially planned to defend itself vigorously against the action. Its defence rested on several arguments: Canadian troops are not trained or equipped to run a prison camp; the Charter of Rights doesn't apply to foreigners outside Canada; halting transfers could cause more Canadian casualties; and the unsubstantiated claims of torture made by *The Globe and Mail* should not be admissible as evidence.[17] Perhaps the most revealing claim Ottawa intended to make was that halting the transfers would interfere with the government's ability to wage war.[18]

Notwithstanding the arguments Ottawa planned to advance to stop the injunction, the government evidently concluded either that it would lose or that it would be publicly embarrassed by the court. On the day the injunction was to be heard, official Ottawa blinked. The government announced that a new detainee transfer agreement had been concluded with the Government of Afghanistan. It had been signed that very day—May 3, 2007. The new agreement was entered into the court as an affidavit to stay the proceedings. The boil had been lanced. The new agreement would contain better safeguards and protections for transferred detainees than the Dutch, British, or Danish agreements. Canada now had a detainee transfer agreement with Afghanistan that featured the most stringent human rights protections of any agreement.

Canadian government representatives were now accorded full and unfettered access to detainees, including private interviews. Human rights groups and "the UN system" were also to be given access. Notification to Canada of the status and location of detainees was required. The Government of Afghanistan would no longer be permitted to transfer a detainee handed over by Canada to a third state without written permission from Ottawa. And Kabul was now required to investigate all allegations of abuse and mistreatment of prisoners.[19] Rick Hillier admitted publicly that circumstances had changed and that the agreement he had signed in late 2005 was no longer adequate. The Canadian Forces now thought that a new agreement with tough monitoring provisions and rigorous human rights protections was in Canada's interest.

In reality, only one thing had changed. The media had shone a spotlight on the original agreement. Its shortcomings had provoked a political crisis for the government, and public support for the Canadian mission in Kandahar would surely have declined had this issue not been put to rest quickly. The Harper government moved quickly to seize the reins from the military and put in place an agreement that would reduce its vulnerability on its signature policy. Civilian oversight on at least some part of the government's Afghanistan policy seemed to have been restored. And when Prime Minister Harper visited Kabul in May 2007, his host, President Karzai, helped him put out the fire. Karzai stated in public that the stories reported in the Canadian press were false and that no prisoner abuse was going on in Afghan jails.

The problem of protecting the rights of detainees, however, has not gone away. The deputy chair of the Afghanistan Independent Human Rights Commission, Ahmad Fahim Hakim, was adamant that he could not guarantee that detainees were not being tortured in Afghan prisons. The new agreement was an improvement, he said, and the commission had a better relationship with the National Directorate of Security that manages the prisons. But the commission employs too few monitors, the monitors need more training, and there can be a twenty-day gap between when the commission is notified and when the first visit to a detainee takes place.[20]

Protecting the detainees from abuse, Hakim argued, should not be the responsibility of any one NATO member acting alone. It is a collective problem that all NATO members share. "Maybe so," replied General Dan McNeill, the commander of ISAF, "but most NATO members are not willing to share that responsibility. No collective solution to detainees is possible. It will not happen."[21] Ray Henault, now chairman of the NATO Military Committee in Brussels, reacted emphatically when asked whether NATO would consider establishing and running prison facilities in Afghanistan. "No. NATO developed an explicit policy on detainees in December 2005. It was developed by SACEUR [the Supreme Allied Commander in Europe] and approved by the NATO Council.... Detainees are handed over to the Afghan government, conditioned by national decisions."[22] The major troop contributors in the south—Holland, Britain, Canada, and the United States—may well meet together with the commission and the National Directorate of Security on a regular basis, but even improved coordination cannot guarantee that detainees are not tortured.

Hakim is realistic about what can be done to protect the rights of detainees. He is grateful that Ottawa insisted on improving its agreement with Kabul and that better protections have been put in place. The Afghan Independent Human Rights Commission now gets easier access to detainees than it did before. "Our conversation with the Afghan authorities is much better," Hakim said, "in part because they know how important the issue is to Canada." Important though they are, better relations with Afghan authorities and unimpeded and more frequent monitoring are only the first steps. "If there were not an ongoing problem with human rights," Hakim concluded in his soft-spoken but determined manner, "the coalition forces would not have to be in Afghanistan."

FIFTEEN

THE THREE *DS* IN AFGHANISTAN

C anada is a country of more than thirty million people, a wealthy country endowed with resources and blessed with skills, talent, and diversity. People from all over the world come to Canada to make it their home. With this kind of talent and these kinds of assets, Canada should be among the best in what it does in the world, a leader and an innovator.

We're not. Again and again, leaders from every political party and government officials across departments lament that Canada is punching below its weight—it could be doing much better in Afghanistan. Canada's soldiers have fought with extraordinary bravery in Afghanistan. They have shown skill, commitment, and dedication. The problem lies elsewhere. Countries with fewer resources than Canada are doing better. Their development assistance programs are more effective, and their ministers work together to identify and plug gaps in security and peace building. Why Canada is underperforming is a large and complicated question, but the damage is at least partly self-inflicted.

When Paul Martin became prime minister, he accelerated a review of Canada's international activities that had begun under the Chrétien government. The International Policy Statement that came out of that review developed the concept of the Three *D*s—defence, development, and diplomacy—that would work together in "a whole of government" approach to focus all of Canada's assets in a coherent strategy.[1] The three arms of government abroad—the Department of National

Defence (DND), the Department of Foreign Affairs and International Trade (DFAIT), and the Canadian International Development Agency (CIDA)—would work closely together to reinforce one another's objectives. Foreign Affairs was given a new Global Peace and Security Fund to support the objectives of Canadian foreign policy around the world.

Afghanistan was the first real test of the Three *D* policy, and officials from all three departments do not think that Canada has done as well as it could. The Three *D*s are not working well together and some are not working well alone. In Ottawa, words like *dysfunctional*, *debilitated*, and *broken* are common descriptions of the institutions at the centre of Canadian foreign policy. These descriptions come not from hostile outsiders but from people who have spent years working within one of the three big departments—Defence, Foreign Affairs, and CIDA—that are Canada's face to the world. The balance among those three departments has shifted markedly in the last three years. Defence has been reinvigorated under strategic and focused leadership, while the other two have largely lost their way.

The First *D*: Defence

The Canadian Forces have flourished under the charismatic leadership of General Rick Hillier, who has redefined the strategic purposes of the military and articulated a clear set of challenges. Afghanistan is the face of the future, Hillier argues, and the Canadian Forces will be deployed more and more to failed and failing states far from Canada's shores. In a globally integrated environment, Canada's forces have to move nimbly and be capable of fighting.

Hillier's leadership, because it is so strong, so strategic, and so focused, has unbalanced the relationship between civilians and the military, as well as the relationship between Defence and other departments. Some allege that Canada's military now lacks sufficient civilian oversight, either by the Department of Defence or across the

Government of Canada. It is the military that is forging policy. Yet that is not the way it is supposed to be in a mature parliamentary democracy. Civilian oversight matters. Policy is made better by it. The military benefits from it.

The military is also prodding the other two departments, constantly expressing irritation at their slow pace and bureaucratic culture. Canada's military is at war in Kandahar and is understandably intolerant of all the usual excuses. It wants real partners. Those on the front line, in combat, cannot understand the pace at which the other two departments work, their emphasis on process, and the culture of consultation that delays decisions by months.

The Department of National Defence is not without its critics. General Hillier has said repeatedly that the Canadian Forces will be focusing on failed and failing states that threaten international peace and security in unstable and dangerous parts of the world. Yet the policy directorate in the Defence Department continues to concentrate on its traditional concerns: NATO, NORAD, and the Canada–U.S. relationship. In 2003, John McCallum became the first Canadian minister of defence in twenty years to visit China, yet Canadian defence ministers routinely travel to NATO meetings in Europe several times a year. To put it mildly, policy knowledge in Defence is lagging badly behind strategic planning.

The most serious criticism of the Canadian Forces came from senior advisers around Prime Minister Martin, who accused the military of working with their friends in Washington to drive policy in the direction they wanted it to go. Senior military officers and civilian staff worked with their counterparts south of the border, sputtered one of Canada's most experienced civil servants, to lobby the government to join the war in Iraq and to participate in Ballistic Missile Defence. "It's unthinkable for the Canadian Forces," he insisted, "to behave that way."[2]

There is truth to this charge. Canada's military missions were largely, if not exclusively, determined on the basis of Ottawa's relationship with the United States. Canada's military leaders saw Afghanistan out of the corner of their eyes as they looked squarely at Washington, at what Washington wanted and at what Washington might accept. The Canada–U.S. relationship framed every major recommendation that Canada's military leaders made to their minister. Afghanistan was never the subject but only the object, the terrain in which the Canadian Forces operated as they struggled with an assertive Bush administration. Afghanistan could have been anywhere. It was no more than a spot on the map.

It is not surprising that Canada's political leaders would pay attention to military advice framed within the larger context of the Canada–U.S. relationship. "Every Canadian prime minister," said John Manley, "has two overriding priorities. The first is national unity. The second is managing Canada's relationship with the United States."[3] The two economies and the two societies are so intermingled that it would be surprising if Ottawa did not consider—and consider carefully— what Washington wanted. Canada's economy is so dependent on the United States, and the personal ties between Canadians and Americans are so dense, that it would be irresponsible in the extreme if leaders in Ottawa did not seek to help the United States when it needed help. And paying attention to the wishes of the United States goes beyond self-interest. Deep bonds of kinship and friendship connect the two societies.

But Washington's reactions tended to be the exclusive consideration in almost all of the discussions about Afghanistan. So much was refracted through the lens of the Canada–U.S. relationship that Canadian leaders found it difficult to "see," to really see Afghanistan. Much was ignored: Afghanistan's history, its traditions and accomplishments, its social structure, its strengths and fault lines, its tribal and ethnic divisions, the devastation of its social and physical infrastructure after thirty years of fighting, its deeply rooted patterns of warfare, and its long history of expelling foreign armies that thought they had come to stay.

The anticipated reaction of the United States repeatedly shaped Canada's choices. Nowhere is this more evident than in the constant stream of advice the military gave to the political leadership about the negative reaction in Washington were Canada to act in a particular way. The preoccupation with what the United States—and in particular the White House—would think, what it would do, bordered on the obsessive. This obsession is born of years of intimate relationships among senior officials in the two militaries.

The advice, often phrased as Cassandra-like warnings, was consistently wrong. Senior military officers and civilian officials in the Department of National Defence and Foreign Affairs exaggerated at every step the negative reaction in Washington if Ottawa were to pursue a different path, if Canada were not "onside," and if it were not visibly onside. That refrain echoes at every important decision point.

When he looked back on his time in Canada, the U.S. ambassador to Ottawa did not share this talk of catastrophe. In a stunning revision of the history that he helped to make, Paul Cellucci put the relationship between the two countries in a larger perspective. In an interview two years after the controversy over BMD, Cellucci was far more sanguine than he was at the time. "There is no strain in the relationship," he insisted. "The relationship between Canada and the United States is government-to-government, person-to-person, family-to-family, military-to-military. It's a very old and very complicated relationship and crises never disrupt for very long. These strains are grossly exaggerated. It's overwhelmingly in our interest to work with you."[4] This from one of the most vocal critics of Canadian policy when he was ambassador. Perhaps once he was away from the daily maelstrom of controversy and pressure and had time to reflect, Cellucci came to a more measured judgment.

Military leaders and civilian officials in Ottawa did not behave as if the Canada–U.S. relationship were a mature one, strong enough to manage differences, even substantial differences. Before Prime Minister Chrétien made his final decision on whether to join the United States in the invasion of Iraq, he was warned repeatedly about the damaging consequences of saying "No" to Washington. It was simply inconceivable to some military leaders that Canada would not be part of the coalition. Prime Minister Martin was pressed even harder on the Ballistic Missile Defence program. The consequences would be "catastrophic," some officials in Defence claimed, if Canada refused to participate. The consequences were not catastrophic. Certainly among military officers and defence officials of the two countries there was disappointment, chagrin, an occasional snide remark and a snub, even a temporary exclusion from a club. But at the highest political levels, the decision barely caused a ripple.

The advice that Canada's political leaders received from officials in National Defence was persistently wrong and consistently immune to correction even when the evidence didn't fit. What explains this obsession with the United States?

The seduction of privileged access to the latest technology, the most up-to-date weaponry, and the most up-to-the-minute military intelligence is undoubtedly a big part of the story. The U.S. military is the best in the world and Canadian officers understandably find it impossible to resist the lure. But that is not the whole story.

Government after government cut the budget of the military. In the first five years of his term, Prime Minister Chrétien and Finance Minister Martin deepened the cuts. Only in 1999 did Chrétien reverse the trend and inject about seven hundred million dollars into the defence budget to improve the "quality of life" of soldiers. Chief of the Defence Staff Rick Hiller described the 1990s as the "decade of darkness" for the Canadian Forces.[5] Starved of new equipment, new technology, and without enough recruits, the Canadian Forces became a dependant of the U.S. military, getting there what they could not get at home. In 2007, for example, the Canadian military borrowed wholesale from U.S. doctrine on counterinsurgency to train its soldiers for Afghanistan. The CF relies on the U.S. military not only for doctrine but also for technology, equipment, training, and, most of all, for approval. Hillier is more respected among senior officers for having been deputy commander of Fort Hood, Texas, than for being commander of ISAF in Kabul.

Prime Minister Martin had a different view of the Canadian role in its relationship with the United States. "Canada has to play a role in the world," he insisted. "We shouldn't always be the rump end of a British or American army. Canada can take the lead. My view on Canada's foreign policy is that we benefit no one by being handmaiden to the great. There's no payback, as Tony Blair has learned. There is a Canadian perspective on the world which is important to the exercise of our sovereignty."[6] When Prime Minister Martin committed the Canadian Forces to Kandahar in 2005, he made it clear that Afghanistan would be only one of several priorities in Canadian policy. On the others, Canada would take the lead and would go where the United States didn't want to go or was unwelcome. Martin understood that as a friend of the United States, Canada would occasionally speak with its own voice on international issues, and that when it did, Washington would appreciate the help even if it did not always agree with the advice.

Paul Wolfowitz, at the time a prominent member of the Bush administration and a leading neoconservative, suggested to Bill Graham, then the minister of defence, that Washington valued Canadian military contributions in places the United States wouldn't go, especially in Africa. Paradoxically, were Wolfowitz to try to make this argument in Canada, he would have a tough time convincing some Canadians that the ties between Canada and the United States are far more resilient than officials in DND tend to think. They can stretch to accommodate differences, partnership, and a smart division of labour.

The Second *D*: Development Assistance

"Successful counterinsurgencies are as much about the political and economic issues," observed Colonel Bernd Horn, when he came back from his tour of Canadian forces in Kandahar, "as they are about military action." Military action to ensure security is a struggle, an uphill battle, he continued, without economic and political progress. "No amount of patrolling or sweeps through the mountains alone can solve the problem of providing useful employment for the unemployed disenfranchised young men of the country, who represent a limitless pool of potential insurgents."[7] But political and economic progress in Afghanistan has been slow.

Generally, international spending on the military has dwarfed spending on development and reconstruction. The international community has spent only eight percent of the total funds it committed to Afghanistan between 2002 and 2006 on development and poverty relief.[8] The conventional wisdom is diametrically opposed: Eighty percent of the spending should go to economic, political, and social development. The question of how much development assistance Afghanistan can absorb in a relatively short time is very real, but the current balance is clearly badly off.

Although there has been significant progress since 2001, the challenges remain daunting, particularly in southern Afghanistan, where the insurgency is growing. Nationally, unemployment was estimated at thirty-three percent in 2006—it is probably higher—and most adult-age workers are getting by on short-term employment. There is no safety net for those without work. "Poverty," concluded a recent report that looked at progress in Afghanistan, "is fuelling anger towards the central government and motivating young men to rearm and fight in the insurgency or with local illegal armed groups to earn cash."[9] What makes the challenge so difficult in Afghanistan is that nation-building and economic development must take place in the midst of an ongoing war.

Afghanistan is one of the poorest nations in the world. Its per capita annual income is only $230, life expectancy is forty-three years, almost half of children under the age of five are moderately or severely underweight, and one-quarter of all children die before they reach the age of five. Afghanistan has the second-highest infant mortality rate in the world, literacy is only twenty-three percent, and more than twenty percent of the people do not have adequate nutrition. Kabul was virtually destroyed by vicious fighting during the civil war, its buildings reduced to rubble, its roads pockmarked by shells that had exploded. Life is even more difficult for Afghans who live in rural areas. Agriculture had declined after years of drought, and until recently, when some of the major roads in the south were rebuilt and reopened, farmers could not export the crops they harvested. Under the Taliban, many of the schools and clinics run by women were forced to close and health services deteriorated alarmingly. Fighting destroyed eighty percent of Afghan schools and only ten percent of the population had access to health care facilities.

Immediately after the United States ousted the Taliban, donors convened an international conference in Bonn in December 2001 and pledged significant funding for development. But the G-8 countries had no plan, no strategy. "The first discussion we had about establishing some sort of government in Afghanistan," said John Manley, "was at the Foreign Ministers' meeting at the United Nations General Assembly in November of 2001. Until then, the mission had been to defeat al-Qaeda and capture bin Laden."[10] Sarah Chayes, an intrepid journalist who lived in Kandahar at the time, remembered the confusion and the improvisation. "There was no strategy for targeting reconstruction dollars," she claimed, "so as to produce the greatest possible domino effect. Worse, there was not even a clear notion of what the desired 'end state' in Afghanistan was ... It was as though it had never occurred to anyone to think about what would happen once the Taliban were defeated."[11]

World leaders had given little thought to what came after the Taliban, but what they had learned, they acknowledged, was that they neglected Afghanistan at their peril. Four years later, some lessons had been learned. On January 31, 2006, in London, the Afghan government and sixty donor nations signed the Afghanistan Compact, which established precise benchmarks for both the government and the donors. They also put in place a Joint Coordinating Monitoring Board that would meet regularly to evaluate progress.

Much has been accomplished in a very short time. Within five years, more than six thousand schools have been rebuilt and six of thirteen million children—two million girls—are now in school. Roads and bridges have been repaired, new roads have been built, and new wells have been dug. Access to health clinics is vastly better than it was five years ago and the infant mortality rate is beginning to drop. Programs in rural transportation, safe drinking water, irrigation, and schools are among the twenty thousand projects that are now underway. The Ministry of Rural Rehabilitation and Development (MRRD) and the Ministry of Public Health have improved their capacity to deliver basic social services. These are real achievements.

Perhaps most encouraging is the success of the National Solidarity Program (NSP), led by the Afghan minister of rural rehabilitation and development, working with non-governmental organizations. More than sixteen thousand locally elected community development councils now dot Afghanistan, and elected leaders choose projects that meet their priorities.[12] Women either sit on these councils or, in the south, form separate councils. Participation in these councils has given women some standing in their communities, the ability to speak at council meetings, and a voice in the shaping of village priorities.

One of these council meetings was held in May 2007 in a local mosque outside Kabul, in District 15. A woman sitting against the wall rose to her feet during the meeting and told the men how important it was to her and the other women that a woman as poor as she had a voice in the development of her village. What she and the other women wanted, she said, was to learn to read. If they couldn't read, she explained, they couldn't help their children. And, she continued after a moment's pause, women who couldn't read were cut off, isolated. She asked for a teacher, a literate woman who could teach the women in the village. The men acknowledged her request, one made a note, and the meeting moved on to talk about the funding that was available. At the end of the meeting, the women received some of the money to pay the one literate woman in the village to teach them to read.

Canada has been a significant part of this success. CIDA's mandate is long-term development and it has chosen to focus its resources on building the state in Afghanistan, on extending its reach and deepening its hold. Without an effective state that can reach down and reach out, CIDA's leaders argue, nothing else will succeed. Nipa Banerjee, a young CIDA official at the Canadian embassy in Kabul in the early days, pushed hard to secure the funding for the National Solidarity Program, and Canada became one of its earliest and largest donors. In two years, from 2003 to 2005, CIDA spent more than $150 million to help rebuild Afghan national institutions, disarm Afghan militias, and establish microfinance facilities.[13] The ability to borrow small amounts of money has mattered enormously to the women of Afghanistan. Canada was ahead of other donors, ahead of the curve. But the focus was always on national programs, on building the institutions of the Afghan state, not particularly on the south.

Progress has been slow in the southern provinces of Kandahar, Helmand, and Oruzgan, the epicentre of the insurgency. At the end of 2006, more than four hundred community development councils were operating in Kandahar, but Afghans themselves are much less optimistic about reconstruction and development than they were even a year ago. A villager from Kandahar province put it bluntly: "Since the international community's involvement five years ago, there has been no reconstruction work. The international community promised us it would bring security and development. It promised to build schools, irrigation systems, roads, hospitals, and to provide work opportunities for the Afghan people. Five years ago we were happy and optimistic of the future," he said. "But five years later, there is no security, no sign of reconstruction and no improvement in living standards. The international community has repeatedly broken its promises. We don't trust foreigners anymore. We don't have any income and are forced to join the Taliban. The monthly income to join the Taliban is US$200 per month. Afghan people need money."[14] As the insurgency has grown in the south, travelling to schools and clinics has become much more difficult. Attacks against girls going to school have increased and many of the reopened schools in the south have been forced to close. Some

Afghan parents are afraid to send their children to school and women again report feeling afraid to leave their homes.[15]

Money is not the immediate problem. If anything, aid came too quickly for the Afghan government to manage. In 2005 and 2006, the Afghan government spent only forty-four percent of the funds that it received for development.[16] The ministries and their partners simply did not have the capacity to implement the programs that were being funded.[17] In a review of what has worked well and the challenges ahead, the Monitoring Board created by the Afghanistan Compact recently identified four "elephants in the room," four critical problems that could put at risk all the hard-won gains: weak governance, corruption, the opium economy, and security.

Canada faced all these challenges when it made Afghanistan the largest recipient of Canadian aid. Since 2001, the Canadian government has committed one billion dollars in development assistance to Afghanistan, or one hundred million dollars a year for the decade. Prime Minister Harper pledged an additional two hundred million dollars for reconstruction in 2007, and Canada is now one of the five largest bilateral donors to Afghanistan. Even though Canada is a large and significant donor, its development assistance is only one-tenth of what it is spending on the military effort in Afghanistan. This is a strange skewing of priorities.

Much of CIDA's development assistance in Afghanistan is deliberately invisible, for good reasons. Just over a third of the money is channelled through multilateral agencies to avoid duplication and waste. Canadian funding for food aid, for example, goes to the World Food Program, which manages the distribution of emergency rations within Afghanistan. Forty-three percent of the money goes to the Afghan government, so that there is an Afghan face on development. It is this money that supported the National Solidarity Program and microfinance. CIDA is invisible for a second reason: Its funding goes principally to long-term development, not to short-term "hearts and minds" programs. The results of most of its funding will only be visible in years, if not decades. It is hard to find a Canadian flag in any development project in Kabul or Kandahar. Quite right, say CIDA's leaders. There should be no Canadian face. Development must be Afghan-led.

Only twenty-eight percent of CIDA's funding goes to the south. It is only very recently that CIDA has deepened its programs in the south without cutting back on what it is doing nationally. "We have gone national," explained Stephen Wallace, the head of the Afghanistan Task Force at CIDA, "to reach down locally."[18] Yet there is a gap, an obvious and important gap, in Canada's assistance program in the south. CIDA simply does not do "quick impact reconstruction," projects that are visible and are likely to have an impact on Afghan "hearts and minds." It does not help villagers to dig a well or repair a road or build a school. These kinds of projects are not within its mandate, CIDA officials insist. They are correct, but that still leaves a growing gap. The military has repeatedly said that it cannot succeed without an effective reconstruction program, one that has a quick and visible impact on the lives of Afghans in the south. CIDA insists that it does development work, not reconstruction projects, and needs secure conditions before it can do development.

There is merit to the argument that development needs security, but the reflexively repeated distinction between "development" and "reconstruction" is invisible to Afghans who are struggling to feed their families and survive. When Bill Graham, then the minister of defence, visited Kandahar in the fall of 2005, the Governor of Kandahar and other local leaders urged Canada to fund projects in Kandahar—vocational training schools, cement factories, agricultural processing plants, hospitals—that would improve the quality of life for Afghans and provide an attractive alternative to the promises of the Taliban.

It is no surprise that the military is frustrated. They complain that there is "no Canadian flag" on funding for Afghanistan, that Afghans cannot see what "we" are doing. Brigadier General David Fraser, the feisty commander of Task Force Afghanistan in the south during

Operation Medusa, was scathing in his criticism of Canadian development assistance. He distinguished among projects that can be accomplished in weeks, months, years, and generations. He understood that CIDA was investing in the future, in projects that would show results in generations, but he was facing a challenge in 2006. The Taliban were shooting at his men. He asked CIDA, with some frustration, "Where is your tool kit, your procedures, to get us from here to fifteen years from now?" If the Taliban were not kept at bay, he insisted, women and girls would not be in school fifteen years from now no matter how much long-term funding CIDA provided. "We support microfinance," he said with some bitterness, "but we do not support microdevelopment. Why not? CIDA only delivers at the long-term end of the spectrum. And it is the military that is picking up the slack. CIDA has to move into the twenty-first century!"[19]

British General David Richards, the commander of ISAF in 2006, agreed. He complained that it had taken months for Canada to deliver assistance in some parts of the Panjwai district after the heavy fighting in Operation Medusa. "The Canadian commander here had to search around for money to do the things he wanted to do," said General Richards. "Will we meet the race against time? ... We're on track to do it. But it's a very important issue."[20] He argued that Canada needed to increase the speed of its assistance by giving more money to military commanders for quick projects.

The military's complaint is borne out on the ground. In the poorest areas, in the remote villages and refugee camps in Kandahar, people have not seen a foreigner or received any food or other assistance.[21] Southern Afghanistan receives proportionally less food aid than the rest of Afghanistan and the system to distribute food is woefully inadequate. CIDA contributes to the World Food Program, which does not participate directly in the distribution of food. It is the Afghan government and the Provincial Disaster Management Committee that are responsible for distributing food, and they turn to the International Committee of the Red Cross and the Afghan Red Crescent Society

(ARCS). ARCS is doing the best it can, but its capacity is limited and it relies on volunteers to reach remote areas; these volunteers themselves depend on irregular bus services because of the insecurity of the roads. Provincial officials estimate that almost seventy percent of food aid is diverted before it reaches those who need it most.

In a review of food aid, the Senlis Council, a non-governmental organization, was bitterly critical—somewhat unfairly—of CIDA. Only a small number of the people dislocated by the fighting are receiving the food they need. Their survey found that eighty percent of Afghans in the south worry about feeding their families.[22] The World Food Program dissented strongly. CIDA is its largest donor, they asserted, and doing its best. It is the absence of security on the roads that prevents the trucks from reaching people in need. What is true is that Canada's participation in this long chain is several times removed from people who are displaced, dislocated by fighting, and hungry. Its aid is invisible to those who need it most, who are poorest and most desperate. It is precisely these angry and embittered people who become ready recruits for the Taliban.

CIDA and Defence officials see their challenges and responsibilities very differently. In meetings with Defence and Foreign Affairs, CIDA officials insist that their responsibility is to put an "Afghan face," not a Canadian flag, on development assistance. The Afghan minister responsible for reconstruction agrees with CIDA. "Canadian aid is channelled through the government budget. Our highest priority," insisted the minister of rural rehabilitation and development, Mohammed Ehsan Zia, "is to rebuild the institutions of the state. Parallel programming without the face of the Afghan government is dysfunctional. It is not what we want."[23] Afghanistan's leaders understand how important it is that their people see their own government helping. CIDA's programming reflects that priority.

General Hillier minimized the differences between the military and CIDA, and insisted that the relationship has improved significantly in 2007. "The beginning was hard," he said, "but things are much better in Ottawa than they used to be. We do development—through our quick-impact projects—and CIDA does development too."[24] His commanders in the field are much less charitable. They react with incomprehension, at times bordering on rage, to CIDA's dismissal of the short-term projects designed to win hearts and minds in southern Afghanistan—the projects the military so badly want—as "force protection." The label infuriates Canada's top soldiers, as does CIDA's argument that these kinds of projects are properly the responsibility of the military.

Not enough CIDA funding, military commanders complain, is going directly or indirectly, to the south of Afghanistan, where they are fighting a deadly insurgency. CIDA officials respond that the amount of money being programmed in the south tripled in 2006; in 2007, almost a third of Canadian aid would be going to the south. Not enough, the military answers, to meet the needs of those in the south who are most likely to join the Taliban.

The soldiers who are fighting the insurgency in the southern provinces understand the urgency of helping people today, of meeting their needs now, to separate them from the Taliban and to deny the Taliban what they need to operate effectively. "When I was commanding our forces in the south," Brigadier General David Fraser said with some asperity, "I was the biggest warlord in the south. I had the guns and I had the money. When an Afghan leader wanted something done, I listened and I got it done. That's what makes the difference in an insurgency."[25] The Senlis Council shared this sense of urgency. It recommended that CIDA be relieved of its responsibility for Kandahar and that a special envoy be appointed to coordinate Canada's development, diplomatic, military, and civilian volunteer resources in the south.[26]

There is more than a tinge of rivalry here, of institutional leaders working at cross-purposes, with different cultures, different procedures, and different time horizons. Underneath these departmental rivalries and the difficulty of integrating programming, however, are serious differences. There is no way of squaring this circle. Unless the Afghan state develops properly, controls corruption and brutality, and builds functioning institutions, people will not support the government. Yet that is a project of decades and progress comes in very small steps. "It's a fact that there are corrupt practices," Mohammed Ehsan Zia acknowledged, "that this government has inherited from a failed state. We have suffered from a failed state for thirty years. We are moving to correct it. But it will take time."[27]

Controlling corruption is not only a long-term necessity for a viable Afghan state, but it is also an immediate, short-term objective in the provinces in the south and the east, where the insurgency is growing. If tribal elders see only a corrupt government, with a brutal police force, it is easy to understand why joining the Taliban becomes an acceptable, even attractive, option. General Hillier expressed his deep concern about governance in Afghanistan. "CIDA delivers development. We deliver security and reconstruction. Who delivers governance? We don't have a toolkit for governance. My great concern is that we have not built the governance that Afghanistan needs, the efficient, effective functioning ministries. Sometimes I think that the Afghan government is Karzai with a cell phone. Where is the UN in all of this? The failure to build governance is our feet of clay."[28]

There are no obvious answers, no easy formulas to settle what Canadian aid should look like and where it should go. "There is a legitimate discussion," said a senior CIDA official, "about how much development assistance should have a Canadian flag and how much should have an Afghan flag. We have to find the right balance."[29] The balance Canada had in 2006 was clearly not right. At the end of the year, CIDA began the funding of some "quick impact" projects in Kandahar, but not quickly enough and not with enough impact to satisfy the military. The military now runs a small Civil-Military Cooperation (CIMIC) program, but more and more, the dispute between CIDA and the Canadian Forces is shifting the burden of responsibility for reconstruction to the military. As General Dan McNeill, the commander of

ISAF, put it with a hint of steel in his voice: "NATO forces are not about development. They are about reconstruction. In Afghanistan, it is reconstruction that is pulling development forward."[30]

wouldn't you need both

The Three *D*s in Action:
The Provincial Reconstruction Team in Kandahar

The Provincial Reconstruction Team (PRT) that Canada sent to Kandahar in 2006 was a critical test of the Three *D*s, an example of the "whole of government" approach working together in "a single integrated battle space." The PRT brought together development officers, military personnel, civilian police officers, correctional services staff, and diplomats in a single unit in Kandahar to develop, monitor, and focus Canadian strategy in southern Afghanistan. Their job is reconstruction.

The PRT has a dedicated "force protection" team that allows military officers to move around "outside the wire," in armoured convoys. It has twelve combat engineers who manage the PRT's reconstruction projects to win local support. "We write up a contract [with a village council] on a field message pad," said Major Steve Murray, deputy PRT commander in 2006, "and do it so it's enforceable."[31] The team found an Afghan contractor and began repairs on dilapidated Afghan police stations, started building new stations, and worked on improving checkpoints in the city. It bought winter jackets made by war widows for children in the local orphanage and blankets made by imprisoned Afghan women. The PRT also hired a local contractor, who in turn hired two hundred unemployed, fighting-age young men to clean the city streets and pick up the garbage. While they were working, Murray explained, they were less likely to support the Taliban. The pace of the PRT is accelerating as the team works together. In the first half of 2007, Lieutenant Colonel Bob Chamberlain asserted, the projects planned or completed were double those of the previous year.[32]

Where does the PRT get the money to fund these projects? "I asked my commanding officer for the money," explained a senior Canadian officer, "and he gave me more money than I needed. I didn't have people to program and manage all the money that I had to spend." The funding goes directly from Canadian soldiers to Afghans. It bypasses the Afghan government and is wrapped in the Canadian flag. "One step at a time," said Captain Bob Wheeler, "one village at a time."[33] Villagers come to know the face of Canada through the officers who provide the funding that helps them dig wells and repair houses.

"The military is picking up the slack and doing the work," said a senior military officer, "and CIDA hates it."[34] As Rick Hillier famously said, "There is a Three *D* policy and the military does all three of the *D*s." Not so, retorts CIDA, with some testiness. "We made $2 million available to the Canadian Forces which they were unable to program." CIDA contributes five million dollars to the operations of the PRT. It has three officers that review and monitor the activities of its partners in Kandahar, and it plans to increase that number. "They are our spotters on the ground," a CIDA official explained. "They help us identify the programming we need to do." "Yeah," replied a senior military officer, "but CIDA officials don't go outside the wire. They have no additional [life or disability] insurance, so their field officers can't get out in the field." At times, the military can barely conceal its impatience with Foreign Affairs and CIDA. "I find it criminal," said a senior officer, "that only forty-four percent of last year's development budget for Afghanistan was spent. Damn it! What we really need to do is create employment now. Let's build a f— school or clinic, as long as we create jobs for Afghans. We need to change CIDA's rules. Many Afghans can't even read, much less write a business plan. Authority to spend the money in the field is our biggest issue."[35]

Canadian officials on the ground in Kandahar are all well intentioned and work hard to smooth out the wrinkles among their departments. But the differences in culture, objectives, and style grow stronger the farther one is from Kandahar and the closer one gets to Ottawa. "We knew we had a big problem with the police in Kandahar," said a senior military officer. "We pulled together everybody in the

PRT and we settled it in five minutes. We pitched the idea to Ottawa of a new police training academy in Kandahar that would focus on middle level police officers." RCMP Superintendent Dave Fudge, the senior civilian police officer in the PRT, waited over six months to get approval from Ottawa.[36] The merits of this proposal were crystal clear to the PRT in Kandahar, but, at home, the RCMP and the Department of Foreign Affairs were going through procedures. Their pace—and CIDA's—is still far too slow to keep up with events on the ground. Ottawa is light-years away from Kandahar.

The military is not alone. Certain officials at Foreign Affairs are scathing in their criticism of what they see as CIDA's long-standing unwillingness to share information, to collaborate, and to work as part of a team. The Department of Foreign Affairs, in an effort to improve coordination of Canadian policy in Afghanistan, submitted a strategy document on behalf of all three departments—Defence, Foreign Affairs, and CIDA—which Cabinet approved in 2002. But as an official from Foreign Affairs said with some frustration, "It was put on the shelf. It had no afterlife."[37] A small task force of only four officers within Foreign Affairs then monitored policy.

Foreign Affairs tried again in 2005. The deputy minister chaired the Committee of Deputies to monitor Canada's performance in Afghanistan and make its policy coherent. "In the beginning," said a knowledgeable member of Foreign Affairs, "CIDA did not contribute in any meaningful way to the development of an integrated strategy in Afghanistan. CIDA was hopeless in bringing to the table what they were accomplishing on the ground. They couldn't provide information about their programming. Only in 2006 did this change. For a long time CIDA fought the military's program of reconstruction. CIDA has little experience in quick impact programs. Quick is an oxymoron to CIDA."[38]

The criticism does not stop with officials. In its report on Canada's development assistance in Africa that it released in February 2007, the Senate Foreign Affairs Committee described CIDA as "ineffective, costly, and overly bureaucratic." Over eighty percent of CIDA's employees work in Ottawa and staffers in the field, the committee found, have almost no authority to make decisions and allocate funding. This is precisely the complaint that military leaders have been making. The committee's frustration was palpable. It recommended that CIDA either be drastically changed or abolished and that its staff and authority be transferred to Foreign Affairs.[39]

"The Three D policy makes no sense if you haven't thought through how you do it on the ground," said a senior Canadian official.[40] A military officer stationed in Kabul was even more scathing. "Three D was never anything more than Chris Alexander [Canada's first ambassador in Kabul] and General Andrew Leslie tearing around town in a jeep."[41] The "whole of government" approach requires Canadian soldiers to understand the culture of other Canadian agencies that are working in the field—Foreign Affairs, CIDA, the Royal Canadian Mounted Police, who are training Afghan policemen, as well as a large number of non-governmental organizations. To say that the cultures of Foreign Affairs and the Canadian Forces are different is to put it mildly. CIDA personnel have traditionally kept their distance from both, and non-governmental organizations delivering humanitarian assistance and working on development do not want their independence and impartiality compromised by an association with the military.

Working together in practice is not easy. "The greatest problem," said an officer who has just returned from Afghanistan, "is one of ignorance. None of the players fully understand who the other participants are; what they do; their mandates, or how they actually operate." This is a Canadian military officer talking about knowledge of other Canadian—not Afghan—institutions. "Other government departments and civilian agencies," he continued, "are normally not accustomed to military directness or command structures. In addition, ironically, they are most often nowhere near as flexible, more bureaucratic and more risk averse than the military."[42] Timelines, procedures for approval, and organizational styles are all different, and people from one institution do not know or understand the procedures of another. Canadians working in Afghanistan—and likely elsewhere—are far removed from the ideal of the Three *D*s in an integrated space.

These institutional rivalries are lamentable. They have serious consequences for Canada's performance on the ground. But they should not mask the underlying contradictions. Counterinsurgency, development, and peace are not always mutually reinforcing objectives. Each has its own requirements, its own imperatives, and its own dynamics. Ask a CIDA official and a military officer working in the PRT in Kandahar about their priorities and the differences will be obvious. Achieving more of one may mean achieving considerably less of another.

More than two years after Canada's most important institutions began working together in Kandahar in the midst of a growing insurgency, they still differ in their interpretation of Canada's priorities and in their capacity to move forward together. The military, which gives priority to containing the insurgency in the south, wants significant funds to go to the short-term projects that will produce visible quick wins and legitimate the presence of foreign soldiers. It wants reconstruction.

CIDA, meanwhile, gives priority to building the capacity of the state, to strengthening the Afghan ministries that deal with social, economic, legal, and policing issues. It is trying to strengthen and to deepen the state, to push the state down into the Afghan provinces. This disagreement about priorities among Canada's institutions is still going on. "The PRT," ruefully observed a CIDA official in Ottawa, "is a concept in motion."[43]

The Third *D*: Diplomacy

Foreign Affairs, the third in the triad, does not escape criticism from its other two "partners." "By the time the Department makes a decision in Ottawa," a senior military commander complained, "the opportunity has gone by. The Department moves at a glacial pace." Prime Minister Martin thought much the same. "Foreign Affairs is debilitated," he said. One of his officials elaborated. "There has been an unbelievable erosion of the policy capacity of Foreign Affairs." A senior leader at CIDA added that Foreign Affairs has no experience in team building. "It's not in their DNA. They're articulate critics," he concluded, "not operational team builders."

This is a sad indictment of a once-great institution. How and why has Foreign Affairs—at one time home to the cream of the federal civil service—become a shadow of its former self? Foreign Affairs no longer has the ability or even the willingness to challenge Defence on the big policy issues. Defence made the strongest contribution, Prime Minister Martin acknowledged, to the International Policy Statement. It would have been unthinkable, even a decade ago, that Defence would be the leading edge of a policy debate on international issues.

Part of the explanation for the weakness of Foreign Affairs was the recurrent budget-cutting in the 1990s. "The financial challenges within the department," said a former deputy minister in Foreign Affairs, "are huge."[44] More to the point, government after government have refused to fund civilian benefits for officials who are sent to Afghanistan. "National Defence," says an embittered Foreign Affairs official, "provides tax-free benefits for its soldiers. We have not been able to provide any funding package for our civilians—insurance, rest and recreation—who go to Afghanistan. The government refuses to recognize the concept of 'war zones' for civilians. Kandahar is a war zone. We are putting our civilians into a war zone. Civilians working with the U.S. and Dutch governments get danger pay. Not us, even though we say over and over again that this war cannot be won by the military alone."[45] Only in the spring of 2007 were special arrangements made for Foreign Affairs officers who work in danger zones. Even though the Harper government extended the military mission in Kandahar until 2009, no long-term funding had been authorized by mid-2007 for the Global Peace and Security Fund in Foreign Affairs— the fund that supports some of the most important "quick impact" activities in southern Afghanistan. `Stupid!`

There is also an imbalance in the face of government that Canadians see and the voices they hear. Military leaders are free to talk to the public, and Canadian journalists are embedded with the military in Kandahar. Yet officials from Foreign Affairs—and CIDA—under orders from Prime Minister Harper's office, are forbidden to talk to the public. These constraints undoubtedly deepen the demoralization within Foreign Affairs.

Still, Foreign Affairs tends to manage rather than to lead, as one of Prime Minister Martin's political staff concluded. "Steady state stagnation," said another. The weakness of Foreign Affairs is serious, for it no longer provides a strong counterweight to the Department of National Defence. The absence of strong, focused institutions with critical and independent voices deprives the government of advice it needs when it has to make decisions about committing its forces to war. In 2006, the deputy minister of foreign affairs, Peter Harder, pushed hard to establish a more robust task force that would span the important government ministries and institutions—National Defence, Foreign Affairs, CIDA, the RCMP, Corrections Canada—that could contribute to the reconstruction effort in Afghanistan. The assistant deputy ministers agreed, but when their superiors, the deputy ministers, met, the response was, as a member of the Department said, "No bloody way!" Senior officials in Foreign Affairs were angered by the lack of a strong mandate from Prime Minister Martin to create an integrated task force that would assemble the very best Canadian experts. Frustrated, Foreign Affairs expanded its task force on Afghanistan from four to twelve officials.

Only in 2007 was an experienced senior official, David Mulroney, moved back to Foreign Affairs to coordinate policy on Afghanistan across all the departments. Mulroney sent a veteran diplomat to Kandahar, a "senior civilian coordinator," to push forward the integration of Canada's programs in the south. And all major changes in policy—including military policy—now go through the Afghan Task Force, which Mulroney heads. The not-so-hidden agenda was to wrest control of policy in Afghanistan back from the military and return it to the civilians. "At last," said a retired veteran, "someone has the authority to crack some eggs in order to make this omelette."[46]

ALL GOVERNMENTS have some rivalry among their institutions, but the endless bickering and the institutional quarrels that have hobbled Canada's capacity to make a difference abroad are of a different order of magnitude. Few solid bridges span the three most important departments. Senior officials rarely move back and forth among CIDA, Foreign Affairs, and Defence. Because they don't travel across these departments, it is harder to understand the others' cultures, to bridge the solitudes between Venus and Mars, to break down the language barriers that exist between the departments, and to cross-pollinate their thinking. In a healthy democracy, civilians know enough to challenge the military, especially when the military gives advice on the political consequences of military options and the military understands the diplomatic and political consequences of their action on the ground. Those responsible for development assistance recognize that in a war zone, reconstruction matters as well as development. Each is literate about the concerns of the others. These kinds of shared understandings, an ability to think outside an institutional box, are not yet what they need to be in Canada.

Going to Kandahar has given Canadians an opportunity to take a hard look at themselves. The failure of our most important institutions to work closely together is easy to see. Britain puts its money for all three departments in a single "crisis pool" for each mission and all three departments compete for funding. The result is much more tightly integrated programming. Holland sent its three ministers—Development, Foreign Affairs, and Defence—together on a mission to Oruzgan province in Afghanistan in 2006 to identify the gaps in their programs and work together to plug the holes. In the dying days of the Martin government, there was discussion of that kind of visit, but Canada's three ministers have yet to travel together on a shared mission to Kandahar. On the contrary, the institutional bickering in Canada continues.

SIXTEEN

CANADA IN KANDAHAR: MAKING CHOICES

J ohn Manley stepped off the plane in Kabul airport on May 13, 2007, after a long trip from Ottawa. A short two months after the Taliban had been ousted, Foreign Minister Manley had flown to Kabul from Islamabad to meet with newly installed President Karzai. After a week in Afghanistan, far longer than his eight-hour visit five years earlier, Manley was asked: "What's changed? How is Afghanistan different from what it was five years ago?"

"You can see the differences," he answered. "When I first came to Kabul, I saw nothing but destroyed buildings, rubble on the streets, cratered roads. The city was in ruins. Now the streets are bustling with people, the markets are humming and there are new hotels, new schools, girls going to school, and construction everywhere. In 2002," he continued, "I visited the CARE project for widows and orphans, one of the few projects that continued to run under the Taliban. Today, the field is crowded with non-governmental organizations that are working with the Afghan government to provide education and social services."[1]

"Would you have done anything differently in 2002," Manley was asked, "if you could go back and do it over? Would you still send the Canadian Forces to Afghanistan?" Manley thought back to his visit to Kabul five years earlier. Since then, the unrelenting violence in Iraq has coloured perceptions about the insurgency in Afghanistan. But the conditions that led to "regime change" in Afghanistan in 2001 were very different.   *Yes to go*

The United Nations had sanctioned the invasion of Afghanistan as a just war. Al-Qaeda had planned the attack on the United States in sheltered space provided by the Taliban. The United Nations approved the military operation by the United States in September 2001; in early October, NATO, for the first time in its history, invoked the obligation of all members of the alliance to come to the assistance of a member state that had been attacked; and the United Nations Security Council authorized the International Security Assistance Force (ISAF) on December 20, 2001. In a rare moment of global convergence, international law and international institutions sanctioned military action.

The United States also had the approval of its allies and friends. Riding a wave of sympathy after 9-11, Washington received widespread political support for the invasion of Afghanistan. Governments around the world offered their help, both before the invasion and after the Taliban were overthrown. Thirty-seven countries contributed to the military mission and sixty countries have helped with development and reconstruction. The Afghan mission was quintessentially multilateral and all the necessary pieces were in place for effective post-war reconstruction. Yet more than four years later, the Canadian Forces were fighting a resurgent Taliban in the south in an escalating insurgency.

What went wrong? Ignorance, arrogance, and ordnance.[2]

When Canada first sent its forces to Kandahar with the expectation that they would be "early in, early out," the government, like many others, did not understand how badly the years of warfare had damaged the physical and social infrastructure in Afghanistan. The new government in Kabul, unlike most of its predecessors, had only a small representation of Pashtuns. Unless Hamid Karzai's government could provide security and basic services, and unless it could attract significant Pashtun support and participation, the Taliban would be able to draw again on the sympathy and support of the Pashtuns in the

what went wrong?

south. The challenges facing the new government were enormous. Karzai's fragile administration needed protection from warlords like Marshal Fahim Khan, with his seventy thousand–strong militia, who wanted to overthrow the new, weak government. ISAF was limited by UN resolutions to "Kabul and its environs," an area of about 3,600 square kilometres, for nearly two years.[3] President Karzai was dependent in the early years on the warlords and their militias; some of the warlords with private armies that benefited from the trade in opium were members of his new government. The writ of Karzai's government did not extend beyond the capital, and the international forces spoke about Karzai as the "Mayor of Kabul." There was no national army or police, nor a functioning state to referee the struggle among the ethnic groups and the tribes.

Once Osama bin Laden had disappeared, once he was "on the run," the Americans lost interest in the long, difficult, and painstaking process of reconstruction in Afghanistan. Within a year, their attention was badly distracted by their planning for the invasion of Iraq and they looked to hand off responsibility for Afghanistan to others. But the Taliban were not gone. They had retreated to the mountains and over the seamless frontier with Pakistan, which they treated as their own, as part of Pashtunistan. They were regrouping, reorganizing, refinancing, and training new recruits. It became far easier to recruit after the United States invaded Iraq, at long last fulfilling Osama bin Laden's fantasy. It was only a matter of time until the Taliban emerged again to attack NATO forces in the south.

Once again, money, guns, ammunition, and recruits—ordnance—began to flow through Pakistan, at first a trickle, and then a deluge. The Taliban could again draw on allies in the tribal areas along the border and, more and more, on people who were tired of the fighting, tired of the insecurity, tired of the violence, and infuriated by the corruption of the government in Kabul. When Canadian forces returned to Kandahar for the second time, in 2006, they inherited a legacy of ignorance, arrogance, and ordnance. The three are an explosive mixture, fertile ground for an insurgency.

america lost interest

Today, the insurgency in southern Afghanistan is growing and the cycle of violence is spreading beyond the south and encroaching on the capital. "The noose around Kabul," said one long-time resident, "is tightening. The roads in and out of the city are no longer secure."[4]

The signs are ominous. In 2006, suicide bombings more than quintupled, from 27 a year earlier to 139; roadside explosions more than doubled from 783 to 1,677; and direct attacks nearly tripled from 1,558 to 4,552. Thirty-six Canadian soldiers and one diplomat died that year, and untold numbers of Afghan civilians, caught in the growing conflict, were killed. In the first half of 2007, another 22 Canadian soldiers were killed. Although the Taliban—disrupted by ISAF attacks that decapitated their leadership—were unable to launch their long-expected "spring offensive," they attacked more widely in much smaller groups. "[It has] gotten worse from the standpoint that the types of attacks the Taliban have used have changed dramatically. They're no longer meeting us on the battlefield, so to speak," said Brigadier General Tim Grant, then the commander of the Canadian Forces in ISAF. "So the use of suicide bombers and roadside bombs has increased dramatically since last year."[5]

As the insurgency spreads, the number of Afghans killed in the fighting by NATO forces is rising. Afghans are losing trust in their government because of the escalating violence, and they are losing trust in the international community because of the slow pace of reconstruction. There are important exceptions to this generally downward trend. The economy is growing, even though it is not yet generating significant employment; access to health care and basic needs is much better, except in the south; infant mortality is dropping, and the lives of women have improved significantly, although less so in the south.[6] These are real achievements, but they are not enough. A report by the Senate Committee on Defence was gloomy. "The Taliban have time and geography on their side,"[7] they concluded.

Security in the southern provinces, where the Canadian Forces are deployed, is now much worse than it was in 2001, immediately after the Taliban were ousted. Insurgents are taking advantage of a weak government, of a corrupt police force, and of a poppy eradication program that has eradicated political support for the government but failed to stop poppy-growing. Makeshift refugee camps now dot the province of Kandahar, as tens of thousands flee the fighting and the bombardments. Many people are not getting enough food, enough water, or enough medicine.[8] Poor, dissatisfied, and dislocated villagers and townspeople become the foot soldiers of the Taliban.

Yet there is resistance to the Taliban, even in the Pashtun south. After the Taliban had consolidated power in Afghanistan, their stringent Islamic orthodoxy antagonized many Pashtun who lived comfortably with both *sharia*—codified Islamic law—and *Pashtunwali*—the unwritten, oral customary law that has governed the Pashtun for centuries. The zealotry of the Taliban challenged this unwritten tribal code and alienated many of their young supporters, as well as the tribal elders. Even today, an overwhelming majority of the Pashtun in Afghanistan do not want the Taliban to return. Public opinion polls are notoriously unreliable, particularly in the south, but they are one barometer of Afghan opinion. One survey found that nearly half of those surveyed in the south believed that ISAF would be unable to "defeat" the Taliban.[9] Another poll, completed a few months earlier, just after the intense fighting in the south in 2006, showed that an overwhelming majority of Afghans—ninety-two percent—had a negative opinion of the Taliban, and eighty-six percent thought that the overthrow of the Taliban was a good thing for their country.[10] These results are not inconsistent. Afghans in the south do not want the Taliban to return but are losing confidence in the international forces. In Terin Kowt, in southern Afghanistan, Mullah Maulwai Harmdullah appealed to NATO forces at the end of his blessing of a newly built trade school. "We're surrounded by Taliban," Harmdullah said. "We need more security." The town's mayor, Mohamed Kabir, pleaded for special protection for the girls' school in the town, which is now providing an education for girls for the first time in years. "On the other side of the river, there's a lot of difficulties there," he added.[11]

Afghanistan is not Iraq. While millions have fled Iraq to seek refuge in neighbouring countries, millions of Afghans have come home. Kabul has doubled or tripled in size—no one knows for sure—in the last five years. "We have been with the Taliban," said a Pashtun elder, "and have seen their cruelty. People don't want them back."[12] When Afghans turn to the Taliban, they do so largely out of disgust with the behaviour of the government they have or despair about what they do not have.

"When you look back now, would you have sent the Canadian Forces to Afghanistan," Manley was asked again. "Yes," he answered without hesitation, "but we would have had a plan to stabilize Afghanistan. Now we know that there was no effective governance."[13]

Going to War

The most difficult decision any government in Ottawa makes, the one most fraught with responsibility, is to send its young people to war. This decision is so difficult, so grave and fearsome, because soldiers kill and are killed. Those kinds of decisions must be made with the utmost care, with the best information and superb judgment. Yet it is common in history that leaders do not foresee the consequences of their decisions. Prime Minister Chrétien's government, John Manley explained, did not understand the scope of the challenge it faced in Afghanistan.[14] When Prime Minister Martin approved the deployment of troops to Kandahar, a mission he knew to be dangerous, he did not expect war. Nor did the then chief of the defence staff, who resigned in 2008. "Nobody predicted the resurgence of the Taliban," General Rick Hillier said. "It came as a surprise."[15] Canada's NATO allies fared no better. John Reid, the British secretary of defence when British forces moved into Helmand, said at the time that he would be happy if British forces completed their mission "without a shot being fired."[16] Canada and Britain slid into a war in southern Afghanistan that they did not expect.

Even after it became apparent that Canada was at war, political leaders deliberately denied the obvious. Although casualties were escalating in Kandahar, members of Harper's Cabinet were forbidden to use the word *war*. Only in September 2006 did Prime Minister Harper finally acknowledge that Canada was fighting a war in Afghanistan.[17]

That Canada slid into this war does not make the war either unjust or wrong. "There's no doubt about it," argued Bill Graham. "We've watched this mission evolve differently from when we got into it. But I don't think the moral underpinning is any different."[18] What is necessary is a clear understanding of the changing nature of war in the twenty-first century and the choices ahead. Most important, any government owes its citizens a clear, compelling, and honest explanation of why its soldiers are fighting and dying.

Canada is fighting in Afghanistan because an Afghan government supported those who planned and executed an attack against the World Trade Center and the Pentagon. That the Taliban mistreated women and violated their basic rights in ways that are deeply repugnant to many around the world was not material to the decision. The Taliban stoned women to death for years while most of the world looked the other way. Afghanistan drew attention only after September 11, when the world stood in solidarity with the United States, Canada's closest ally and friend. The Taliban that supported al-Qaeda was removed by force very quickly, and Canada sent its troops to Kandahar in 2002 to stabilize a peace, to help the Afghan people recover, not to fight a war.

But war found Canada. The Canadian Forces are fighting to prevent the Taliban from retaking Kandahar to use as a launching pad for a broader offensive against the Karzai government. General Rick Hillier put it bluntly: "The Taliban wants to impose their extreme views on Afghans and aided and abetted by al-Qaeda, they are prepared to use force to regain power."[19] Stripped of all the rhetoric, Canada's soldiers are at war to prevent the re-establishment of a Taliban government in Afghanistan. Canada continues to fight in Kandahar because the Government of Afghanistan asks for its continued presence and support.

But the burden of the fighting is not distributed fairly. This mission is the first important "out-of-area" operation for NATO and it is not a happy story. Canada, together with Germany, persuaded NATO to become engaged in Afghanistan in 2003. It is Canada, along with Britain and the United States, which is now on the front lines of this war against the Taliban. Ottawa has committed to stay in Afghanistan until 2011, as have the British. The Dutch are committed only to 2010.

Other NATO allies are in Afghanistan, but they are not fighting. Their troops are not in the south and east, where the insurgency is, and they refuse to allow their troops to move to where the battle is. Some NATO members have refused to let their forces in Afghanistan move south, even when NATO commanders badly needed them in the field. The caveats that the French and the Germans have placed around their forces are so restrictive that, for all intents and purposes, their forces do not fight. Canada and the United States have asked again and again for these restrictions to be lifted.

At every NATO meeting, then-Foreign Minister Peter MacKay urged NATO members to allow their forces to move south when they are needed. "We want to see other countries with greater capacity come into the south," he argued, "whether it is with more troop deployments, more training, more equipment."[20] At the NATO summit in Riga in November 2006, members "softened" restrictions on the movement of their forces in an emergency.[21] The commander of ISAF would decide when a situation was *in extremis*.[22]

General Ray Henault, formerly chief of the defence staff in Canada and now chair of the Military Committee in NATO, was optimistic that these changes would make a difference. "There was strong recognition at Riga of the need to commit forces in the event of an *in extremis* situation. Many nations now allow their forces to be moved from one region of Afghanistan to another. I can personally attest to these commitments since I was privy to the discussions where these commitments were made."[23] Henault added that half the caveats have been reduced, especially those that restrict the movement of forces. "There is now much better burden sharing," he insisted, "within the alliance."

His colleagues are far less sanguine. General Hillier dismissed the changes as cosmetic. "Pragmatically *in extremis* means absolutely nothing," he said. "The plans, the rotary wing aircraft, and the troops are not available when we need them."[24] General Dan McNeill, the commander of ISAF in 2007, was also not impressed. "*In extremis* doesn't mean a hell of a lot. I have to negotiate with NATO contributors. The Italians, the Spanish, and the Portuguese have been helpful. The Germans have not." McNeill worried openly about NATO's capacity to meet the challenge in Afghanistan. "We see the signs of political failure," he said, "the restrictive caveats, the failure to source to force [to provide the numbers of troops that countries promised], even to the agreed-upon levels, and the failure to agree on what the problem is. It is difficult to believe, but the Germans deny that there is an insurgency here. They insist that the problem is only reconstruction."[25]

Canadian officials who have watched NATO's performance with chagrin mutter under their breath that it is not only Afghanistan's future that is at stake, but the future of NATO as well. The capacity of NATO to act as an alliance is on trial, said a senior diplomat, and it is not doing very well. "Afghanistan is a test," he said, "of whether NATO has any relevance at all to the security challenges of the next generation."[26]

The war Canada's soldiers are fighting in Kandahar is not an anomaly. "The here and now of Afghanistan, Iraq, and dozens of lower-profile conflicts," writes James Travers, "make those titanic struggles [on the last century's industrialized battlefields] as much a relic of the past as the rotary telephone."[27] Much about war will look very different: its purposes and strategies, the weapons, the terrain, and its length. Insurgents will explode bombs, and soldiers, while they are fighting, will help villagers to build schools and clinics. They will not try to defeat the insurgents but to contain them, to narrow their zones of operation and restrict their ability to harass. There will be no decisive military victories. Victory will go to those with strategic patience and endurance.

It is this kind of war that will shape the future. The war in Afghanistan is a foretaste. It is to this kind of war that Canada will be summoned by its allies and by international institutions. In this kind of war—in Kandahar, and elsewhere when the war in Afghanistan is a distant memory—Canada has choices.

Canada had to decide very quickly whether it would stay in Kandahar after 2009 and, if it chose to stay, what kind of contribution it would make to Afghanistan. The genius of insurgency, this book has argued, is to create difficult if not impossible choices. "Effective coun- terinsurgency operations are not rocket science ... they are actually much harder than that," a former Canadian Forces officer said ruefully. General Rick Hillier spoke bluntly about the difficult challenges and the long timeline before the results would be clear. "If this were easy," he said, "it would have been done a long time ago. We face an enor- mous challenge. President Karzai told me that Afghanistan is a country in a hurry. 'We need to do in four or five years,' he said, 'what you did in several hundred.' Afghanistan will not be rebuilt in a year, or two, or five. It's going to take a long, long time. It's going to take a generation or more."[28] Canada found itself approaching a crossroads where there were no good choices, only choices that were least bad. Damned if you do, damned if you don't ...

In this long struggle, Canada had at least three broad options. Which of these three choices Canada made depended in part on factors that were largely beyond Canada's control. Some the Government of Afghanistan could control. Would the performance of the Afghan government improve as it gained experience and maturity? "The people ... at the provincial and local level [in government]," said Sarah Chayes, a journalist who now lives in Kandahar and runs a successful cooperative, "are just raping the country.... You cannot get any administrative task performed without coughing up money.... It is a terrible indictment of the post-Taliban experiment in nation building that we are unable to put up a government that has a minimum of respect for its citizens."[29] Would the Afghan National Police—currently the most hated institution within the Afghan government—become less brutal and less corrupt? Did President Karzai have enough political capital to force that kind of change? Was he willing to use the political capital he had to reform the police and rein in the warlords? Canada's generals worry actively about the effectiveness of Afghanistan's political institutions.

The kind of state outsiders are trying to help build would also be telling. CIDA officials speak about a "strong" state, an "effective and efficient government," a "state that reaches down from the national level to the provinces and districts." This is not a state that many Afghans would recognize, especially those who live in the south and have traditionally kept the state at a distance. "There has never been a discussion," said Chris Eaton, a Canadian who works with the Aga Khan Foundation in Afghanistan, "of what kind of state Afghans want, of what kind of state suits Afghan society."[30] The Afghan state has never reached down into the districts and villages. It has kept its distance, stood apart, and intervened only to mediate disputes among tribal leaders that were spinning out of control. When it intervened inappropriately, it provoked violence and conflict. "I was safe on my long walk across Afghanistan," said Rory Stewart, author of a brilliant chronicle of the Afghan countryside, "because I was handed from village to village. Afghanistan is a country of villages. It does not want or need a 'modern' western state. Governance has to fit the society."[31] It is no accident that the sixteen thousand community development councils enabled by the Ministry of Reconstruction and Rural Development have taken root in Afghanistan. This kind of "governance" is deeply familiar. Much of what international donors today call "governance" threatens this delicate relationship between tribe and state in southern Afghanistan. Especially in the south, outsiders need a deep appreciation of the subtle balance that fits the Afghan political tradition.

What foreign governments who have come to help the Afghan government do would also matter. Would the United States abandon its pressure to eradicate the cultivation of poppies, which is alienating the Afghan population in the south? An aggressive campaign of aerial spraying—an option that is under discussion in Washington—would doom NATO's mission in southern Afghanistan.

How the government of Pakistan handles the problem of restricting Taliban training camps and the financing and recruitment of Taliban sympathizers within its territory is crucial. Today, Taliban leaders walk openly in the streets of Quetta, the capital of Baluchistan in western Pakistan; the Taliban *shura,* or council, meets regularly in the city, and Mullah Omar's spokesman holds press conferences. Afghan and Pakistani Taliban leaders run training camps along the five-hundred-mile border of the tribal areas from Baluchistan in the south to Bajaur in the north. Pakistan's former minister of the interior, Aftab Khan Sherpao, acknowledged that suicide bombers were being trained in the tribal areas. The religious parties in the frontier areas appear to be supporting the Taliban and so are elements of the Pakistan Intelligence Services (ISI), as they did a decade ago. Some go much farther and charge Pakistan with deliberate instigation of the insurgency. "It's really important that you understand [that] what's happening in southern Afghanistan," said Sarah Chayes with urgency in her voice, "is not so much an insurgency—that is, an indigenous uprising by the locals—but rather ... a kind of invasion by proxy of Afghanistan by Pakistan, using Afghans. Fundamentally, this so-called insurgency is being orchestrated, organized, financed, trained, and equipped across the border in Pakistan."[32] Even if the insurgency did not have official support, the Taliban would have little difficulty in raising funds from the Pashtun and in recruiting young men from the *madrassas* in Pakistan. A safe haven in which they can regroup and organize, and a protected area from which they can launch their insurgent attacks, are of extraordinary value to the Taliban. Insurgencies with this kind of asset are much more difficult to defeat.

Ending the flow of men and money from Pakistan will not be easy. The writ of Pakistan's government does not extend to the Pashtun tribal areas that border Afghanistan, and even if it did, Pakistan has deep suspicions of the intentions of the Afghan government. The intelligence services distrust the government in Kabul and see it as the spearhead of India, supported by the United States. The ISI have also long resented Afghan support for Pashtun and Baluch nationalists inside Pakistan, who have called for an independent or autonomous Baluchistan and Pashtunistan. These issues go to the core of Pakistan's national security.

The safe haven Pakistan gives to the Taliban is not a border problem, isolated from the broader relationship between Pakistan and Afghanistan. For the first time in twenty years, the former prime minister of Pakistan, Shaukat Aziz, asked the three million Afghan refugees living in Pakistan to go home so that refugee camps would no longer provide sanctuary to insurgents. President Karzai responded with a proposal to convene two *jirgas,* assemblies of tribal representatives, from both countries to try to improve relations between them. Pakistan's support for the Taliban can only be addressed as part of a much larger bargain between the two, a bargain that reassures Pakistan as well as Afghanistan about core security needs. "Outsiders" will have to work hard with both governments to open space for that kind of political compromise.

Making Choices

If many of these trends continued to be negative, as they may well be, Canada can do little on its own to reverse the factors that would cripple any prospect of success. And if there was no reasonable chance of containing the insurgency, then it would be impossible to justify to Canadians a continuing military commitment and the loss of the lives of Canadian soldiers. Even if the answers to most of these questions— and others—were encouraging, if some of the important trend lines were positive, the Taliban would still be a continuing threat. But the prospects of their return to power would be diminishing, not increasing. Canada would then face a very difficult decision, with no obvious and easy choice. Damned if you do, damned if you don't ...

Canada could extend its commitment in Kandahar and continue its combat role at the same time as it increases the resources it devotes to quick

Can't actually be eradicated though?

and visible impact projects in the south. This choice would have significant implications for Canada's military, for its development assistance program, for its foreign policy, and for how Canada sees itself in the world.

Were Canada to decide to recommit to a combat role, it would have to reconfigure its military and its development assistance program, as well as the way its departments work together outside Canada. The Canadian Forces would have to deepen its strategic understanding of insurgency, develop its doctrine, and adjust its training. Assistance programs would have to make space for reconstruction as well as development. The choice is not either one or the other, but both; the two are essential to a country struggling with insurgency. Institutional changes may seem arcane, boring, tedious, but they matter. "A country like Canada that aspires to be a contributor to global order," said Peter Harder, the deputy minister of foreign affairs throughout much of this story of Canada in Kandahar, "needs a global platform. We are not a major player and we never will be, so agility and focus matter. They matter more in our foreign policy than they do in larger and stronger countries. We have too many institutions that do not work well enough together and so we lose both agility and focus."[33] That loss comes at a high price to Canada in the world.

Were Canada to extend the mission, political leaders would have to speak clearly to the public. Was the purpose of the mission, as Defence Minister Gordon O'Connor said more than once, "retribution," or was it "war-fighting," or was it "reconstruction?" No country can afford to go to war with this confusion of purpose. Canada's leaders would need to make compelling arguments for why Canada is fighting far away from home, why the outcome of this war matters. In the past, Canadians have been willing to listen, but political leaders have not been willing to speak. Governments would have to tell the public why Canada has chosen Afghanistan as one among many possible commitments. They would also have to tell Canadians that we are there for a generation. Our commitment would be a test of our strategic patience. This is the choice that Canada made in autumn 2007.

Canada had a second choice. By 2009, Ottawa could have legitimately claimed that it had done its share. One of only a handful of NATO members, the Canadian Forces have fought bravely and well in Kandahar and it would be time to hand off to another NATO partner. Prime Minister Harper suggested, at least by implication, that Canada will do just that. He affirmed that this mission ends in February 2009 and that any extension would have to be approved by Parliament. "From my perspective," he continued, "I would want to see some degree of consensus around that. I don't want to send people into a mission if the opposition at home is going to undercut the dangerous work that they're doing in the field."[34] The three opposition parties have all demanded the withdrawal of Canada's combat forces no later than the end of the mission—a withdrawal that more than half of the Canadian public supports—and it seemed unlikely at the time that Harper's minority government could muster a parliamentary majority for another extension.

Which NATO member would take over from Canada is far from obvious, given the current difficulties in persuading members to free their forces from their national caveats. In practice, Canada would be responsible for finding the replacement nation among NATO members to substitute for its forces. Not so, said then Minister of Defence O'Connor. "This is NATO's problem, not our problem. We would leave it to NATO. And anyway," he continued, "the Afghan Army is our replacement. We have one 'kandak' [Afghan battalion] with us now and five more have been offered to us to train. They will replace us." But will they be ready by February 2009, he was asked. "They're natural fighters and brave people," O'Connor answered, "and it's their country. We will do the best with what we have."[35]

The withdrawal of the Canadian Forces could have had potentially grave consequences for NATO's mission in Afghanistan and for the alliance more generally; it could have turned the fault lines within NATO into an open fissure. The fragility of NATO—the weak commitment to ISAF by most member states—would have been visible to the naked eye. Ottawa has a long-standing strategic interest in the future integrity of NATO, but it cannot—alone—be responsible for sustaining NATO's mission in Afghanistan.

Canada could have persisted and insisted that it was time for others to shoulder the burden. Even if Canada had withdrawn its combat forces completely from southern Afghanistan, however, it could still have continued—and accelerated—its development assistance. Its commitment to Afghanistan would not have ended, but changed.

Or Ottawa could have argued not only that it wanted others to shoulder the burden but also that it wanted to shift its burden. Canada could have withdrawn its combat troops from ISAF but offered a second Provincial Reconstruction Team (PRT) that would have deployed elsewhere in Afghanistan, not on the front lines, and kept its team in Kandahar as well. It could have left its Strategic Advisory Team (SAT), a team of military officers—along with one official from CIDA—seconded to ministries in the Afghan government to help build their capacity. "SAT teaches ministers and ministries how to manage," explained Gordon O'Connor, "and we don't take advantage of it. The Afghan government trusts us."[36] The team has established extraordinary relationships with ministers and ministries in the Afghan government, and other NATO countries have expressed interest in adding a member to Canada's team. It could also have committed a significant number of army and police officers to train the Afghan National Army and the Afghan National Police, two institutions that are urgently in need of assistance. NATO's problems would have remained, as would have Afghanistan's challenges, but the likelihood of the Canadian Forces engaging in combat would have been significantly less. Here, too, Canada could have expanded its development assistance and made a long-term commitment to fund Afghan institutions.

No matter what Canada chose to do, there was no guarantee of eventual success. The Taliban will almost certainly be part of the future of Afghanistan, in one way or another. They are an organic if militant part of the Pashtun tribes that have spilled across an artificial border for generations. The epicentre of the insurgency is in Kandahar, but the solution is in Kabul.

President Karzai has already begun informal negotiations with the Taliban to explore the possibility that "soft" Taliban leaders could join the government. At the provincial level, the governor of Helmand negotiated with the Taliban and the British in 2006 for all forces to leave the village of Musa Qala and allow a council of tribal elders to govern. That experiment lasted a short three months. The Taliban, led by Mullah Ghafour, who was enraged because his brother had been killed a few days earlier in a NATO air strike, stormed the village, pulled down walls around police headquarters, forced the elders out, and dug in. Residents of the village fled, expecting NATO retaliation. Ghafour was subsequently killed by an air strike and the Taliban left the village without a battle.

Negotiation and fighting generally go hand in hand in Pashtun culture. Some of the more militant Taliban clearly place themselves outside the culture of limited goals and limited means. "Negotiating with the present leadership … Mullah Omar … is not acceptable," said Ahmed Rashid, an expert on the Taliban.[37] The leaders who are based in southern Afghanistan and move in and out of the insurgency are more likely partners. Negotiation will not work if there is no capacity to fight, but combat will not succeed unless there is negotiation to reach out to those leaders in Afghanistan who must be part of the political solution.

Some ISAF leaders are reserved, to put it mildly, about a political solution. Canada's military attaché in Kabul, Jordan Elms, was skeptical. "We are walking away," he said "from those kinds of deals in Helmand. They failed."[38] Others disagree. Negotiations at the national level between President Karzai and Taliban leaders are ongoing. "There is no military solution to this conflict, no economic solution," said Chris Eaton, "only a political solution."[39] But, he worried, "are ISAF and the Afghan National Army prepared to open up the space for a political solution?" In insurgencies, opening the space for a political solution is always difficult and always necessary.

Looking Back and Looking Forward

The decision Canada's leaders made about their commitment in Kandahar will certainly have an impact in Afghanistan. It will also have an impact on how Canadians see themselves in the world. In the last forty years, the image of Canadians as peacekeepers has superseded their image as warriors in earlier periods of history. This picture of Canadians as peacekeepers is now being chipped away as the world throws new challenges Canada's way. "We will face insurgencies again," said Gordon O'Connor. "This is our future, whether it is in Kandahar, Darfur, or Somalia. We are going to use our army."[40] Who are Canadians in this difficult world, where the boundary between at home and away is blurring, where Canadian soldiers build schools as well as fight, and civilians throw bombs?

The debate about Afghanistan in Canada is part of a much larger conversation, a conversation about the shape of the world, its cracks and fault lines, about what is possible. Since the first troops went to Kandahar, Canadians suspended disbelief and took for granted that if Canada, if NATO, got it right—if they committed enough troops, if they stayed long enough, if they spent enough money on the "right" kind of development—they could succeed, and the Taliban could be contained. But is that reasonable?

Are there limits to what outsiders can accomplish in any society and therefore to what they should try? "Ought," said Rory Stewart, "must be shaped by can. We are under no obligation to do what is not possible, what cannot succeed."[41] To put the question bluntly, has the time passed when a Western army can intervene with force outside its own society? Have those who argue, for example, for the use of military force to end the crimes against humanity being committed in Darfur been overtaken by history? Is it possible that any outside intervention, no matter what its purpose, no matter how principled its intent, is doomed because it will be seen as a white, Western expedition that forces its way where it is unwanted? Is outside intervention doomed because it disrupts and destabilizes, with very limited capacity to replace what it breaks?

It is perhaps too early to glimpse the answers, but not too early to ask whether we are approaching the limits of the liberal imagination. When Canada commits to rescue failed and failing states, its political leaders are asking for an extraordinary act of imagination, one that asks Canadians to accept that they share a common fate, a destiny, with people who live halfway around the globe. Those in Britain who led the anti-slavery movement in the nineteenth century made this heroic leap, and saw their own humanity bound up with the humanity of slaves. When Canadian soldiers go to Kandahar—or to Darfur or to Haiti—Canadians must be able to make this same leap. It has been a struggle of centuries to stimulate this kind of imagination, and we have failed more often than we have succeeded.

Writing about the history of Afghanistan, Roger Morris concluded that "it was all there ... the consummate folly of corrupt clients, the false valour of historical ignorance, and the presumption once again to conquer the unconquerable in what the Greeks called 'the land of the bones.'"[42] There is no intention to conquer in Canada's mission in Kandahar, but Canada has struggled with both the consummate folly of corrupt clients and the false valour of historical ignorance. Both have exacted a heavy price.

In this struggle, perhaps we have not listened to others who see us, at times with reason, as alien, oppressive, strange, impatient, self-interested, threatening, or disrespectful. Who do they see when they look at us? Who are we in their eyes? The fate of soldiers who leave home to help others depends on the answers to these questions. If those we have come to help see us as helpful, as patient, as listeners, then they may open the door just a crack. But if they see us as strange or rapacious or impatient, they will simply wait for us to go home. They will endure, and then Canadian soldiers will not succeed, no matter where they go, what they do, and what assistance they bring.

If we cannot meet their eyes and listen to their voices, they will turn away from us. And when they do, we will retreat to fortress North America and Europe and live in a self-imposed cocoon. We will comfort ourselves that it is they, not we, who have failed, and then we too will turn away. It is in the meeting of eyes and the sharing of voices that the end of the story of Canada in Kandahar will be written.

Afghans were hopeful after the ouster of the Taliban that they would have a safer, easier life, where their children could go to school, where women could learn to read and go to work, and they could go to a clinic when they were sick. The vast majority of Afghans resented the brutality of the Taliban and hoped for better days. In the last several years, as the insurgency has spread and corruption continues, they have lost a great deal of that hope. On the last day of John Manley's visit to Kabul in 2007, the former foreign minister asked a group of Afghans about their hopes and fears. What did they think of their government? Did they want ISAF in Afghanistan?

There were common threads that ran through all their answers, a surprising consistency. Everyone talked about what has been achieved in a very short time, but also about their frustrations, their disappointments. Wagma, an educator, insisted that much has been accomplished: "Under the Taliban, the education system collapsed completely. Only in the last few years has education come alive, both in the rural and the urban sectors." Nevertheless, the challenges are large. "The security system is fragile," she said. "My husband and I used to visit my in-laws outside of Kabul once a week. Now they worry and ask us not to come because the roads are no longer safe. Why can't ISAF," she asked, almost plaintively, "deal with the outsiders that are interfering and provide the security that we so badly want?" Kabor, a financial administrator, spoke bluntly: "The most important thing is to create employment. All these insurgencies are because people are jobless and cannot feed their families." Farid, who works with Afghans to build emergency shelters, began by speaking of progress, of hope, of change. "There are a great many positive changes in Afghanistan," he said. "In 2002, one U.S. dollar bought over 1000 Afghanis. Today, $1 buys 50 Afghanis, and the currency is stable." Like his colleagues, he too mourned the lost chances. "We missed many opportunities. We failed to train the Afghan army and police early. We need to invest seriously in peacebuilding activities. The government is corrupt," he added, "and needs to improve. We have made mistakes. In the province of Paktika, local leaders are strong, and if they decided to support the government, they could push the Taliban out. But the government is corrupt," he said, his voice tailing off.

The conversation turned to ISAF, to the presence of Western forces in Afghanistan. What did Afghans think? What did they want? Here, the consensus was remarkable. "I am thirty-five years old and since I was five," said Wagma, "I remember nothing but war. In the last twenty-five years, the whole system of Afghanistan collapsed. Our institutions broke, our buildings collapsed, and we all struggled to feed ourselves. We need time. You must give us time. But it is not hopeless if you stay. If the international forces leave, we will kill each other. A terrible civil war will break out that will engulf the whole region." Kabor chimed in quickly, as if to emphasize the point. "We ask you not to repeat the mistakes you made in the 1990s," he pleaded, "not to abandon Afghanistan again. If the international forces withdraw, Afghanistan will descend into chaos."

There was a moment of silence and then Farid began to speak, his eyes flashing and his voice rising. "If the international forces leave," he argued passionately, "the central government will collapse, millions of people will be displaced. For the time being, nation-building in Afghanistan is like a child. If you do not support a child, teach it how to walk, it cannot stand on its own two feet. Afghanistan is your child."[43]

Those Afghan voices still haunt the Canadians who were listening that morning.

NOTES

ONE: EARLY IN, EARLY OUT

1. Art Eggleton, cited in Allan Thompson, "Six-Month Relief Mission Eyed," *Toronto Star*, November 16, 2001, p. A6.

2. Interview with John Manley, November 17, 2006.

3. Interview with General Ray Henault, March 30, 2007.

4. Interview with General Ray Henault, March 30, 2007.

5. Interview with General Ray Henault, March 30, 2007.

6. Civil libertarians argued that the legislation did not adequately protect civil liberties as a result.

7. Interview with John Manley, November 17, 2006.

8. Interview with John Manley, November 17, 2006.

9. Stockwell Day, "Oral Question Period." In Canada, House of Commons, Legislative Debates (Hansard). 37th Parliament, 2nd session (online) (September 17, 2001). Available at: http://www2.parl.gc.ca/HousePublications/Publication.aspx?Language=E&Mode=1&Parl=37&Ses=1&DocId=653212 [July 2, 2007].

10. Interview with John Manley, November 17, 2006.

11. See Eugene Lang, "General Versus Economist," *The Globe and Mail*, Comment Section, March 2, 2006, p. A19.

12. Interview with John Manley, November 17, 2006.

13. The precise date of the deployment remains secret; however, Eggleton publicly confirmed the JTF2 deployment was two months old at the end of January 2002.

14. Art Eggleton, cited by Daniel Leblanc, "Elite JTF2 Goes into Kandahar War Zone," *The Globe and Mail*, December 20, 2001, p. A1.

15. Since the beginning of the Mulroney government, there have been thirteen defence ministers. Of the thirteen, four have left the portfolio under a cloud of controversy; three have lost their seats in elections; and one, Kim Campbell, went on to become one of the shortest-serving prime ministers in Canadian history.

16. Clinton apparently viewed the extraordinarily expensive BMD project as "bullshit," as a system that would never work, but he accepted the political reality that the Democrats had to go forward with BMD so that they would look strong on national security.

17. Interview with former senior defence official involved in the NORAD trip, October 4, 2006.

18. One example illustrates the point. Defence Minister John McCallum tried urgently to reach a senior admiral at NDHQ and was put on hold and told to call back later, as the admiral in question was on the line with the Pentagon.

19. Interview with former senior defence official, October 4, 2006.

20. Art Eggleton, cited by Sheldon Alberts, with files from Chris Wattie, "Six Months and Out for Our Troops: Ottawa: Analysts Warn of Losses," *National Post*, November 16, 2001, p. A1.

21. Art Eggleton, cited by Brian Laghi, "Eggleton Plays Down Combat Role for Troops," *The Globe and Mail*, November 16, 2001, p. A1.

22. Allan Thompson, "Six-Month Relief Mission Eyed," *Toronto Star*, November 16, 2001, p. A6.

23. Jane Gadd, "Mission Begins Without Canadian Soldiers," *The Globe and Mail*, January 2, 2002, p. A1.

24. Sheldon Alberts and Robert Fife, "Troop Talks with U.S. Hit Crucial Stage: Afghanistan Security Force," *National Post*, January 4, 2002, p. A6.

25. Interview with former senior defence official, October 4, 2006.

26. Art Eggleton, cited by Daniel Leblanc and Jill Mahoney, "Going to War: Canada Opts for Combat Role in Kandahar Region," *The Globe and Mail*, January 8, 2002, p. A1.

27. Interview with John Manley, November 17, 2006.

28. Interview with Paul Cellucci, January 18, 2007.

29. General Ray Henault, cited by Valerie Lawton, "Canada Joins al-Qaeda Hunt," *Toronto Star*, January 8, 2002, p. A1.

30. This incident prompted Prime Minister Chrétien to establish a formal inquiry, headed by former chief of defence staff Maurice Baril.

31. The Chrétien government had provided six hundred million dollars in aid to Afghanistan over seven years, making the country Canada's single-largest aid recipient.

TWO: "WE DON'T KNOW ANYTHING ABOUT THIS COUNTRY"

1. Louis Dupree, *Afghanistan*. Princeton: Princeton University Press, 1980, pp. 57–65.

2. Stephen Tanner, *Afghanistan: A Military History from Alexander the Great to the Fall of the Taliban*. New York: Da Capo Press, 2002, p. 1.

3. Olivier Roy, *Afghanistan: From Holy War to Civil War*. Princeton: Darwin Press, 1995, p. 65.

4. Ali A. Jalali and Lester Grau, *Afghan Guerilla Warfare: In the Words of the Mujahideen Fighters*. Minneapolis: MBI Publishing Co., 2001, and Tanner, *Military History of Afghanistan*.

5. Roy, *Afghanistan*, p. 65.

6. Richard Shultz and Andrea J. Dew, *Insurgents, Terrorists and Militias: The Warriors of Contemporary Combat*. New York: Columbia University Press, 2006, p. 190.

7. Interview with a mujahideen commander, in Jalali and Grau, *Afghan Guerilla Warfare*, p. 299.

8. Olivier Roy, in *Afghanistan: From Holy War to Civil War*, discusses the taboos in the Afghan concept of warfare and the importance of private space.

9. Olivia Ward, "Where the Taliban Breeds," *Toronto Star*, February 18, 2007, p. A10.

10. Olivier Roy explains this disconnect between tribal war-fighting and postwar politics. See his brilliant book *Afghanistan: From Holy War to Civil War*, p. 70.

11. Shultz and Dew, *Insurgents, Terrorists, and Militias*, pp. 151 and 179.

12. Lawrence Wright, *The Looming Tower: Al-Qaeda and the Road to 9/11*. New York: Knopf, 2006, p. 228.

13. Ahmed Rashid, *Taliban: Militant Islam, Oil, and Fundamentalism in Central Asia*. New Haven: Yale University Press, 2000, p. 212.

14. Rashid, *Taliban*.

15. Rashid, *Taliban*, pp. 93–94.

16. Sally Armstrong, *Veiled Threat*. Toronto: Penguin, 2002.

17. Interview with Dr. Sima Simar, 2001.

18. Osama Bin Laden, *Declaration of War Against the Americans Occupying the Land of the Two Places*. August 23, 1996.

19. Wright, *The Looming Tower*, p. 267.

20. Wright, *The Looming Tower*, p. 331.

21. Cited by Stephen Sestanovich, "Is It All Yeltsin's Fault? Fifteen Years Later, the Legacy of a Russian Reformer," *Washington Post*, December 24, 2006, p. B07.

22. Cited by Rashid, *Taliban*, p. 103.

THREE: STAY THE COURSE

1. Boudria was appointed public works minister in January 2002 to clean up the sponsorship programs in that department. He lost credibility when it was revealed that he had spent a weekend at the luxury country home of the owner of Groupe Everest, a company on contract to Public Works and Government Services Canada.

2. Interview with John McCallum, October 17, 2006.

3. Graham lost the 1988 election by fewer than one hundred votes.

4. Conversation with Herb Gray shortly after Graham's appointment to Foreign Affairs.

5. One would be hard-pressed to find a Defence Department anywhere that has ever acknowledged that it has sufficient resources to do the job. NDHQ is no exception to this general rule.

6. This project, which began in the late 1970s, was frustrated and delayed by the Liberals once they came to power in 1993.

7. This was an expensive and dubious proposition, with marginal utility, that was controversial even within the Department of Defence. The civilian side of the department opposed the project, and the army and navy were also against it, because they realized it would leave little money for their capital priorities. But "strategic airlift" was the air force's top priority, and both the chief and vice chief of the defence staff were airforce men. Hence, it was near the top of their priority list. The Harper government has moved forward to acquire these planes.

8. Both civilian and military leaders within the Department of Defence were vigorous supporters of Canada's joining BMD, and they wanted to tender their advice on this subject as soon as possible to try to influence the new minister's thinking. At that time, the Ministry of Foreign Affairs was opposed to BMD and former president Clinton had expressed his reservations about the project to Prime Minister Chrétien.

9. Interview with John McCallum, October 17, 2006.

10. Interview with John McCallum, February 7, 2007.

11. Interview with John McCallum, February 7, 2007.

12. When this issue was first raised with McCallum, the military leadership suggested that Foreign Affairs would probably support a continuing Canadian Forces presence in Afghanistan at a modest level, but there was no certainty of this.

13. He had already met with the newly minted finance minister, John Manley, the day before to begin a conversation on the subject.

14. Interview with John McCallum, October 17, 2006.

15. Interview with Bill Graham, January 30, 2007.

16. Bloodworth subsequently served as national security adviser to Prime Minister Harper and is now deputy clerk of the Privy Council.

17. Department of National Defence, *Overview Brief for Visit of Minister McCallum to Washington, D.C.*, December 12, 2002. Obtained through the *Access to Information Act*.

18. Interview with John McCallum, October 17, 2006.

19. Interview with John McCallum, February 7, 2007.

20. Interview with John McCallum, October 17, 2006.

21. Interview with John McCallum, February 7, 2007.

22. Interview with John McCallum, October 17, 2006.

23. Interview with John McCallum, October 17, 2006.

FOUR: WALKING A TIGHTROPE

1. Jean Chrétien, "Oral Question Period." In Canada, House of Commons, Legislative Debates (Hansard). 37th Parliament, 2nd Session (online) (November 19, 2002). Available at: http://www2.parl.gc.ca/HousePublications/ Publication.aspx?Language=E&Mode=1&Parl=37&Ses=2&DocId=571223 [July 2, 2007].

2. Cited by Allan Thompson, "Graham Opens Door Wider for Joining War on Saddam: May Be Situations Where Mandate Is Not 'Feasible,' Axworthy Charges Liberals Cozying Up to Americans," *Toronto Star*, January 11, 2003, p. A10.

3. Cited by Sheldon Alberts, "Chrétien Gives Conditional Support for War," *National Post*, January 24, 2003, p. A2.

4. Cited by Thomas E. Ricks, *Fiasco*. New York: Penguin Press, 2006, p. 95.

5. Cited by William Walker, "Canada May Fight Without U.N. Vote," *Toronto Star*, January 10, 2003, p. A1.

6. Interview with John McCallum, October 17, 2006.

7. Cited by Daniel Leblanc, "Some Liberal MPs Leery of Joining War on Iraq Without UN," *The Globe and Mail*, January 11, 2003, p. A4.

8. Daniel Leblanc, "Some Liberal MPs Leery of Joining War on Iraq Without UN," *The Globe and Mail*, January 11, 2003, p. A4.

9. Vice Admiral Greg Maddison before the House of Commons Standing Committee on Procedure and House Affairs, February 26, 2002.

10. Interview with John McCallum, February 7, 2007.

11. Interview with John McCallum, February 7, 2007.

12. Chris Wattie, "Forces' Last Chance to Show Country What They Can Do," *National Post*, January 10, 2003, p. A5.

13. Interview with John McCallum, February 7, 2007.

14. Interview with General Ray Henault, March 19, 2007.

15. Memo to Vice Admiral Greg Maddison from Joint Staff Steering Committee, January 7, 2003. Obtained through the *Access to Information Act*.

16. Interview with John McCallum, October 17, 2006.

17. Interview with Bill Graham, January 30, 2007.

18. This story is told in great detail in Ricks, *Fiasco*, pp. 115–16.

19. Interview with John McCallum, February 7, 2007.

20. Interview with John McCallum, February 7, 2007.

21. Interview with John McCallum, February 7, 2007.

22. Interview with Bill Graham, January 30, 2007.

23. Interview with John McCallum, February 7, 2007.

24. Interview with Bill Graham, January 30, 2007.

25. Interview with Bill Graham, January 30, 2007.

26. Sheila Copps, on *The Agenda with Steve Paikin*, October 4, 2006.

27. Interview with John Manley, November 17, 2006.

28. Interview with John McCallum, February 7, 2007.

29. Interview with John McCallum, February 7, 2007.

30. Interview with John McCallum, February 7, 2007.

31. Interview with John McCallum, October 17, 2006.

32. John McCallum, "Oral Question Period." In Canada, House of Commons, Legislative Debates (Hansard). 37th Parliament, 2nd Session (online) (February 12, 2003). Available at: http://www2.parl.gc.ca/House Publications/Publication.aspx?Language=E&Mode=1&Parl=37&Ses=2&DocId= 695956 [July 2, 2007].

FIVE: HALF PREGNANT

1. See Eddie Goldenberg. *The Way It Works.* Toronto: McClelland & Stewart, 2006, p. 295.

2. Goldenberg, *The Way It Works*, p. 295.

3. Interview with Paul Cellucci, January 18, 2007.

4. Goldenberg, *The Way It Works*, p. 1.

5. Cited by Goldenberg, *The Way It Works,* p. 8.

6. Goldenberg, *The Way It Works*, p. 290.

7. Interview with John McCallum, October 17, 2006.

8. Interview with Bill Graham, January 30, 2007.

9. Interview with Bill Graham, January 30, 2007.

10. Interview with Paul Cellucci, January 18, 2007.

11. Interview with Paul Cellucci, January 18, 2007.

12. Interview with Bill Graham, January 30, 2007.

13. Interview with Bill Graham, January 30, 2007.

14. Interview with Bill Graham, January 30, 2007.

15. Cited by Bob Woodward, *Plan of Attack*. New York: Simon & Schuster, 2004, p. 373. This is the only reference to Canada in the book.

16. Interview with General Ray Henault, March 19, 2007.

17. Interview with Bill Graham, January 30, 2007.

18. Interview with John Manley, November 17, 2006.

19. Paul Koring and Daniel Leblanc, "Canadian Will Run Persian Gulf Naval Task Force," *The Globe and Mail*, February 11, 2003, p. A1.

20. Paul Koring and Daniel Leblanc, "Canadian Will Run Persian Gulf Naval Task Torce," *The Globe and Mail*, February 11, 2003, p. A1.

21. Daniel Leblanc, "Navy Will Pitch in If War Starts in Iraq," *The Globe and Mail*, February 14, 2003, p. A10.

22. Interview with General Ray Henault, March 19, 2007.

23. Interview with John McCallum, February 7, 2007.

24. Interview with Bill Graham, January 30, 2007.

25. Cited by Allan Thompson, "Sailors Would Not Hand Over Iraqis," *Toronto Star*, April 9, 2003, p. A12.

26. Cited by Allan Thompson, "Sailors Would Not Hand Over Iraqis," *Toronto Star*, April 9, 2003, p. A12.

27. Interview with John McCallum, February 7, 2007, and interview with Bill Graham, January 30, 2007.

28. Interview with General Ray Henault, March 19, 2007.

29. Interview with General Ray Henault, March 19, 2007.

30. Interview with John McCallum, February 7, 2007.

31. Natynczuk is now vice chief of the defence staff.

32. Interview with John McCallum, February 7, 2007.

33. Interview with Bill Graham, January 30, 2007.

34. Interview with General Ray Henault, March 19, 2007.

35. Interview with John McCallum, February 7, 2007.

36. Interview with senior government official, January 7, 2007.

SIX: PULLING IT TOGETHER

1. North Atlantic Treaty Organization, *Communiqué*, Madrid NATO meeting, June 3, 2003.

2. Interview with John McCallum, February 7, 2007.

3. Department of National Defence, *Briefing to JSSC*, p. 12, January 7, 2003. Obtained through the *Access to Information Act*.

4. Interview with John McCallum, February 7, 2007.

SEVEN: TRANSITION

1. Interview with John McCallum, October 17, 2006.

2. Cited by Sheldon Alberts, "President Not 'a Statesman,' Minister Says," *National Post*, March 20, 2003, p. A8.

3. Sheldon Alberts, "President Not 'a Statesman,' Minister Says," *National Post*, March 20, 2003, p. A8.

4. Interview with John Manley, November 17, 2006.

5. Cited by Joseph Brean and Sheldon Alberts, "U.S. Loses Faith in Canada," *National Post*, March 26, 2003, p. A1.

6. Interview with Scott Reid, October 20, 2006.

7. Interview with Tim Murphy, February 1, 2007.

8. Interview with Paul Martin, February 7, 2007.

9. And he was prescient. Today, military experts such as retired Major General Lewis McKenzie are making the same argument. See Lewis McKenzie, "Go Big, Go Bold and Get It Done," *The Globe and Mail*, November 22, 2006, p. A25.

10. Barry Cooper, "Martin's Cabinet Picked for PR," *Saskatoon Star-Phoenix*, December 22, 2003, p. A10.

11. Interview with Paul Martin, February 7, 2007.

12. In contrast to Pratt, the military establishment didn't particularly like or respect John McCallum. He was too independent of mind, too willing to challenge the reigning orthodoxy and received wisdom in the military and the department. He didn't genuflect in the presence of serving or retired generals—in short, he wasn't one of "them." And while some thought he was prone to making mistakes, he did manage to get the military its largest funding increase in fifteen years to that point in time.

13. Interview with John Manley, November 20, 2006.

14. Interview with John Manley, November 17, 2006.

15. Interview with John Manley, November 17, 2006.

16. Interview with John Manley, November 17, 2006.

17. Report of the Standing Committee on Foreign Affairs and International Trade, *Partners in North America: Advancing Canada's Relations with the United States and Mexico,* December 2002.

18. Interview with Bill Graham, January 30, 2007.

19. Russia has reverted to opposing BMD due to American plans to base interceptors and radars in Eastern Europe.

20. Cellucci was referring to a comment Chrétien had made criticizing Bush's profligate fiscal policy and suggesting that the president was less conservative than Chrétien when it came to managing the finances of his government.

21. Interview with Bill Graham, January 30, 2007.

22. Rumsfeld's reply read as follows: "Dear Minister Pratt: Thank you for your recent letter regarding cooperation between the United States and Canada on missile defense. As you noted in your letter, the United States and Canada have been partners in the defense of North America for over 50 years. In light of the threat involving the proliferation of ballistic missiles, I agree that we should seek to expand our cooperation in the area of missile defense. I am supportive of the approach to missile defense cooperation that you outlined in your letter and agree that this should be the basis on which we move forward. Thank you again for your letter. I look forward to continuing the long-standing defense cooperation between the United States and Canada. Sincerely, Donald Rumsfeld." For the text of both letters, see http://www.forces.gc.ca/site/Focus/Canada-US/letter_.asp [July 8, 2007].

23. Interview with Bill Graham, January 30, 2007.

24. Interview with David Pratt, October 23, 2006.

25. Interview with Paul Martin, February 7, 2007.

EIGHT: TOWARD A NEW AGENDA

1. Interview with Paul Martin, February 7, 2007.

2. Interview with Paul Martin, February 7, 2007.

3. Interview with Tim Murphy, February 1, 2007.

4. James Travers, "Graham Still in the Picture," *Toronto Star*, July 22, 2004, p. A21.

5. Conversation with Bill Graham, winter 2005.

6. Interview with Bill Graham, January 30, 2007.

7. Interview with Chris Alexander, March 2, 2007.

8. Eugene Lang, "We Never Discussed the Real Afghan Option," *The Globe and Mail*, May 19, 2006, p. A15.

9. Interview with Bill Graham, January 30, 2007.

10. Interview with General Ray Henault, March 30, 2007.

11. Interview with Bill Graham, January 30, 2007.

12. Interview with Bill Graham, January 30, 2007.

13. Interview with General Ray Henault, March 30, 2007.

14. Interview with General Rick Hillier, May 22, 2007.

15. Interview with Bill Graham, January 30, 2007.

16. Interview with Paul Martin, February 7, 2007.

17. Bloodworth was moved from Defence and appointed deputy minister of public safety, a new superministry created by the Martin government and headed by Deputy Prime Minister Anne McLellan.

18. Interview with Bill Graham, January 30, 2007. There was a historical precedent for such thinking inside DND. The last defence policy paper written in 1994, while the government was mired in a forty-billion-dollar deficit, would have cost an enormous amount of money to implement. It was developed without much reference to the government's financial condition at the time. As a result it was never fully implemented.

19. *Purple* is the term used for trades or positions that are not directly employed in any of the three military elements.

20. Interview with Bill Graham, January 30, 2007.

21. Had John McCallum been minister of defence at this time, Leslie would have become chief of the defence staff. When Leslie was a one-star general, McCallum had identified him as his preferred successor to Henault (and he told Graham so). McCallum was not at all concerned about breaking with tradition or precedent in this way; he felt that military traditions like service rotation and defined lengths of tenure for the CDS should be broken. He believed these traditions acted as political constraints that prevented necessary change and reform. McCallum thought that Leslie was the most competent, visionary, and impressive of the senior officers, and he believed that Leslie would shake up a tired institution and drive the kind of radical reform that the minister of defence thought was needed. McCallum would often say he believed in the "Gord Nixon theory" of institutional leadership. When McCallum was chief economist at the Royal Bank, Gord Nixon, a man in his early forties at the time, was

appointed CEO. The bank needed vibrant new leadership that would force change on the bank's conservative institutional culture, but the new CEO had to be young enough to serve for several years to see that change through. McCallum believed the Canadian Forces needed that kind of basic institutional change, and he saw Leslie as the only senior officer who was energetic, visionary, and young enough to be able to force change and serve the length of term necessary to see reform through.

22. He has since publicly embraced the purchase of the Boeing C-17s, since the Harper government committed to acquiring these aircraft.

23. Hillier used this term publicly in the press conference announcing the government's intention to buy the Mobile Gun System on October 30, 2003.

24. The army never disposed of the thirty-year-old Leopards, "the millstone" around Hillier's neck. Many army commanders rejected Hillier's arguments and tenaciously held on to the tanks until there was an opportunity to deploy them. In 2006, that opportunity arose. Today a squadron of the Leopards is in Kandahar, on its first foreign deployment since coming out of the Canadian garrison in West Germany in the early 1990s. In April 2007, the Government of Canada announced that it would be acquiring up to one hundred surplus Leopard 2 tanks from the Netherlands to replace the existing fleet, as well as securing the loan of twenty Leopard 2A6 tanks from Germany for use in Afghanistan over the summer of 2007.

25. Interview with Paul Martin, February 7, 2007.

NINE: NAVIGATING BMD

1. The papers from the Ministry of Trade and CIDA came in for equal criticism at the Centre. After reviewing one of the final drafts of the trade paper, Peter Nicholson remarked with real frustration, "We have no trade policy." Conversation with Peter Nicholson, winter 2005.

2. Interview with Paul Martin, February 7, 2007. Michael Pitfield was Pierre Trudeau's clerk of the Privy Council during the 1970s and early 1980s.

3. Interview with former senior official, January 7, 2006.

4. Interview with Tim Murphy, February 1, 2007.

5. Graham Fraser, "A New Face for Foreign Policy," *Toronto Star*, March 19, 2005, p. F1.

6. Interview with Paul Martin, February 7, 2007.

7. Government of Canada, *Canada's International Policy Statement—A Role of Pride and Influence in the World-DEFENCE-Summary.* Ottawa: Department of National Defence, 2005, p. 3.

8. Interview with Paul Martin, February 7, 2007.

9. Conversation with Peter Nicholson, February 2005.

10. Interview with Scott Reid, October 20, 2006.

11. Doug Bland, a professor of Defence Management at Queen's University and a former colonel in the Canadian Forces, had written a book called *Canada Without Armed Forces*. He, like many others, argued that the Canadian Forces had been so badly run down for so long that no amount of new resources could repair the damage and restore their lost glory.

12. Cited by Amy O'Brian, "Forces Budget Demands 'Unrealistic,'" *The Vancouver Sun*, February 27, 2003, p. A3.

13. Interview with Paul Martin, February 7, 2007.

14. Interview with Tim Murphy, February 1, 2007.

15. Some MPs equated Ballistic Missile Defence with Star Wars, the anti-ballistic missile program started by the Reagan administration. The NDP had dubbed BMD as "Son of Star Wars." There are few similarities between the objectives of Star Wars and BMD. Star Wars had the science fiction–like and technologically infeasible goal of defending the United States against a full-scale Soviet intercontinental nuclear missile attack. BMD is intended to intercept one or two missiles fired at North America from North Korea or al-Qaeda. Star Wars would have changed the basic nature of nuclear deterrence and undermined the international arms control regime.

16. Interview with Paul Martin, February 7, 2007.

17. Interview with Bill Graham, January 30, 2007.

18. Interview with Paul Martin, February 7, 2007.

19. Interview with Paul Cellucci, January 18, 2007.

20. Interview with Paul Cellucci, January 18, 2007.

21. Cited by Tim Harper and Susan Delacourt, "Missile Pitch Stuns Martin: Controversial Defence Scheme Raised in Talks with Prime Minister," *Toronto Star*, December 1, 2004, p. A1.

22. Interview with Paul Cellucci, January 17, 2007.

23. Interview with Paul Martin, February 7, 2007.

24. There was one proposal being promoted by Raytheon, a large corporation that was heavily involved in the development of BMD, that would have put a BMD radar system in Goose Bay, Labrador, at a cost of several hundred million dollars to Canada.

25. Interview with Paul Martin, February 7, 2007.

26. Interview with Scott Reid, October 20, 2006.

27. Interview with Bill Graham, January 30, 2007.

28. Interview with Scott Reid, October 20, 2006.

29. Interview with Scott Reid, October 20, 2006.

30. Interview with Tim Murphy, February 1, 2007.

31. Interview with Tim Murphy, February 1, 2007.

32. They advanced these arguments despite the fact that senior Defence officials now conceded that BMD would not be located in NORAD, but would

more likely be housed either in NORTHComm or StratComm, two command structures that did not include Canadians.

33. Gilles Duceppe, "Oral Question Period." In Canada, House of Commons, Legislative Debates (Hansard). 38th Parliament, 1st Session (online) (February 2, 2005). Available at: http://www2.parl.gc.ca/HousePublications/Publication.aspx?Language=E&Mode=1&Parl=38&Ses=1&DocId=1594887#Int-1099785 [July 2, 2007].

34. Jack Layton, "Oral Question Period." In Canada, House of Commons, Legislative Debates (Hansard). 38th Parliament, 1st Session (online) (December 1, 2004). Available at: http://www2.parl.gc.ca/HousePublications/Publication.aspx?Language=E&Mode=1&Parl=38&Ses=1&DocId=1519808#Int-1044349 [July 2, 2007].

35. Interview with Bill Graham, January 30, 2007.

36. Chantal Hébert, "Missile Defence PM's Major Irritant," *Toronto Star*, February 4, 2005, p. A19.

37. Conversation with Ward Elcock, February 2005.

38. Cited by Aileen McCabe and Anne Dawson, "PM to Say 'No' to Missile Shield," *Ottawa Citizen*, February 23, 2005, p. A1.

39. Interview with Paul Martin, February 7, 2007.

40. Interview with Tim Murphy, February 1, 2007.

41. Interview with Scott Reid, October 20, 2006.

42. Interview with Paul Martin, February 7, 2007.

43. Interview with Bill Graham, January 30, 2007.

44. Interview with Paul Martin, February 7, 2007.

45. Interview with Paul Cellucci, January 18, 2007.

46. Interview with Tim Murphy, February 1, 2007.

TEN: FROM KABUL TO KANDAHAR

1. Conversation with Bill Graham, 2005.

2. Cited by Bill Schiller, "The Road to Kandahar," *Toronto Star,* September 9, 2006, p. F1.

3. Interview with Tim Murphy, February 1, 2007.

4. Interview with Paul Martin, February 7, 2007.

5. See David Rothkopf, *Running the World.* New York: Public Affairs, 2005, p. 431.

6. Department of National Defence, Briefing Note on Deputy Minister–Level Meeting on Afghanistan, January 24, 2006, p. 4. Obtained through the *Access to Information Act*.

7. Interview with Bill Graham, January 30, 2007.

8. Interview with Chris Alexander, March 2, 2007.

9. Bill Schiller, "The Road to Kandahar," *Toronto Star*, September 9, 2006, p. F1.

10. Interview with Paul Martin, February 7, 2007.

11. Interview with Paul Martin, February 7, 2007.

12. Interview with Paul Martin, February 7, 2007.

13. Interview with Tim Murphy, February 1, 2007.

14. Interview with Paul Martin, February 7, 2007.

15. Canada did not contribute to this UN force because, as Prime Minister Harper stated at the time, the Canadian Forces were committed in Afghanistan.

16. Interview with Paul Martin, February 7, 2007.

17. Bill Schiller, "The Road to Kandahar," *Toronto Star*, September 9, 2006, p. F1.

18. Interview with Paul Martin, February 7, 2007.

19. Interview with Scott Reid, October 20, 2006.

20. Interview with Paul Martin, February 7, 2007, and interview with Tim Murphy, February 1, 2007.

21. Bill Schiller, "The Road to Kandahar," *Toronto Star*, September 9, 2006, p. F1.

22. Interview with Tim Murphy, February 1, 2007.

23. Interview with Tim Murphy, February 1, 2007.

24. Interview with Paul Martin, February 7, 2007.

25. Interview with Tim Murphy, February 1, 2007.

26. Cited by Bill Schiller, "The Road to Kandahar," *Toronto Star*, September 9, 2006, p. F1.

27. In September 2006, the Canadian Centre for Policy Alternatives estimated that Canada accounted for over forty percent of non–U.S. casualties in Afghanistan during 2006; and, when adjusted for the relative size of troop commitments, a Canadian soldier in Kandahar is nearly three times more likely to be killed in hostile action than a British soldier, and four and a half times more likely than an American soldier in Afghanistan.

28. Cited by Stephen Thorne, "'Our Job Is to Be Able to Kill People,' Top Soldier Says," *Edmonton Journal*, July 16, 2005, p. A12.

ELEVEN: SCUMBAGS AND DUTCHMEN

1. Fowler had previously been deputy minister of national defence.

2. They wouldn't be returning to Canada after the mission was over. Hillier made it clear that this was a permanent donation, not a loan.

3. Interview with Bill Graham, January 30, 2007.

4. Interview with Tim Murphy, February 1, 2007.

5. Bill Graham, "The Canadian Forces' Mission in Afghanistan: Canadian Policy and Values in Action," Ottawa: Department of National Defence, p. 7.

6. Bill Graham, "The Canadian Forces' Mission in Afghanistan," p. 3.

7. Hillier usually did not speak from a prepared text. Nor did he generally consult Graham on the content of his speeches, but spoke extemporaneously.

8. Interview with Bill Graham, January 30, 2007.

9. Interview with Bill Graham, January 30, 2007.

10. Eugene Lang and Philip DeMont, "Following Rumsfeld's Lead," *Toronto Star,* October 23, 2006, p. A21.

11. Interview with Bill Graham, January 30, 2007.

12. Interview with former defence official, January 11, 2007.

13. Interview with former defence official, January 11, 2007.

14. Interview with Bill Graham, January 30, 2007.

15. Interview with former defence official, January 11, 2007.

16. Interview with Bill Graham, January 30, 2007.

TWELVE: THE CHALLENGE OF INSURGENCY

1. Interview with Paul Martin, February 7, 2007.

2. Interview with General Rick Hillier, May 22, 2007.

3. Rupert Smith, *The Utility of Force: The Art of War in the Modern World.* New York: Alfred A. Knopf, 2007.

4. Interview with General Rick Hillier, May 22, 2007.

5. Emanuel Adler, paper presented to the 2006 Annual Meeting of the American Political Science Association, Philadelphia, September 2006.

6. Interview with Colonel Bernd Horn, November 16, 2006.

7. The three incidents occurred on February 17 and February 27, 2007. Graeme Smith, "Bombing, Bullets Herald Deadly Spring," *The Globe and Mail,* February 28, 2007, p. A9.

8. Interview with Colonel Bernd Horn, November 16, 2006. See also his *Full Spectrum Leadership Challenges in Afghanistan,* unpublished paper, November 2006, pp. 8–9. Colonel Horn conducted seventy-eight interviews in Afghanistan from October 5 to 25, 2006.

9. Cited by the Senlis Council, *An Assessment of the Hearts and Minds Campaign in Southern Afghanistan,* Autumn 2006, Chapter 2, p. 8.

10. Cited by Barry Bearak, "Karzai Calls Coalition Careless," *The New York Times,* June 24, 2007.

11. Interview with General Dan McNeill, May 16, 2007.

12. Email from David Kilcullen to George Packer, November 2006, cited in "Knowing the Enemy," *The New Yorker,* December 18, 2006, p. 63.

13. Interview with Chris Alexander, March 2, 2007. See also Gordon Smith, *Canada in Afghanistan: Is it Working?* Calgary: Canadian Defence and Foreign Affairs Institute, 2007.

14. Interview with Farid, a CARE leader who manages emergency shelters in Kabul, May 19, 2007.

15. Interview with Chris Alexander, March 2, 2007.

16. Cited by Peter Pigott, *Canada in Afghanistan: The War So Far.* Toronto: Dundurn Press, 2007, p. 170.

17. Conversation with Brigadier General David Fraser, Commander of Task Force Afghanistan/AEGIS/Regional Commander South from February to November 2006, on January 7, 2007.

18. Interview with senior Canadian officer, January 15, 2007.

19. Peter MacKay, Gordon O'Connor, and Josée Verner, *Canada's Mission in Afghanistan: Measuring Progress, Report to Parliament*. Ottawa: Government of Canada, February 2007, p. 8.

20. Interview with General Rick Hillier, May 22, 2007.

21. Colonel Bernd Horn, *Full Spectrum Leadership Challenges in Afghanistan*, unpublished paper, November 2006.

22. Cited by Graeme Smith, "Inspiring Tale of Triumph over Taliban Not All It Seems," *The Globe and Mail*, September 23, 2006, p. A15.

23. Sarah Chayes, *The Punishment of Virtue: Inside Afghanistan After the Taliban*. New York: Penguin, 2006. Chayes argues that the United States was instrumental in securing Shirzai's appointment in the days after the Taliban fell.

24. Cited by Graeme Smith, "Ashamed of Corruption, Afghan Offers to Quit," *The Globe and Mail*, November 14, 2006, p. A22.

25. Interview with senior Canadian military officer, January 17, 2007.

26. Interview with General Rick Hillier, May 22, 2007.

27. James Glanz and David Rohde, "U.S. Report Finds Dismal Training of Afghan Police," *The New York Times,* December 4, 2006, p. A1.

28. Seema Patel and Steven Ross, *Breaking Point: Measuring Progress in Afghanistan*. Washington: CSIS, 2007, p. 36.

29. Interview with Colonel Bernd Horn, January 17, 2007.

30. Conversation with Brigadier General Greg Young, May 16, 2007.

31. Conversation with Brigadier General Greg Young, May 16, 2007.

32. Cited by Graeme Smith, "Chief Cracks Down on Kandahar Police," *The Globe and Mail*, January 24, 2007, p. A15.

33. David Rohde and James Risen, "C.I.A. Review Highlights Afghani Leader's Woes," *The New York Times*, November 5, 2006, p. A14.

34. Interview with Colonel Bernd Horn, January 17, 2007.

35. Interview with General Dan McNeill, May 16, 2007.

36. Cited by David Rohde and James Risen, "C.I.A. Review Highlights Afghani Leader's Woes," *The New York Times,* November 5, 2006, p. A14.

37. United Nations Office on Drugs and Crime and the World Bank, "Afghanistan's Drug Industry," November 2006, http://www.unodc.org/pdf/Afgh_drugindustry_Nov06.pdf estimates opium GDP in the range of $2.6–$2.7 billion of a total GDP of $6.7 billion in 2006. It constitutes thirty-six percent of licit GDP.

38. Report of UN Office of Drug Control, November 29, 2006, cited by James Glanz and David Rohde, "U.S. Report Finds Dismal Training of Afghani Police," *The New York Times*, December 4, 2006, p. A1.

39. Cited by Elizabeth Rubin, "In the Land of the Taliban," *The New York Times Magazine*, October 22, 2006, p. 92.

40. Cited by the Senlis Council, *Five Years After Their Removal from Power: The Taliban Are Back.* Senlis Council News Release, September 5, 2006. Available at: http://senliscouncil.net/modules/media_centre/news_releases/68-news [July 25, 2007].

41. Interview with General Dan McNeill, May 16, 2007.

42. Cited by George Packer, "Knowing the Enemy," *The New Yorker*, December 18, 2006, p. 63.

43. Cited by George Packer, "Knowing the Enemy," *The New Yorker*, December 18, 2006, pp. 63 and 67.

THIRTEEN: HARPER'S WAR

1. As of February 1, 2007, the CDS sent a Canadian Forces General Message reminding CF and DND members that the "Canada First" policy was still in draft form and evolving.

2. "Risk to Troops in Afghanistan Exposed," *New Scientist Magazine*, September 9, 2006, p. 6.

3. Interview with General Rick Hillier, May 22, 2007.

4. Interview with Bill Graham, January 30, 2007.

5. Interview with Gordon O'Connor, July 4, 2007.

6. Interview with Gordon O'Connor, July 4, 2007.

7. In Germany, during the late 1970s, then–Lieutenant Colonel Gordon O'Connor was commander of the Royal Canadian Dragoons. Coincidentally, then-Captain Rick Hillier was one of the men he commanded.

8. Interview with senior government official, July 4, 2007.

9. Interview with Gordon O'Connor, July 4, 2007.

10. Interview with Bill Graham, January 30, 2007.

11. Interview with General Rick Hillier, May 22, 2007.

12. Interview with Gordon O'Connor, July 4, 2007.

13. Interview with Gordon O'Connor, July 4, 2007.

14. This was so-called A-base funding that was not used to finance missions. Overseas missions were funded centrally from the fiscal framework of the government.

15. See, for example, Eugene Lang, "We Never Discussed the Real Afghan Option," *The Globe and Mail*, Comment Section, May 19, 2006, p. A15.

16. Gordon O'Connor before the Standing Senate Committee on National Security and Defence, May 8, 2006.

17. Interview with General Rick Hillier, May 22, 2007.

18. Interview with Bill Graham, January 30, 2007.

19. Interview with Paul Martin, February 7, 2007.

20. Interview with Paul Martin, February 7, 2007.

FOURTEEN: THOSE VEXATIOUS DETAINEES

1. *Arrangement for the Transfer of Detainees Between the Canadian Forces and the Ministry of Defence of the Islamic Republic of Afghanistan*, Article 7, says that "The Participants will be responsible for maintaining accurate written records accounting for all detainees that have passed through their custody." Paul Koring, "Canada Loses Track of Afghan Detainees," *The Globe and Mail*, March 2, 2007, pp. A1 and A8. The agreement also specified that "Participants recognize the legitimate role of the Afghan Independent Human Rights Commission within the territory of Afghanistan, including in regard to the treatment of detainees, and undertake to cooperate fully with the Commission in the exercise of its role."

2. Fahim, who was always considered a threat to the stability of the Karzai government, had been forced out of Afghanistan by the Americans. It was rumoured that the Americans had threatened to seize his assets, which were in foreign banks, unless he left Afghanistan. Fahim agreed on the pretext that he needed to seek medical attention in the West due to deteriorating health. He has since returned as an adviser to President Karzai.

3. Interview with Bill Graham, January 30, 2007.

4. Interview with General Rick Hillier, May 22, 2007.

5. Interview with senior official, Department of Foreign Affairs, May 28, 2007.

6. Alex Neve, the head of Amnesty International in Canada, met with Bill Graham later that November and told the minister that the Dutch would be following the lead of the Danes.

7. This 2006 report was released publicly through the *Access to Information Act* with all the references to abuse by Afghan authorities redacted from the text. An unexpurgated version of the report was subsequently leaked to the media.

8. Cited by Alan Freeman, "Human Rights Weren't on Tory Radar: MacKay," *The Globe and Mail*, June 15, 2007. Available at: http://theglobeand mail.com/servlet/story/RTGAM.20070615.wdetainees15/BNStory/Afghanistan [July 25, 2007].

9. Alan Freeman, "Human Rights Weren't on Tory Radar: MacKay," *The Globe and Mail*, June 15, 2007.

10. The allegations of prisoner abuse by Canadian soldiers were based on documents obtained by Professor Amir Attaran through the *Access to Information Act*. Paul Koring, "Military Investigates Claims Canadians Abused Detainees," *The Globe and Mail*, February 6, 2007, p. A1.

11. Paul Koring, "Canada Loses Track of Afghan Detainees," *The Globe and Mail*, March 2, 2007, p. A1.

12. The commission has since stated publicly that it lacks both the necessary access to Afghan prisons and the staff resources to monitor transferred detainees.

13. Cited by Paul Koring, "Red Cross Contradicts Ottawa on Detainees," *The Globe and Mail*, March 8, 2007, p. A1.

14. Alex Dobrota, "O'Connor Acknowledges Error on Detainees," *The Globe and Mail*, March 9, 2007, p. A13.

15. Graeme Smith and Campbell Clark, "Top Soldier Changes Tack, Expresses Doubt on Deal," *The Globe and Mail*, May 3, 2007, p. A1.

16. Paul Koring, "Court to Hear Transfer Injunction Arguments Today," *The Globe and Mail*, May 3, 2007, p. A8.

17. Paul Koring, "Court to Hear Transfer Injunction Arguments Today," *The Globe and Mail*, May 3, 2007, p. A8.

18. Paul Koring, "Court to Hear Transfer Injunction Arguments Today," *The Globe and Mail*, May 3, 2007, p. A8.

19. Arrangement for the Transfer of Detainees Between the Government of Canada and the Government of the Islamic Republic of Afghanistan, Ottawa: Government of Canada, May 3, 2007.

20. Interview with Ahmad Fahim Hakim, deputy chair, Afghanistan Independent Human Rights Commission, May 16, 2007.

21. Interview with General Dan McNeill, May 16, 2007.

22. Interview with General Ray Henault, March 19, 2007.

FIFTEEN: THE THREE DS IN AFGHANISTAN

1. Government of Canada, *Canada's International Policy Statement—A Role of Pride and Influence in the World*. Ottawa: 2005.

2. Interview with senior civil servant, January 16, 2007.

3. Interview with John Manley, May 14, 2007.

4. Interview with Paul Cellucci, January 18, 2007.

5. Speech by Chief of the Defence Staff Rick Hillier to the annual meeting of the Conference of Defence Associations, Ottawa, February 16, 2007.

6. Interview with Paul Martin, February 7, 2007.

7. Interview with Colonel Bernd Horn, November 16, 2006.

8. The Senlis Council, *An Assessment of Hearts and Minds Campaign in Southern Afghanistan*, Autumn 2006, Chapter 3, p. 11. Available at: http://www.senliscouncil.net/modules/publications/017_publication [July 25, 2007].

9. Seema Patel and Steven Ross, *Breaking Point, Measuring Progress in Afghanistan*. Washington: CSIS, 2007, p. 57.

10. Interview with John Manley, May 14, 2007.

11. Sarah Chayes, *The Punishment of Virtue: Inside Afghanistan After the Taliban*. New York: Penguin, 2006, p. 151.

12. Peter MacKay, Gordon O'Connor, and Josee Verner, *Canada's Mission in Afghanistan: Measuring Progress, Report to Parliament*. Ottawa: Government of Canada, February 2007, p. 14.

13. Interview with Stephen Wallace, vice-president, Afghanistan Task Force, CIDA, May 8, 2007.

14. Cited by the Senlis Council, *An Assessment of Hearts and Minds Campaign in Southern Afghanistan*, Autumn 2006, Chapter 3, p. 10.

15. Human Rights Watch, "Lessons in Terror: Attacks on Education in Afghanistan." Available at: http://www.hrw.org/reports/2006/afghanistan0707/afghanistan0706webfullwcover.pdf [July 2006].

16. Real income per capita in Afghanistan was thirteen dollars in 2005. Barnett Rubin, "Saving Afghanistan," *Foreign Affairs*, January–February 2007, p. 66.

17. Jonathan Goodhand and Mark Sedra, *Bargains for Peace? Aid, Conditionalities and Reconstruction in Afghanistan*. Netherlands Institute of International Relations, Clingendael Conflict Research Unit, August 2006, p. 3.

18. Interview with Stephen Wallace, May 8, 2007.

19. Conversation with Brigadier General David Fraser, May 30, 2007.

20. Cited by Graeme Smith, "Extra Troops to Bolster Canadians in Afghanistan," *The Globe and Mail*, January 27, 2007, p. A21.

21. The Senlis Council, *An Assessment of the Hearts and Minds Campaign in Southern Afghanistan*, Autumn 2006, Chapter 1, p. 19.

22. The Senlis Council, *Canada in Afghanistan: Charting a New Course to Complete the Mission*, Ottawa: May 28, 2007.

23. Interview with Mohammed Ehsan Zia, December 4, 2006.

24. Interview with General Rick Hillier, May 22, 2007.

25. Interview with Brigadier General David Fraser, May 30, 2007.

26. The Senlis Council, *Canada in Afghanistan: Charting a New Course to Complete the Mission*, Ottawa: May 28, 2007, p. 4.

27. Interview with Mohammed Ehsan Zia, May 17, 2007.

28. Interview with General Rick Hillier, May 22, 2007.

29. Interview with senior CIDA official, January 17, 2007.

30. Interview with General Dan McNeill, May 16, 2007.

31. Cited by Christie Blatchford, "Rebuilding Afghanistan, One Project at a Time," *The Globe and Mail*, December 16, 2006, p. A27.

32. Murray Campbell, "One Step at a Time, One Village at a Time," *The Globe and Mail*, May 21, 2007, p. A13.

33. Murray Campbell, "One Step at a Time, One Village at a Time," *The Globe and Mail*, May 21, 2007, p. A13.

34. Interview with senior military officer, January 11, 2007.

35. Interview with senior Canadian military officer, March 17, 2007.

36. Cited in Graeme Smith, "Afghan Suspected in Killing Is Again Locked Up," *The Globe and Mail*, January 20, 2007, p. A1.

37. Interview with official from Foreign Affairs, February 22, 2007.

38. Interview with official from Foreign Affairs, February 22, 2007.

39. Standing Senate Committee on Foreign Affairs and International Trade, *Overcoming 40 Years of Failure: A New Roadmap for Sub-Saharan Africa.* Available at: http://www.senate-senat.ca/africa.asp [February 15, 2007].

40. Interview with senior Canadian diplomat, January 10, 2007.

41. Interview with Canadian military representative, Kabul, May 16, 2007.

42. Interview with senior Canadian officer, January 11, 2007.

43. Interview with CIDA official, May 8, 2007.

44. Interview with official from Foreign Affairs, February 22, 2007.

45. Interview with official from Foreign Affairs, February 22, 2007.

46. Interview with retired official from Foreign Affairs, April 2007.

SIXTEEN: CANADA IN KANDAHAR: MAKING CHOICES

1. Interview with John Manley, Kabul, May 18, 2007.

2. Rami Khouri, editor of the *Beirut Star*, used this phrase in an email circulated to members of a Middle East study group.

3. UN Resolution 1510 (2003) expanded the ISAF mandate to the entire country at the request of the Afghan government on October 13, 2003. The German-led PRT in Konduz came under ISAF command as of December 31, 2003, as a consequence of that resolution.

4. Interview with senior Afghan official, May 18, 2007.

5. Cited by Graeme Smith, "As More Blood Spills, the Military Sees Progress," *The Globe and Mail*, July 2, 2007, p. A10.

6. Seema Patel and Steven Ross, *Breaking Point: Measuring Progress in Afghanistan.* Washington: CSIS, 2007, p. 51 and p. 60.

7. Senate Committee of National Security and Defence, *Canadian Troops in Afghanistan: Taking a Hard Look at a Hard Mission*, interim report, 2007, p. 5.

8. Seema Patel and Steven Ross, *Breaking Point*, p. 38, and the Senlis Council, *Losing Hearts and Minds in Afghanistan: Canada's Leadership to Break the Cycle of Violence in Southern Afghanistan.* Ottawa: October 2006.

9. The Senlis Council, *Canada in Afghanistan: Charting a New Course to Complete the Mission.* Appendix I, p. 20. Ottawa: May 28, 2007.

10. The Program on International Policy Attitudes (PIPA), University of Maryland, in collaboration with the Afghan Center for Social and Opinion Research, Kabul, *Afghan Public Opinion Amidst Rising Violence—A WorldPublicOpinion.org Poll*, December 14, 2006. Opinion in the provinces of Zabol and Oruzgan was excluded for security reasons. Available at: http://www.worldpublicopinion.org/pipa/pdf/dec06/Afghanistanrpt.pdf (December 2006).

11. Murray Brewster, "Dutch-Australian Unit in Afghan Region Virtually Surrounded by Taliban," Canadian Press, February 17, 2007.

12. Cited by Barnett Rubin, "Saving Afghanistan," *Foreign Affairs*, January–February 2007, p. 61.

13. Interview with John Manley, Kabul, May 18, 2007.

14. Interview with John Manley, Kabul, May 18, 2007.

15. Interview with General Rick Hiller, May 22, 2007.

16. Cited in "A Double Spring Offensive," *The Economist*, February 22, 2007, pp. 28–30.

17. Cited by Peter Pigott, *Canada in Afghanistan: The War So Far*. Toronto: Dundurn Press, 2007, pp. 111 and 129.

18. Interview with Bill Graham, January 30, 2007.

19. Interview with General Rick Hillier, February 20, 2007.

20. Cited by Tim Harper, "Bush Promises More Soldiers for Afghanistan, Seeks Help," *Toronto Star*, February 16, 2007, p. A10.

21. Email correspondence from James Appathurai, NATO spokesperson, March 1, 2007.

22. Interview with General Ray Henault, March 19, 2007.

23. Interview with General Ray Henault, March 19, 2007.

24. Interview with General Rick Hillier, May 22, 2007.

25. Interview with General Dan McNeill, May 16, 2007.

26. Interview with senior official, Department of Foreign Affairs, February 22, 2007.

27. James Travers, "We've Lost Sight of the Mission's Purpose," *Toronto Star*, February 3, 2007, p. F1.

28. Interview with General Rick Hillier, May 22, 2007.

29. Testimony of Sarah Chayes before the Standing Committee on Foreign Affairs and International Development, House of Commons, Ottawa, Evidence 58, May 29, 2007.

30. Interview with Chris Eaton, May 16, 2007.

31. Interview with Rory Stewart, Turquoise Mountain Foundation, May 17, 2007.

32. Testimony of Sarah Chayes before the Standing Committee on Foreign Affairs and International Development, House of Commons, Ottawa, Evidence 58, May 29, 2007.

33. Interview with Peter Harder, February 22, 2007.

34. Cited by Gloria Galloway and Ingrid Peritz, "Troops Won't Stay Unless All Parties Agree, PM Says," *The Globe and Mail*, June 23, 2007, p. A1.

35. Interview with Gordon O'Connor, July 4, 2007.

36. Interview with Gordon O'Connor, July 4, 2007.

37. Cited by Olivia Ward, "Where the Taliban Breeds," *Toronto Star*, February 18, 2007, p. A10.

38. Interview with Jordan Elms, May 16, 2007.

39. Interview with Chris Eaton, May 16, 2007.

40. Interview with Gordon O'Connor, July 4, 2007.

41. Interview with Rory Stewart, Turquoise Mountain Foundation, May 17, 2007.

42. Roger Morris, "Afghanistan: Another Ill-Fated Attempt?" *The Globe and Mail*, March 1, 2007, p. A19.

43. Interviews with Wagma, Kabor, and Farid, May 19, 2007.

ACKNOWLEDGMENTS

1. Thomas Axworthy, "To Go Ahead, Canada Must Know Its Past," *Toronto Star*, June 15, 2007, p. A15.

ACKNOWLEDGMENTS

Canadians generally know little about their country's history. Without memory, without knowledge of what Canada has done in the past, its citizens are poorer. "History is to citizenship," writes Thomas Axworthy, "what mathematics is to science—the key to unlocking competence. For self-governing men and women to decide where they want to go, they must first know where we have been."[1]

It is in this spirit that we came together to tell the story of Canada in Afghanistan, the story of how Canada's leaders chose to commit our military forces and our development funds, our people and our treasure, to a country unknown to most Canadians, ancient and remote, halfway around the globe. By 2006, Canada's soldiers were fighting and dying in a war that no one in Ottawa had anticipated when they first committed the Canadian Forces in 2001. Afghanistan is Canada's unexpected war.

History rarely walks a straight line, but often meanders along the side roads and occasionally takes a sharp detour. When the Canadian Forces first went to Afghanistan, they knew little about the country, its history, its complexity, its struggles, its secrets. They also knew little about their colleagues in government departments who would work with them. As Canada's diplomats, development experts, police, and non-governmental organizations joined the Canadian Forces in Kabul and Kandahar, together they learned not only about Afghanistan but also about one another and about their country. In Afghanistan, we have learned about ourselves, about how we work together in the world, about our weaknesses as well as our strengths. Canadians from many different departments in Ottawa agree: Much is not right and much can be done better. This history of Canada in Afghanistan sets the stage for important choices that Canadians will have to make in the future, long after Canada's mission in Kandahar is a distant memory.

We came to know each other through one of the threads woven through this book. During the heated controversy over Ballistic Missile Defence, one of us was inside government, the chief of staff to the minister of defence, and the other was in the privileged sanctuary of the University of Toronto. At an academic conference in Washington, a senior Pentagon official expressed impatience with the endless delays in Ottawa on whether or not Canada would participate in the program. It was not terribly important to Washington, the Pentagon official said, whether Canada joined or not; Washington would not care much and Canada would pay no price for saying "No." All that the Pentagon wanted was a decision.

The message was so counterintuitive, so different from the heated rhetoric in Canada, so at odds with official statements and the consensus within the federal government. At a chance meeting at the University of Toronto, we talked about the message, its variance with what we were both hearing, inside and outside government. So began a friendship, and the first of many conversations about Canada in the world. These conversations and that friendship led to the decision to tell this story together, a story that belongs to Canada's citizens.

We owe so much to so many Canadians, inside and outside government, who were extraordinarily generous with their time and their wisdom. We would like to thank especially those who granted us interviews, sometimes repeatedly as we went back again and again to confirm what we were told, and who agreed to speak "on the record."

The Honourable John Manley, former minister of foreign affairs and former deputy prime minister; the Honourable Bill Graham, former minister of foreign affairs and minister of national defence; and the Honourable John McCallum, former minister of national defence, went over the record with us many times as new questions arose and new information became available. They were generous with their time, analytic, and invaluable to the reconstruction of this story. The

Honourable Gordon O'Connor made time in his busy schedule as minister of defence to talk about the mission in Afghanistan. The Right Honourable Paul Martin, former prime minister of Canada, spent several hours with us as we struggled with the big questions. Tim Murphy, former chief of staff to Prime Minister Martin, and Scott Reid, former director of communications to Prime Minister Martin, were extraordinarily helpful and thoughtful.

Leaders in all of Canada's departments went out of their way to be helpful. General Ray Henault, former chief of the defence staff and currently chair of the NATO Military Committee, made himself available from Brussels for several discussions. His adviser and director of the international staff, Colonel B.A. Boudreau, facilitated these conversations as well as interviews with other NATO officials. General Rick Hillier, chief of the defence staff through much of the critical period, answered our questions with his customary candour and vigour. Brigadier General David Fraser, commander of Task Force Afghanistan /AEGIS/Regional Commander South from February to November 2006, provided important information and context about Operation Medusa, the major battle in 2006. Lieutenant General Andrew Leslie, chief of the land staff, shared his knowledge of both Canada's military and of Afghanistan. Colonel Bernd Horn at the Royal Military College was extraordinarily generous with his interviews in Kandahar, his research, and his analytic insights. Jordan Elms, currently Canada's military attaché in Afghanistan, spoke about Canada's performance in Afghanistan.

Leaders at the Canadian International Development Agency (CIDA) were no less generous with their time. Robert Greenhill, the president of CIDA, made time to talk with us about Afghanistan and the way CIDA worked with its partners. Stephen Wallace, vice-president, Afghanistan Task Force, provided a detailed analysis of CIDA's programming in Afghanistan and discussed the challenges with clarity. Diana Youdell, CIDA's talented representative in the Canadian embassy in Kabul, went above and beyond the call of duty to educate us about the challenges in the field and to arrange interviews with CIDA's Afghan partners.

The Department of Foreign Affairs was welcoming and helpful. Peter Harder, a former deputy minister, reviewed the history of Canada's engagement and sketched the broad landscape of Canada's policies in Afghanistan, its accomplishments, and its shortcomings. Ambassador Arif Lalani, currently Canada's ambassador in Kabul, not only spent time but also extended his personal hospitality so that we could meet with Canada's representatives in the field. David Sproule, Canada's former ambassador in Kabul, shared the "lessons learned."

Many, many Canadians who serve their government spoke to one or the other of us at length, but did so "off the record." They did so because they were public servants or serving officers and, understandably, felt constrained. Nevertheless, they wanted to tell the story, to ensure its accuracy, and to inform the debate. Their contribution to this book is beyond calculation and we thank them all.

The Honourable Paul Cellucci, the U.S. ambassador to Canada during much of this story, spoke to us with surprising frankness. Lieutenant General Dan McNeill, commander of the NATO International Security Assistance Force in Afghanistan, somehow found an hour in his day to talk about the strategic challenges in Afghanistan. Chris Alexander, formerly Canada's ambassador to Kabul and currently the United Nations Secretary-General's Deputy Special Representative to Afghanistan, spent several hours talking about Canada's role in Afghanistan and then opened his home in Kabul to ensure a broad cross-section of perspectives. Lieutenant General Jo Gooderij of the Netherlands analyzed with clarity the Dutch approach to counterinsurgency operations in southern Afghanistan.

We also owe a special debt of gratitude to Afghans who talked to us, often passionately, about their country. Dr. Sima Simar, the chair of the Afghan Independent Human Rights Commission, was her usual extraordinary self: wise and passionate in her commitment to human rights. The deputy chair of the Afghanistan Independent

Human Rights Commission, Ahmad Fahim Hakim, detailed with exhaustive care the challenges the commission faces and its need for Canadian help. The dedicated staff at the CARE Afghanistan office taught us so much about Afghanistan; it is the voices of Wagma, Kabor, and Farid, all senior Afghan leaders at CARE, that close this story.

Two remarkable foundations in Afghanistan, the Aga Khan Foundation and the Turquoise Mountain Foundation, opened their doors to us. Chris Eaton, a Canadian with the Aga Khan Foundation, was unusually blunt and perspicacious. Rory Stewart, who now heads the Turquoise Mountain Foundation, walked with us through his restoration of part of old Kabul and shared his deep understanding of Afghanistan.

The minister of reconstruction and rural development, Mohammed Ehsan Zia, spoke about his vision for Afghanistan, his hopes, his worries, his pressing needs. He too extended his hospitality to make certain that we met Afghans who are struggling to ensure a better future for their country.

We owe a special debt of gratitude to Gordon Smith, former deputy foreign minister of Canada and currently the director of the Centre for Global Studies at the University of Victoria, to Sally Armstrong, who has been to Afghanistan countless times over the last decade, and to Senator Hugh Segal, who brings wisdom and judgment to his analysis of Canadian foreign policy, for reading the manuscript for us. They caught as many errors as they could, but the responsibility for all those that remain is, of course, ours.

Shane Diaczuk—a former official in the Department of National Defence and aide to the minister of national defence—brought his extraordinary knowledge, diligence, and expertise to the search for documents and sources. Shane was a source both of knowledge and wisdom about Canada's mission to Afghanistan and the complex psychology of the military–civilian relationship.

Max Shapiro carefully checked sources and notes, and Sharon Yale read proofs with intelligence and precision to avoid the embarrassment that comes with error. We hope they succeeded.

This book would not be without Diane Turbide, our editor at Penguin. From the moment we first spoke to her, Diane enthusiastically embraced the telling of the story of Canada in Afghanistan. She charmed, cajoled, encouraged, but always with just a hint of steel, and then pushed us much further than we would have been able to go on our own. The book is far better because of her keen eye and sensitive ear. A special thank you to Elizabeth McKay who managed us—our multiple drafts and our electronic files—with quiet competence and warm assurance. Sharon Kirsch was a compassionate copy editor, and Sandra Tooze held our hands through the production of this book. Working with the team at Penguin was a wonderful experience. Michael Levine, as usual, contributed to this story in every way possible. He is incomparable.

Above all we are grateful to our spouses, Camielle and Michael. They suffered our odd writing habits—before dawn or painfully late at night—with patience. They did many of the chores each of us normally does as we stole time to write. We could not have written this book without their generosity, their warm encouragement, and their unfailing willingness to do more than they should have at home, almost always without complaint.

Writing this story has been a remarkable journey. When Canada first went to Kandahar, the book argues, we knew very little about Afghanistan, but we also did not know enough about ourselves. Through Canada's mission in Afghanistan, we now see ourselves more clearly. We hope Canadians will come with us on this journey, "as self-governing men and women" who must decide where they want Canada to go in the future and what they want Canada to do in the world.

Janice Gross Stein, Toronto
Eugene Lang, Ottawa
Canada Day, 2007

INDEX

U

V